Illustrations

PLATES

good specimen of the elegance and comfort of Oriental life . . .
the centre building, or pavilion, contains the drawing-, dining-
and sitting-rooms, on one floor; the sleeping apartments are
in the cool and well-shaded circular bungalow on the left; the
kitchen, the servants' quarters, stabling, etc. stand in the
detached buildings on the other side—the former communicat-
ing with the pavilion with a covered way.'
(J. Deschamps, *Scenery and Reminiscences of Ceylon*, 1845)

In the background of the sacred peak tea pluckers are shown
working on a plantation in the Maskeliya district. These
workers belong to an important section of Ceylon's peoples—
immigrants from India who, since the days when tea displaced
coffee as the island's major crop, have been resident there.
(*photograph by courtesy of the Ceylon Tea Centre, London*)

In the twilight before the dawn pilgrims wait on the summit
of the peak held sacred by Buddhists, Hindus and Moslems to
see the sun rise and throw the shadow of the peak on the
western hills.
(*photograph by Ina Bandy*)

The Perahera at Kandy, held in the months of July–August
every year, is the best known of the island's rituals. The Tooth-
relic of the Buddha is borne on the back of an ornately capari-
soned elephant in an impressive procession in which lay
officials of the temple of the Tooth in Kandy, Kandyan chieftains, dancers, acrobats, representatives of the major Hindu
shrines in Kandy and a hundred or more elephants take part.
(*photograph by Edith Ludowyk*)

Colombo Harbour, very much modernized and improved
since 1947, is one of the largest in south-east Asia.
(*photograph by courtesy of the Ceylon Tea Centre, London*)

LINE ILLUSTRATIONS

Marygrove

EX LIBRIS

The Story of Ceylon

Uniform with this book

*

Statue of a king or a sage: Polonnaruva, twelfth century A.D.

THE STORY OF
CEYLON

E. F. C. LUDOWYK

ROY PUBLISHERS, INC.
NEW YORK

Printed in Great Britain

Library of Congress Catalog Card Number
62--19240

TO THE MEMORY
OF FRIENDS IN CEYLON
J.R.B., E.M.G., P.L.J.,
N.M. DE S., AND C.B.S.

Contents

Preface

This book attempts to narrate, without any claim to completeness, the story of the important events and persons crowded into the two thousand years and more of Ceylon's history. Where it seemed wise to simplify the account of turning-points in the story rather than pester a reader unacquainted with complicated details of social distinctions (as in Chapter 12), simplification was preferred.

It would have been impossible to undertake even the simplest rendering of the story of Ceylon without dependence on the work of numerous scholars to whom I have acknowledged indebtedness in the course of the book. In addition I wish to set out with gratitude my special debts to the following, without whose help in discussion and correspondence I should not have been able to complete my undertaking: Dr. G. C. Mendis, sometime Reader in History in the University of Ceylon, for having read and criticized Chapters 1–12 with a historian's patience and tolerance; Bhikkhu W. Rahula for his many helpful suggestions on the first six chapters; Dr. I. H. Van Den Driesen, Lecturer in Economic History in the University of Ceylon, for permission to quote from his Ph.D. thesis 'Some Aspects of the History of the Coffee Industry in Ceylon'; Dr. Kingsley de Silva, Lecturer in History in the University of Ceylon, for the benefit of his knowledge of mid-nineteenth-century Ceylon: Upali Wickremeratne from whose careful reading and criticism of the second half of the book I learnt a great deal; a government official in Ceylon, who wishes to remain anonymous, for his advice on the presentation of the first half of the book; and lastly R. C. L. Attygalle for the stimulating effect of his clearness of mind and memorableness of phrase in his discussion and criticism of its last six chapters.

Mine entirely is the responsibility for the use made of the material they so generously made available to me.

I wish to thank the following for permission to quote from published work: Miss I. B. Horner and the Pali Text Society for extracts from the PTS editions of the *Mahavamsa* and the *Culavamsa*; the University of Ceylon for extracts from the University *History of Ceylon*, Vol. 1, Part II; UNESCO for the version of one of the Sigiri Graffiti by W. G. Archer in *Ceylon* (UNESCO World Art Series); the Hon. the Minister for Cultural Affairs, Ceylon, and Professor Paranavitane for allowing me to render the latter's version of No. 314 of *Sigiri Graffiti* into another form; and the Associated Newspapers of Ceylon for two extracts from *The Life and Times of D. R. Wijewardene* by H. A. J. Hulugalle.

I should like to express my gratitude to the following who helped with the illustrations: Madame Ina Bandy for the frontispiece and Plate 4 (b); *The Times of Ceylon* and Mr. D. C. L. Amarasinghe, CCS, for permission to use the latter's photograph, first published in *The Times of Ceylon Annual 1960*, for Plate 1; The Trustees of the British Museum for Plates 2 and 3; my wife for her photograph of the Perahera used for Plate 5; the Ceylon Tea Centre, and particularly its Librarian, Mr. R. J. Dennis, for Plates 4(a) and 6; Mr. Charles Gunawardena, Press and Information Attaché to the Ceylon High Commission, London, for his help; and Dr. G. C. Mendis for allowing me to reprint the map of old Ceylon which appeared in his *Early History of Ceylon*.

The Search for a Clue

How should the story of Ceylon begin but by fixing its limits, first in place and then in time? The island of Ceylon lies to the south-east of the continent of India (India and Pakistan now) almost alongside its southern extremity, between five and nine degrees above the Equator and nearly midway between the tropics of Capricorn and Cancer. Its northernmost point overtakes the southernmost point of India, so to the casual eye glancing over a map the island appears to be the extrusion of the peninsula, from which it is sundered by a strait so shallow that only ships of the smallest draught can successfully negotiate its hazards. These the voyager sees either as a chain of rocks or the suspicion of a reef unhistorically called Adam's Bridge. If Ceylon is not in Milton's phrase 'India's utmost isle', it is yet an Indian isle. Indeed it is necessary to think of it as of many other islands separated from the continents to which they once belonged. England and Japan come at once to mind. They instruct us how dangerous it is in recounting their stories to isolate island from continent or to force them irretrievably together.

From the south-western lowlands of Ceylon, called the Low-country, mountain ranges rise up to eight thousand feet, all along the centre of the southern half of the island. The mountain barrier which on its south-western slopes receives both monsoons, the south-west and the north-east, makes of the south-west of Ceylon and its central mountainous core an area called the Wet Zone with an annual rainfall of between 100 and 200 inches. To the central plain of the north and the east, cut off by the mountains from the south-west monsoon, only the north-east monsoon brings rain. This plain which slopes from the mountain shelf very gradually to the sea has an annual rainfall of 60 inches and below. High as these figures are when compared with those of England, by comparison with those of monsoon lands they are low, and as a result this area is known as the Dry Zone. The north-central plain through which the largest river of Ceylon, the Mahaveliganga, flows to the sea near Trincomalie was the setting of the country's ancient culture, which depended on the skill of its inhabitants in conserving the water the rains brought to the hills and the rivers carried through the land.

The population of Ceylon is close upon 10 millions and is made up of various groups. The Sinhalese, mainly Buddhist and speaking a language of Indo-Aryan origin, form the major element in it—nearly 70 per cent of the total. The Tamils, mainly Hindus and speaking a Dravidian language spoken by over 20 millions in South India, number just over 10 per cent of the population. In size the Moors come next—about 4 per cent of the population. They are called Moors because the Portuguese who so named them considered all Moslems to be Moors—the North African Mauretanians whom they knew. The Moors of Ceylon are of Indian rather than Arab descent, and came to Ceylon as traders. The language they speak is generally that of the area where they have settled. A very much smaller group of people called Burghers because this was the Dutch term for the townsfolk of their settlements in the East, are Eurasian, the descendants of the various European races in Ceylon since the sixteenth century and the native population. They are mainly English speaking, and still are an urban population. In addition to these groups there is a large group of Indian origin, the majority working on the plantations of tea and rubber, who have lived in Ceylon for two or three generations.

In all these different groups differences are observable—of ethnic origin, of religion, of language and of development. For instance, the Sinhalese of the comparatively prosperous south-western coastal areas is very different from the Kandyan villager, and townspeople, whether Tamil or Moor, are different from their kin in rural areas. What is typical of the population of Ceylon is its diversity, a diversity produced by the historical development of the island.

In time the story of Ceylon compasses two thousand five

hundred years of legend and history. According to one tradition Vijaya, a prince of the lion race (Sinhalas), after whom the island was named, set out from India and landed on the north-western shores of Ceylon on the very day on which the Buddha finally passed away. This was in 483 B.C. Of the aboriginal people of the island living in it prior to the arrival of the immigrant prince we know next to nothing.

Two thousand five hundred years are a long span of time, difficult to see in true perspective and continually eluding our grasp. Its events refuse to fall into coherent patterns. Its long wars celebrated by epic poets, its periods of peace when nothing seems to happen, the scramble of European nations for control of its spices, and then the evolution of modern Ceylon under British auspices make up a temporal sequence of two thousand five hundred years. Its figures—kings, generals, clerics, fidalgos, merchants, proconsuls, even the statesmen of a decade ago—seem in the Kierkegaardian phrase to 'hurry in a perpetual vanishing'. So much has happened, so many peoples have set foot in Ceylon, colonized it, been thrown out of it, and wandered away from it, that in the criss-cross markings on the shore it is hard to pick out one clue which will explain them all.

Time with its fluxes and refluxes has perhaps washed away numerous clues; place which seems more stable is no safer stay. For that too is subject to decay and change, and only in the scale of geology remote from the usual range of imagination could there be events so decisive that they might provide a clue. Perhaps the two most significant events for the future of the island's story antedated its human history: its separation from India and the upthrust of the central mountain mass which gave it its distinctive physical character. Still unchanged are the gradual tilt of the northern and eastern plain away from the mountain mass, the rampart of the mountainous south-centre with its sharp western and southern walls and the western and southern coastal belts. But all this hardly takes us on our way. It gives us the arena, on it the human actors had to appear and perform. Place gives us only the setting.

Perhaps our clue may be given us by a casual detail which should not be neglected because of its triviality. In the unpredictability of history any fortuitous help should not be scorned. Is there anything to be gained by considering the shape of

B

Ceylon—the way the island arrests our attention as we stare at it in the map?

The shape of Ceylon has always been commented on. Descriptions of it have ranged from the picturesque to the prosaic. It has been likened to pear, mango, pearl, chrysalis, and swine's ham. If a variation of one of these is taken up here, let its excuse be not fancifulness but the search for one of the many clues there may be to the unravelling of Ceylon's story.

The shape of the island could be described as resembling the 'mango pattern'—the popular phrase for the conventional artist's motif in one of the most ancient and highly developed of India's arts, its textiles. There is a story, unsupported by any historical evidence, that the Indian craftsman working on *chint* (the Hindi term for a painted or spotted cotton material), instead of painting his design or stamping it on the material with a wooden block, multiplied the pattern in his own primitive way by clenching his fist and using its soft underside as block. Immersing his folded hand in the dye, he rapidly pressed it directly on the woven fabric. The design thus left on the cloth was called the 'mango pattern'. It is also known as the fir-cone pattern. Where the motif originated, whether ages ago in the south, or, as is more likely, in Moghul times in the north, it is distinctively Indian. It is known all over the Western world now as the Paisley pattern, the mills of Scotland having taken over the Indian motif of the decorated whorl, narrow at the top with its beautiful broad base to balance the composition. The island of Ceylon resembles this. The peninsula of Jaffna is the elongated apex; the southern base, slightly aslant, giving a free impression of the rest of the island as it appears on modern maps.

It is permissible to catch even in this mythical account of how a pattern came into being a hint of one mode of looking at the story of Ceylon. That story could be revealed as a design stamped with the strong original dye of Indian culture and bearing the clear impression of an Indian prototype. India was always there, no farther away than a few hours' sailing, always remembered, even at times when the Indian connection has been disavowed and indignantly repudiated. Indian culture spread so widely over Asia that nowhere in that quarter of the world has any country been untouched by it. Indeed it would be as difficult to tell the story of England, ignoring France, as to speak of Ceylon deliberately forgetting India. So that if even out of its physical shape there should be elicited some reminder of its Indian connections, this should not be reckoned as needless elaboration.

The story of Ceylon then could be based, both in place and time, on the fact of its connection with India. Right throughout its history India has left a deep impression on Ceylon—the India of the Buddha, Asokan India, the India of the Guptas, and much nearer home British India too. The various peoples who make up the Ceylonese, with their background of thoughts, beliefs, passions, the languages they speak and the way they have lived, have been people connected with India. The British no less than the Colas and Pandyans came to Ceylon from India. From India have come salvation and also cause of deep offence. In its affinities, as well as in its discords, the relationship of India and Ceylon has been as intimate as that between parent and child. If there is such a thing as the one single clue to the development of the story of Ceylon it might perhaps be found in its Indian heritage, even at those moments when the individuality of Ceylon has been most strongly asserted.

But this clue alone will not take us through the maze. There may be some truth in the exaggeration that hardly anything of importance has happened in Ceylon which has not happened as a result of the fact of India. The Indian connection, Indian influence, the geographical proximity of India have meant much in the story of Ceylon, but it has not been everything. The particularity of the island as distinct from India and from all other regions of South Asia should be borne in mind. At all stages in the history of Ceylon we are aware of India, but of something else too which is not India, but is very definitely Ceylon.

What does this particularity of Ceylon consist of, where might it be found? Does it arise out of a particular geographical setting, something given specifically to the island and not to be found elsewhere? Will it be revealed in a certain stage of human achievement when something not there before, something original, emerges and becomes typical of Ceylon alone? To try to find the uniqueness of Ceylon in a particular part of the country more or less untouched by anything else which might have happened since the Ceylon of history established itself as an entity, is difficult. It is equally difficult to isolate it in any particular group of people, even in those who, compared with others, could still be thought of as originally and uniquely representative of the island. No region in the world is free from change, nor can we claim that any one group of people in a country either represents its original inhabitants or all those others to be found in it. What group, for instance, could claim to be typical of England, even England without Scotland and Wales?

If we search for a part of Ceylon which seems hardly scarred by human history we could not do better than consider the small plateau, known now as the Horton Plains, seven thousand feet above sea level, where damp and low jungle occasionally retreats from grassy patches of plain. Stunted trees hung with moss and lichen wave in the wind like disapproving minor prophets. This small area might be thought of as the survival of the most ancient part of Ceylon—the heart of its once inaccessible mountain region, the 'Malaya' of the ancient chronicles. Some remains of Stone Age man have been found about twenty miles south-west as the crow flies, but so far the plateau has revealed no ancient traces of human settlement. In medieval times water was drawn from it to irrigate fields hundreds of feet below. It may be that nothing has been discovered because no one has searched, but if any part of the island has lain undisturbed for thousands of years it would be this—too high and forbidding for the fugitive, and away from the pilgrim trails of more recent times leading to the sacred Peak on which the footprint of the Buddha is believed to be found, now known to the English reader as Adam's Peak. Its two mountains of Totapola and Kirigalpotta were known and named—probably after the twelfth century A.D. But they do not appear to have entered the story of Ceylon. On this high plateau the *neloo*, a species of bush indigenous to Ceylon, blooms in September, and the wild bee is busy in its thickets as it must have been for millennia.

But even here the difficulty of isolating what is and has been uniquely Ceylon crops up, for in its streams are trout bred during the years of English rule of the island, and not far from its boundaries is the tea bush. This recent importation, with its regular rosettes of green sewn on the hillsides, is a reminder of how close upon the heels of the ancient treads the modern. The

Horton Plains are certainly one Ceylon, one moment of time in the story, but other moments are recalled by it too.

Shall we find what is specifically Ceylon in any group of people? Legends speak of the country as having been first inhabited by demons and snakes (as *Yakkhas* and *Nagas* were translated into the popular imagination) when the first Sinhalese landed on its coast. Were these *Yakkhas* and *Nagas* aboriginal tribesmen, worshippers of demons and snakes, whom invaders from the continent found on the island and forced farther and farther inland? Perhaps in their descendants might be found something which is an integral part of old Ceylon. There used to be in Ceylon a people called the *Veddahs* or hunters. Whoever they were, they have in the course of the last hundred years been assimilated into village communities, as better communications and the opening up of land for increasing population have pushed villages farther and farther into jungle.

The account given of them by Robert Knox, an Englishman who spent eighteen years in Ceylon in the seventeenth century, combines all that folklore and legend asserted about them then. Knox was no scientific observer, nor did he ever come into contact with them. For one moment during his exciting escape from the Kandyan kingdom he was in danger of running into a chattering band of the women of these 'wild men', as he called them. His account of them is as follows: 'For as in these Woods there are Wild Beasts, so Wild Men also. . . . They call them Vaddahs, dwelling near no other Inhabitants. They speak the Chingulays Language. They kill Deer, and dry the Flesh over the fire, and the people of the Countrey come and buy it of them. They never till any ground for corn, their Food being only Flesh. They are very expert with their Bows.'

The *Veddahs* were the subject of ethnological and anthropological study for the first time at the end of the last century. But even then it was difficult to separate the genuine from the fake exhibit. These short and under-developed hunters, who must have been forced into the jungle from the plain by the pressure of people whom they could not resist, hardly maintained themselves as a distinct racial group. Throughout historical times their numbers must have been augmented by fugitives from justice or from the wrath of feudal overlords and kings. Indeed the ancient chronicles rationalize their existence

21

as a group by the fable that they were the children of Vijaya by a *Yakkha* princess deserted by him after he had become ruler of the kingdom he conquered through her aid. The anthropometrist has discovered in them physical traits enabling him to speak of characteristics different from those of other groups with which they have been mixed, but the layman must have been hard put to it to see in them more than the traces of ill health and destitution to which their life in the jungle exposed them. Romance might make play with their primitive life, their skill with bow and arrow and their jungle lore, but these had gone when they were first scientifically examined. The very few who eighty years ago might with some justice have been called *Veddahs* were the most wretched stratum of population on the fringe of the jungle for whom as yet little had been done by British administration.

Of their boasted skill with bow and arrow nothing remained. The Seligmans in 1910 found that all the *Veddahs* they met were bad or indifferent marksmen. Indeed the schoolboy of today playing Indians is probably a better shot with a bow than any of them. As for their nomadic life—although the Seligmans did meet four families who had never practised cultivation and heard of two more—they noted how frequently the *Veddah* was an article on show for the benefit of the tourist. The Danigala *Veddahs*, according to them, were 'the classical "wild Veddahs" of Ceylon described by so many travellers; their descent is pure but their own customs have been almost entirely forgotten, and are certainly ignored at the present day. They live in the park country, have a *chena* and banana garden, and do a good trade in cattle both by herding for the Sinhalese, retaining every fifth calf as is the custom of the country, and also selling those they have bred themselves.'

These words were written fifty years ago. To hope that the *Veddah*, if he were produced, would be the repository of the pristine qualities of the most ancient inhabitants of Ceylon is as vain as looking for an Etruscan in Central Italy or for the contemporaries of Akhnaton among the fellahin of the Nile Valley.

In no single group of people today shall we find what is typical of Ceylon, for in the story of an island close to and influenced by its continental neighbour what must emerge is the essential diversity of peoples who found a home on the island and intermingled with those already there. As an island on the highways of trade of West with East, even in those earlier days when West was India and East China, Ceylon was continually attracting various peoples to its shores. Besides the constant stream from India there were traders and seafarers from Arabia, Africa, from the islands of the Malayan Archipelago, and from China. Trade brought one set of pilgrims, religion another, for by the fourth century of the Christian era the fame of the island as the repository of Buddhist relics was well established. As island, Ceylon was detached from the rest of the continent, but it was also the goal of voyagers in search of trade and religion.

Moreover as tropical island, well-watered, with its lush vegetation and climate tempered by the sea, Ceylon has been a powerful magnet. Its precious stones, their value fabulously exaggerated, were the subject of legends to be found in *The Arabian Nights*. At times the attraction of the island seemed to lie not in the resources which differentiated it from the continent of India, but in its similarities with it. South India in ancient times—the Dravidian country—was flourishing and prosperous. It throve on the trade which took the luxuries of India, China and the East to the Graeco-Roman world. Yet wave after wave of invaders from the continent broke upon the island. Ceylon drew them as it was a country like their own, into which South Indian people were continually pressing.

In the course of time a variety of peoples gradually settled on the island. There were travellers' tales of a Jewish community, of Nestorian Christians—from Iran probably. Traders from imperial Rome and the Grecian kingdoms knew the island and some may have settled. The old truism that there is no racial stock which has not been mixed with several other strains could be illustrated if need be from the story of Ceylon. That same story will also illustrate how easily this can be forgotten. The mixture of racial groups in Ceylon today reveals itself in the frequency of eyes coloured from brown to blue, of crinkly and smooth hair, of flat noses and hooked ones. Such traits will be met with both in towns and in villages.

Since the sixteenth century various other groups of people have come to Ceylon. When invaders from much farther overseas than before appeared on the western coasts of Ceylon in the sixteenth century the spices of a tropical island drew them thither. Once again the resources of the island determined its history, but there is a difference to be noted. As before with gems and elephants, the prospect of gain drew traders and invaders to the island. But things had altered now. These were operators on a larger scale, the scope of their activities was not confined to the Bay of Bengal or to Eastern waters; the commerce they engaged in was so different in degree from that of their predecessors that it was altogether different in kind. The processes of trade which brought the seafaring nations of western Europe to Ceylon in the sixteenth and seventeenth centuries seem continuous with earlier processes whereby Indian, Arab and Malay had found their way to the island. But they soon alter in character and ramifications. They could scarcely be thought of as being the same. The island, its position, its resources, were as meaningful as ever before, but now they were going to be held in a much larger frame, in a setting which included, not intermittently but continuously, great powers whose activities were rapidly changing both worlds—the old and the new—not only on the face of the globe but very markedly within the confines of the island too.

Faced with Ceylon today the observer is aware of many Ceylons, both many Ceylons of place, of time and of persons. Change has altered its landscape not once but several times in the course of the two thousand five hundred years of its story. There have been, and are, various cultures in the diversity of peoples who have made up Ceylon. Even if one group of the variety of its groups were held in suspension in the mind, it would be strange if a paradoxical element in its culture were not sensed. Take the Sinhalese, its major group. Beneath the patina of several centuries of civilization, of considerable sophistication of thought and sensibility there lurks something of an older world, not properly assimilated with what replaced it or with the new, and even now disturbing by its presence. This may be little more than the effect on the observer of the complexity of the culture of a mixed group of people with long and various traditions. But this is no ordinary complexity; it deepens as the major events of a long history are unfolded. At all times there seem to have been continually present in the culture seemingly incongruous and irreconcilable elements.

The entity is not all of a piece. There are disquieting strains and tensions which arise, not as might be expected of rival groupings, or the results of layer upon layer of people who came to Ceylon, fought, settled and lived in it, but from an imbalance, noticeable not only here but running through all strata.

To turn to D. H. Lawrence at this juncture is not to quote authority, for he was in no sense qualified to express the opinion of any kind of specialist on Ceylon, and what he felt was intuition. But it was the intuition of a highly sensitive poet, and in the procession of elephants and dancers organized in Kandy in 1922 in honour of the visit of Edward, Prince of Wales, he sensed the strength of primeval sources of power in people and in country. His poem 'Elephant' conveys his poet's vision of Ceylon. This was his reality of Ceylon. As description it is inaccurate. It is unobjective and even prejudiced. But he responded with the imaginative power of the artist to an old rite and traditional dances in a modern setting. We can, if we will, discount 'blood', 'lust', and 'rage' as Lawrentian idiosyncrasies, but they are the signals of a reaction due to something more than, to put it in the most derogatory terms, an aberration. Lawrence had the visionary power of the great artist, and his words should be pondered:

In elephants and the east are two devils, in all men maybe
The mystery of the dark mountain of blood, reeking in homage,
*   in lust, in rage,*
And passive with everlasting patience. . . .

It is the combination of the 'rage' with the 'patience' which is noteworthy. It seems to echo the tones of a culture difficult to comprehend or to explain, except through the evocation of opposites. It may, of course, as the poem indicates, be found in all men, and not in one group or in all groups in Ceylon and the East.

How then could the particularity of Ceylon, its reality, be seized? A particular moment of time, a particular group of people, may be fallacious clues to what we seek. Whether we can grasp the reality at all has long been the subject of philosophical dispute. Indeed all our human transcriptions of it—in literature, in painting, in sculpture, even in scientific record—

25

do not seem very different from the deliberate imposition of our own arbitrary patterns on the variety of impressions the world leaves upon us. On the ground of what is seen we incise the figure we notice, and history so often becomes the rearrangement of what the historian has elected to treat as fact. Whatever they may be, these facts, they are one person's selection from a mass of unco-ordinated experiences. That is why 'Stick to the facts' seems to be such a futile cry in debates, for one man's facts may not be the same as another's.

Of course, from time to time, believing that one branch of knowledge or the other provides the key which opens all doors, we comfort ourselves with the claim that we have free entry into reality and that we could lead anyone through its mazes. So theology, economics, psychology, have been offered as unimpeachable clues. Though historians, as a result, have regimented everything in the interests of the particular clue they have held fast to, far better this than the alternative of abdicating responsibility at the threat of the chaos of unmanageable fact. We have always been warned that we are far removed from the reality we claim to know, yet it would be wrong to assert that only subjective impressions are possible, that all we know of reality is the inchoate out of which the mind must create something in its own image.

If these are the difficulties which beset the trained historian working according to scientific rule, the task of the humbler narrator, dependent on the work of the scientist, is just as complicated. As for the reality of Ceylon, what it has been, what it has meant to the numerous people who have lived in the island or have only been interested in it from a distance, could never have been, nor can it ever be, a fixed quantity deducible from the shapes fished out of the waters of history or conjecture. Where so little is known, and so much has to be guessed—particularly about its ancient history; at a time like the present when tempers are so easily frayed and susceptibilities can be so deeply wounded, the simple task of telling a story can be fraught with untold dangers. There may be debate about what truly belongs to the material of a story, about how it should be organized, how its highlights and shadows are limned, and about the conclusion to which it tends. Besides, even with material unexceptionably gathered a story can hardly be told, except from the particular angle the story-teller chooses, even if he had no purpose in recounting his tale but his own interest in it. But these are after all the obvious difficulties in the task of seizing any reality or telling any story. It is good to be reminded of them, for it is easy to overlook them.

Ancient Ceylon

CHAPTER 1

Poetry and Myth

That the beginnings of the story of Ceylon are situated in the half-world of poetry between myth and folk-lore, is to be expected. That the vague shapes of legend and tradition have a more compelling reality, even at the present time, than the bright light of day of the world in which the inhabitants of any country live, can be accepted too. To discount these mythical shapes would be unwise, for if they were rejected as unhistorical and patently incredible, it would be impossible to tell the story of the people to whom they were, and are, the truth, nor would it be easy to understand it. To subject the legends to critical autopsy would be possible only when they cease to live as the verbalized statements of dogmatic assertion. To tilt at them with the ardour of the confirmed sceptic is to ignore the force of what is consciously believed, even in the teeth of demonstration to the contrary. The Portuguese in the seventeenth century attempted to demolish the faith of innumerable Buddhists by destroying what they thought was the original Tooth Relic, an object of veneration to Buddhists in Ceylon and in Asia. They possessed themselves of it, and, to their own satisfaction, systematically destroyed it. It is strange that their own worship of images and relics had not taught them that, if the human mind accepts a myth, this alone is sufficient to preserve it from any touch of reality. The relic the Portuguese destroyed was not the Tooth Relic, but that to the Buddhist could no more be destroyed than the worship of the Virgin Mary could have been proved to be idolatry to the Portuguese.

Myths have played, and still play, a significant role in the story of a country. Sometimes they change, at other times older myths are revived, and new ones are added to the old stock, as the social situation demands it. They cannot be left out of the story of a country, whatever private opinions the reader or writer may hold about them, either as fact or fable. It is always necessary to know them, and to look in them for the light cast on the way the story of a country has developed, and the way, too, in which the people of the country have regarded themselves. In the configurations of the myths could be traced the needs they have satisfied, and the world of the men and women whose creations they were.

The oral traditions out of which the perfected myths of Ceylon arose can be handled now only in their much later literary embodiments. But the earlier forms can be guessed at, for there still exist renderings of them in the intermediate stage between story and epic. The final shape of most of these early legends about Ceylon, or Lanka as it was known by its Sanskritic name, was mainly the result of the rage for order of a Buddhist *religieux* or *bhikkhu* of the fifth century A.D. Of all the influences of men and women upon the Sinhalese, his has probably been the strongest. To overestimate it is impossible. This *bhikkhu*, a figure as shadowy as those in the legends in which he dealt, synchronized oral traditions, and an ancient chronicle with legends of the Buddha, and composed the *Mahavamsa*, the Pali Chronicle of the early kings of Ceylon, dealing with the 'history' of the island from the very earliest times to the fourth century A.D.

His story gave the Sinhalese a consciousness of the special Buddhist destiny of the island and of their role as defenders of the faith, both of which are at the present day much more potent than sheaves of facts gleaned from any of the fields of history or economics. The early legends—of the Buddha's visits to Lanka, of Vijaya, the exiled prince of the lion race (the Sinhalas, from *sinha* the Sanskrit for 'lion'), and how he came to Lanka—have exerted a strong pull not only on the story of Ceylon, but also on how it has been told. How decisively these legends have worked will be understood by the general reader if it is stated that they have swayed, and continue to sway, the imaginations, the calculations and the passions of the Sinhalese as vigorously as the vision of Israel has the Zionist.

It is doubtful whether any people could live without myth of some kind to sustain them. Myths of heaven on earth, of the promised land, of the Socialist homeland, of full employment and the welfare state are well known in our own time. If they do nothing else they redeem pawned self-respect, and cushion men and women from the awkward corners of uncomfortable reality. As the myth satisfies the unconscious wishes of people, it would seem that its source is not as material to it as its availability. Indeed without the myth we should be hard put to it to justify our schemes of morality, for if there were no faith or belief in what is not demonstrable, there would scarcely be opportunity for virtues which are not prudential.

Myths are a liability too. They can on occasion be dangerous. There is a dramatic moment of fine intensity in Brecht's *Galileo* when the young Sarti, disgusted at Galileo's betrayal of their cause, turns on his erstwhile teacher with the words: 'Unhappy is the land which has no heroes.' To which the old man replies, not without shame at his own inability to live up to his pupil's expectations, 'Unhappy is the land which needs heroes.'

The justice of this aphorism might be illustrated by the story of Ceylon, for it would appear that its recorded history repeatedly reflects this need. Not only this, but more significantly, the legendary heroes once created to satisfy old needs are still resorted to in the entirely different circumstances of the present. That cultures have their mythical heroes is not surprising, indeed it would be strange if they should lack them. There is a slight distinction to be drawn, however, between this and the need for heroes. Brecht's is a generalization which might be rephrased in this way: where at any stage in the story of a country, its people have felt the need for heroes, then it would seem that the country was expressing dissatisfaction with itself. To have invented what was once required is surely the normal and economical satisfaction of desires, to be met with in the history of individuals as of communities. But to insist on satisfying a recurring need at all times in the same old ways is surely an indication of deep-seated *malaise*. To be, at the present time, dependent on the mythopoeic creativeness of ages long past is to argue an inability to face up to the demands of the contemporaneous. When we continually cry for a cause, for a hero whom we could follow, when we need the sustenance of legendary forefathers, we are most probably showing symptoms, not only of angry unhappiness, but also of retarded adolescence.

If no vivid political and religious colouring had been added

C 33

to the legends of the heroes of Lanka as they exist in the first few chapters of the *Mahavamsa*, a great deal of their sharpness and brilliance would long have been effaced. But what the age demanded fifteen centuries ago as an image of itself still looks us in the eye today. The chronicle, or epic poem, first composed in the fifth century A.D., was taken up and continued thrice later—in the thirteenth, the fourteenth and the eighteenth centuries. It has a notable unity of tone throughout the record it chose to make of the religion of the Sinhalese and their kings. Whatever enters it is at once transformed by the single-minded intention of its various authors.

The author of the first part, called the *Mahavamsa* of the Great Dynasty, was probably the *bhikkhu* Mahanama. He begins with an obeisance to the Buddha, and claims that the ancient originals upon which he drew for his subject matter were 'here too long drawn out and there too closely knit; and contained too many repetitions'. His work, on the contrary, would be 'free from such faults, easy to understand and remember, arousing serene joy and emotion and handed down (to us) by tradition'.

Indeed the background of his first references to Ceylon is composed of the travellers' tales and folklore of countless voyagers, to be met with in accounts of Ceylon early and late. What seems to have been common to them all was the legend that the island, famed for its precious stones and so-called Ratnadipa or 'island of gems', was inhabited by a race of demons, called '*yakkhas*' and '*yakkhinis*' (which could be translated 'demon' and 'demoness'). They were given to luring unwary voyagers ashore and devouring them. As trade inevitably got the better of the unknown terrors of the ocean, these traditional stories end with the worsting of the *yakkhas* and *yakkhinis* by a hero who comes from over the sea.

Against this background the chronicler celebrates a succession of heroes, both religious and secular. His style is in keeping with its extraordinary content. Its language, its repetitions, its address to its audience, all of them recall the tradition of the heroic lay sung by the bard.

The first of the heroic figures whose connection with Ceylon is treated is naturally the Buddha (563–483 B.C.). The chronicle opens with his conquest of Lanka. The theme of the heroic is

34

enunciated in the stories of his three visits to Ceylon. The Buddha comes as conqueror to instil fear into the minds of the *yakkhas*, and to assign them their proper limits. His first visit was both victory and the beginning of a new era of civilization and a new order. The *yakkha*, non-human as he was, was given a definite place among the categories of beings. He was feared and propitiated, but yet accepted as a being who had submitted to the Buddha. He was as real (and still is as real) in the imaginations of the Sinhalese of the fifth century as devils and angels were to medieval Christians.

The second hero celebrated is Vijaya. His name signifies Victorious One. He is a conqueror like the Buddha, but in a very different sense. His story is that of the leader of the first band of Sinhalese to emigrate from India to Ceylon, where like Aeneas in exile from his home he founded a new Troy. The legend probably goes back to the days when a central Indian tribe, of which the lion was the totem, invented a geneaology for themselves.

It tells of a princess of the Vanga country in India of whom it was foretold that she would mate with a lion. 'Very fair was she and very amorous,' according to the chronicle, 'and for shame the king and queen could not suffer her.' Being a young woman of independent spirit she took her own destiny into her hands, disguised herself and joined a caravan travelling into another country. The caravan was attacked by a lion, her companions took flight, but she with regal fortitude followed the tracks of the animal. When she came up with him 'she bethought her of that prophecy of the soothsayers which she had heard, and without fear she caressed him, stroking his limbs'. Unable to withstand this appeal the lion carried her off to his cave where she became his mate. She bore him 'twin-children, a son and a daughter'. The son, whose hands and feet resembled the paws of a lion (*sinha*), was called Sinhabahu, the daughter Sinhasivali. When the boy reached the age of sixteen he tried his strength on the rock with which his lion-father had barred the cave, and proving himself he later escaped with both his mother and his sister. He carried them away, one on the right shoulder and the other on the left.

When they reached a village on the border of the lion's domains they were recognized as being no ordinary fugitives by

35

the miracles which attended their reception by the village folk. The princess, forgetting her lion-husband, married a cousin of hers. In the meantime the lion, missing both his mate and his offspring, ravaged the country until a large reward was offered by the king to anyone who would rid the kingdom of him. Sinhabahu, the son, was twice dissuaded by his mother from undertaking the exploit. When the reward was increased, without waiting to obtain his mother's leave he set out to slay his father.

Three times the undutiful son shot an arrow at his father, but such was the love of the beast for his offspring that the arrow rebounded harmlessly from his forehead. But enraged, as he must understandably have been at these repeated attacks, the lion could not withstand the fourth arrow and was slain. The victorious son, returning to the capital with his father's head, was acclaimed as hero. As the grandson of the king who had just died, he was offered the crown. But he had other ambitions. Installing his mother and her husband in the kingdom of her father as queen, he went off with his sister to the place where he was born, and set himself up there as ruler with his sister as his queen. She bore him 'twin sons sixteen times'. The eldest of these was Vijaya.

The latter grew up a scapegrace prince, angering his father's subjects by his many deeds of violence, until they demanded the young man's death as punishment. Unable to oppose his people's wishes, the king disgraced his son by shaving half his head and the heads of seven hundred of his desperadoes, before he formally exiled them, 'putting them forth upon the sea and their wives and children'. Vijaya tried to establish himself in one haven and failed, because the violence of his followers had set the people there against them. He then set out for Lanka, and landed on the island, on the coppery sands of the shore which stained the palms of himself and his comrades red, on the very day on which the Buddha passed away between the *sal* trees in the grove at Kusinara.

Vijaya, the 'valiant' as the poet called him, was to fare better in Lanka than he ever fared before, because the Buddha as he passed away entrusted him to the care of the king of the gods. He was to be protected and Lanka to which he came was to be under the special surveillance of the latter. It was going to be

36

the home of Buddhism. 'In Lanka, O lord of gods, will my religion be established, therefore carefully protect him with his followers and Lanka.'

The god Upulvan, disguised as a wandering ascetic, met Vijaya and his followers, and wound a charmed thread round their hands to ensure their safety. Not a moment too soon, for one of the *yakkhinis* of the island appeared to the group in the form of a bitch. One of Vijaya's men who argued that the presence of a bitch implied the existence of dogs, a village and human habitations probably, followed her. The bitch led him to her mistress, the *yakkhini* Kuveni. She sat by a pond at the foot of a tree spinning, as a woman-hermit might.

Unable to move because of the spell put upon him by Kuveni, the man was yet able through the power of the god's charmed thread to save himself from being devoured by her. But she seized him and hurled him down a chasm, treating in this way all Vijaya's seven hundred followers who were lured to the pond.

Vijaya, now alone, set out in search of his men. He came to the pond, and noticed that there were footprints of men going into it but not one of a single person coming out. Sure from this momentous deduction that she was no human being but a *yakkhini* who could not resist human blood, he made up his mind quickly. He seized her by the neck and threatened her with death, unless she gave him back his men. She entreated him not to kill her, promising him a kingdom and herself to do with as he wished. Making her swear an oath to keep her promises, he released her. He was conducted by her to the place where his men were safe and unharmed. Here she gave them food, and when Vijaya offered her as guest and equal some of the meal his men had prepared, she assumed the guise of a beautiful sixteen-year-old girl, and made a 'splendid bed, well-covered around with a tent, and adorned with a canopy'. Seeing this 'and looking forward to the time to come', Vijaya took her as his spouse and lay with her on the bed.

Having fulfilled one part of her promise—to do him a woman's service—she likewise kept the other part of her contract and gave him a kingdom, betraying the people of her father's city to Vijaya and his men. She enabled them to slay the *yakkhas* and *yakkhinis* when they were gathered together for a wedding feast,

37

although as demons they were invisible to mortal sight and therefore beyond human power to harm. Through her magic arts she uttered cries, and where they heard the sound of her voice, she instructed Vijaya and his men to strike. Their blows rained on the bodies of the *yakkhas* and *yakkhinis* gathered there and all of them were slain.

So Vijaya was victorious. On the spot where he had landed he founded a city. As he and his followers had come from the country of the king Sinhabahu who had slain the lion, they were called Sinhalas.

Vijaya colonized that part of the land, but he refused to be consecrated as king. In the meantime Kuveni had borne him two children. Vijaya was unwilling to be consecrated or to found a dynasty unless he had a queen of noble birth as his wife. A maiden of a royal house, as well as others for his ministers, were sent for from India, and on their arrival Vijaya parted from Kuveni. He asked her to go away leaving her two children behind. His words to her are worth remembering for the excuse was both incompatibility of temper and sober reasons of state: 'Go thou now, dear one, leaving the two children behind; men are ever in fear of superhuman beings.' The affection of the man for the demoness or sorceress, whom he had loved and who had helped him to power, was overcome by the king's concern for his subjects and the stability of his kingdom. Heroic and legendary adventure had given way to a more prosaic era of nation-building. At such a time it was impossible to add to the strain of living the tensions of insecurity. However, he did ask her to leave the children behind.

Kuveni, in fear of reprisals from *yakkhas* still to be found in other parts of Lanka, if she were deserted by Vijaya, attempted to bribe him with promises of gold. She tried and tried again, failed and went away with her two children to meet the doom she foresaw. She was killed by her own people who mistook her for a spy; her children, saved by an uncle, fled to the mountainous central region and there they lived as husband and wife. From them, according to the chronicle, the wild jungle tribes of Ceylon trace their descent. Like all heroes who grow up into beautiful swans from ugly ducklings, their father Vijaya forsook 'his former evil way of life' and ruled for thirty-eight years over Lanka in peace and righteousness.

For the religious poet there could hardly be human interest in the story he told. In the first place Kuveni was no human being, but a demoness whose instincts led her to destroy human beings. Besides he was not interested in her, but in the founder of the Sinhala race. Among its other attributes the story of Vijaya surely has evidence of the undoubted abilities of the religious to indemnify the hero in advance for his lapses. Vijaya was the instrument of destiny which could not allow the founding father of the island where Buddhism was to be established a *yakkhini* as royal consort. As the primordial ancestor of a line of Sinhalese kings he had to be provided with a wife politically and socially acceptable. This myth of the founder of the line of kings was an article of political faith long after its fabulous events were supposed to have taken place, for we are told of a medieval Sinhalese king who in want of a better title to the crown than any he had to offer, could bolster his claims with reference to his descent from Vijaya.

Other legendary lore held to describe the island of Ceylon is to be found in the *Ramayana*, the Sanskrit epic of the exploits of the hero Rama who used to be an object of worship in the island. It assumed its final form in the fifth century A.D. The story it told of the abduction of Sita by Ravana, the demon king of Lanka, is still well known in Ceylon. Though it has been disputed whether the Lanka referred to in the epic was in fact Ceylon or an island in the mouth of a South Indian river, or whether the whole legend was anything more than a nature myth, the average person, in both India and Ceylon, has no doubt at all that the incidents of the epic are to be connected with the island of Ceylon.

Even at the present day the traveller in Ceylon will be shown places infallibly associated with the legend. Popular etymology has perhaps linked place-names like Sita Eliya with the name of the heroine of the story; the identification of sites described as Ravana's cave, his Asoka garden with places in the island, and such trump cards as the island near Manaar where Hanuman staggered, or the hilltop near Galle which he is reputed to have thrown into position there, have been too strong to have been beaten by higher criticism.

The legend of Rama and Sita, later to be elevated into god and goddess, has not counted for as much in the emotions of the people of Ceylon as that of Vijaya. It was probably not known in the island before A.D. 300. It never received the same religious sanction, the specific Buddhist imprint of the other legend. The *Ramayana*—or that part of it dealing with Sita, her abduction and her rescue—belongs to the consciousness of the Hindu aware of the traditional myths of Hinduism. But as it is Indian and Hindu it enters the consciousness of the people of Ceylon too, irrespective of whether the Lanka of the poem was Ceylon, for into this half-world of myth and legend topography hardly enters.

One of the champions who befriended Rama, Vibhishana, the brother of Ravana, entered the pantheon of Ceylon. He is still worshipped as a guardian deity. He even has a place in the hearts of good Buddhists who know the legends and prize them. He was a god worshipped from ancient times, probably from the pre-Buddhistic era. Later he was believed to have the peculiar power of satisfying his devotees with the gift of offspring, and received poets' recommendations on behalf of royal princesses in need of this boon. That he was not uniformly successful does not appear to have diminished the ardour of his devotees. His statues still stand in the Buddhist fanes of Ceylon.

Repeated in the story of Rama is the victory of the hero from India, a prince upon whom, as on Vijaya, humiliation is placed by his father. He comes to Lanka, is aided by the powerful monkey god and his lieutenant Hanuman, vanquishes the demon-king, and returns home to his own kingdom in India. The best-known features of the story today are of the flight of Ravana from Lanka and back in his aerial chariot; of Sita's desolation as prisoner in Ravana's palace; and of the stratagems of Hanuman who discovered her there. Again in this legend Lanka, the abode of demons, is subjugated by a hero who comes from the mainland of India. But in this case the hero leaves Lanka never to return, though some of the personages in the story were transformed under Buddhist influence into protectors of the island.

With the legends which elaborate the mission of the kinsman of the Indian emperor Asoka to Ceylon we reach another stage, that moment when history begins to emerge from legend. Buddhism which came to Ceylon from its homeland in India was, according to the *Mahavamsa*, first preached in the island by the prince-*bhikkhu* Mahinda, who came bringing salvation to the inhabitants of Lanka. In this case too the mould which had shaped the earlier legends shows traces of its presence. The hero was again victorious, and in consequence of his mission a new order was instituted in Ceylon, the old and the unenlightened having been relinquished.

The strong surface markings of the legends of Ceylon (independent of the *Ramayana*) might now be indicated: the island is both desirable and dangerous; savage beings possessed of magical powers used to destroy human beings who inhabited it; from across the Indian mainland, either by sea or by air, arrives the hero with the special mission; he is victorious; as a result a new dispensation is set up; the island thus is specially blessed or sanctified through the activity of the hero.

If we ask how the mould shaping the legends came into being we would not be far wrong in assuming that it was forged in the troubled times of fifth-century Ceylon. Whatever the earlier form of the legends might have been, the political and social situation of the Ceylon of Mahanama, the poet of the *Mahavamsa*, hammered out its ultimate shape. In it will be felt the hopes and fears of the *bhikkhus* of the Mahavihara at that moment engaged in 'war' with sectarian *bhikkhus*; the wish for a strong king who would at the same time be a champion of orthodoxy and amenable to their control; the remembrance of civil war and invasion only to be withstood by the hero.

Later legend is not as important. The old travellers' tales, from which most legends borrowed something, are seen to be still alive in the array of references to Ceylon to be met with in Arab, Chinese and medieval European records. In all it is the isle of precious stones. To the Arabs it was contiguous with the Garden of Eden, for from its peak Adam took his last look at the terrestrial Paradise he had forfeited. So it came to be known to medieval European travellers as Adam's Peak. The Chinese knew it as the land of Buddhist learning, and through tales of its dangerous old-time inhabitants. Christian friars remembered it as the reputed site of Paradise, distorting the Arab legends.

If Ceylon still turns up, in an age when church-going and hymn-singing are falling into desuetude, in the memories of an older generation of Englishmen as the land where 'every prospect pleases, and only man is vile', then the national honour of

41

the island could be saved by remembering that Bishop Heber who wrote the hymn was speaking neither from personal experience nor from consulting any specific traditional sources. He was propounding conventional dogma about the vileness of human nature in general. To this he casually attached Ceylon because of the myth popular in his time that the potent aroma of its cinnamon was wafted to the traveller approaching its shores. There was not a particle of truth in this belief, as in most of the others referred to here, though it had its uses.

CHAPTER 2

Legend and History—Missionary

In the middle of the third century B.C. history begins to
emerge from tradition and legend. The settlements made by
immigrants from the Indian mainland in the north-west of
Ceylon assumed the character of agricultural communities
under chieftains or rulers who guided the plough themselves.
These communities began to impound water from rivers and
streams for the production of rice, their staple food.

It is the ruler of one of these communities, in his day perhaps
the most important of all others in Indian-colonized Ceylon,
whose name is first connected with history. In his domains one
of the missions sent outside his empire by the Indian monarch
Asoka (269–232 B.C.) achieved the most influential and lasting
results. By comparison with other rulers of ancient India much
is known about the Mauryan emperor Asoka, yet little is clear
about the man and what exactly he believed. From the rock
edicts scattered throughout his range of territories we know
that he was anxious to spread among his subjects and in regions
adjacent to his a *Dhamma* (law) or teaching. Certainly the religion which Mahinda, the son of one of his consorts, brought to
Ceylon was Buddhism.

The stages in the story of the introduction of Buddhism to
Ceylon, as recounted in the *Mahavamsa*, are significant. They
reveal, as the chronicler who described them seven hundred
years after the event intended, the firm outlines of what was one
of the most important single episodes in the whole of Ceylon's
history.

It has to be noted that in the *Mahavamsa* account the knowledge of the teaching of the Buddha was unknown in Ceylon
until it was first preached there by Mahinda, the son (or the
brother) of the emperor Asoka. As in previous accounts of the

43

legendary past of Ceylon, the subordination of fact and probability to the special motive of the chronicle decided everything. In probability Buddhism must long have been known in Ceylon, for there were contacts between the settlers' communities and India where in the fifth and fourth centuries B.C. it spread and had influence. The reason why this was overlooked, or neglected, in the *Mahavamsa* account seems to be clear in the sequence of events recorded, for they indicate that more than the introduction of a new religion to Ceylon is at issue.

The first stage in the story concerns the ruler of Anuradhapura, the capital city founded by a legendary chieftain who captured a *yakkhini* who had assumed the form of a beautiful mare. Aided by her he defeated eight of his uncles in battle, and built himself a new city. In the middle of the third century B.C. his grandson Tissa (250–210 B.C.) was ruler of Anuradhapura. He sent an embassy to the Mauryan emperor Asoka with priceless gifts which were miraculously discovered in his country when he became its head. The embassy returned from Asoka with everything needed for the ceremonial consecration of a king. The dignity of kingship was to be bestowed on the Sinhala ruler.

The second stage of the story is reached when Tissa was consecrated the first king of the Sinhalese according to traditional Indian rites. He had been consecrated before, but these rites were presumably either maimed or insufficient to confer the status of kingship. Whatever the purpose of the second consecration, whether it was the design of Asoka ready to compliment a friendly ruler, or whether it implied a particular relationship between the new kingdom and the Mauryan state, it invested the figure of the man who had sent an embassy to the Mauryan court at Pataliputra with the new and important dignity of royalty. Tissa now came to be known as Devanampiya or 'dear to the gods', a conventional kingly title Asoka had used of himself.

The third stage of the story begins with the message of Asoka which the envoys who consecrated Tissa brought to him: 'I have taken refuge in the Buddha, his doctrine and his Order (the Buddha, the *Dhamma*, and the *Sangha*), I have declared myself a lay-disciple in the religion of the Sakya son; seek then even thou, O best of men, converting thy mind with believing heart, refuge in these best of gems!'

44

In the fourth stage of the story the chronicle relates how Mahinda went on his mission to Ceylon. He had already taken Buddhist vows and was now a *thera* or Elder. He waited till the moment decreed when the king Tissa would be ready to receive the new teaching, and set out for Ceylon accompanied by four *theras*, a *Samanera* or novice and a lay-disciple. He met Tissa, who was out hunting on a hill not far from his capital, Anuradhapura. Mihintale, the traditional place of the meeting of *thera* and king, is now one of the sites of Buddhist pilgrimage in Ceylon. Here Mahinda, having first satisfied himself of the king's ability to understand the Buddha's teaching by testing his powers of intelligence, preached an important Buddhist sermon to him. The king was converted to Buddhism, and he and his retinue declared themselves ready to accept the new religion.

The next stage of the story describes how Mahinda, preaching to gods, court, officials, and common people, secured their adherence to Buddhism. The gods (*devas*) who held the island in their protection were first enlisted. When the *Dhamma* had their acceptance, it was natural that court and people should receive it with equal enthusiasm. With king, gods, court and masses united in their allegiance to Buddhism, the next few stages of the story are instructive.

The king then donated a royal park to Mahinda and his *theras*. Of this gift of the park Bhikkhu Rahula writes: 'This gift expressed in a tangible and visible form the inner religious devotion of the king and assured the material security necessary for the spiritual life of the monks. Mahinda therefore made in public the most important declaration that Buddhism would be established in Ceylon.' The stress, as we shall see, lies in the significance of the word 'established'.

It was in this royal park that the Mahavihara, the seat of the most influential group of *bhikkhus* in Ceylon, was later to be built. Its devotion to Buddhism in Ceylon, the power it was going to wield, through its own members and kings and notabilities who were its benefactors, decided both the actions of kings and the loyalties of Sinhalese in the island. In fact what the Mahavihara decided to celebrate was to become the history of Buddhist Ceylon, or at least as much of that history as is still remembered.

That much was yet to be done is demonstrated by the next

stage in the story. The king asked Mahinda whether Buddhism now 'stood'—whether it was firmly planted in the land. 'Not yet, O ruler of men,' Mahinda replied, 'only O lord of nations when the boundaries are established for the *uposatha* ceremony and the other acts (of religion), according to the command of the Conqueror, shall the doctrine stand.' Within the boundaries would be the residence of the monks where the ceremonies by then traditional in the order—the recitation of the Vinaya, confession of transgression of the rules—could take place at the prescribed times.

At this stage we receive the impression that these sections of the *Mahavamsa* commemorate not the conversion of a king and his subjects to a new religion, but its establishment as the state religion of the kingdom. The importance of this will be examined later; it should be sufficient at this point to quote Bhikkhu Rahula on the conception of Buddhism 'standing' in a particular country—its establishment therein: 'The idea of the "establishment" of Buddhism in a given geographical unit with its implications is quite foreign to the teaching of the Buddha. Such a thing was never expressed by the Master. True it is that the Buddha sent forth his disciples to go about in the world preaching the dhamma for the "good of the many". But nowhere had he given injunctions or instructions regarding a ritual or a particular method of "establishing" the Sasana in a country. Buddhism is purely a personal religion. Once a man realizes the Truth, Buddhism is established in him. Thus, Punna, one of Buddha's own disciples, goes to his home in Sunaparanta—a morally backward country, notorious for its wicked people—and converts a large number of them to Buddhism. . . . But there is no talk at all about the "establishment" of the Sasana there.'

The word *Sasana* is worth dwelling on. Bhikkhu Rahula writes: 'The word literally means "doctrine", "teaching", "message", "order". But to the ordinary man in Ceylon it means "the Buddhist religion with its institutions, monasteries, monuments, the *sangha*, beliefs, customs, ceremonies, etc." Of course the teaching of the Buddha is included too. The majority of people in Ceylon use the words *sasana* or *Buddha-sasana* and *agama* (religion) or *Buddha-agama* as synonymous.'

Whether the establishment of the *sasana* (whatever its wide

46

range of connotations covered) was unusual, or a new departure, the trend of the narrative in the chronicle indicates that
this was intended. The king, as the story continues, insisted that
the boundaries for the monastery where the few rites of the
sangha could take place should be established forthwith, and that
they should take in the city too, for he was determined to 'abide
under the Buddha's command'. This was done, the king himself guiding the plough which furrowed the future boundaries.

What yet remained to be done, according to the *Mahavamsa*
account, was the provision of relics and a branch of the Bodhi
tree beneath which the Buddha had attained enlightenment for
the veneration of king and people. These were sent to Ceylon
from India, Mahinda's sister bringing with her a branch of the
sacred tree which was planted with great ceremony in an enclosure specially prepared for its reception. With her arrival in the
island an order of *bhikkhunis* (female *bhikkhus*) was instituted.

When Mahinda died in Ceylon sixty years after he had been
ordained a *bhikkhu*, it could be said that everything required
for an institutionalized religion in a country had been provided:
a ruler formally and ceremonially crowned head of the country
who voluntarily and intelligently accepts the religion; various
grades of its people, not forgetting its supernatural protectors,
who likewise willingly accept the new teaching; an organization
identified with the religion vested by the king with property and
holding it by right; the symbolical acknowledgement of the
authority of the new institution in the inclusion of the royal
capital in its boundaries; specific objects of worship imported
into the country making it self-sufficient for the religious devotion of the masses.

What is implicit in the *Mahavamsa* is straightforwardly expressed in a commentary contemporary with it. This text of the
fifth century A.D., the *Samantapasadika*, gives another account of
how Mahinda answered the king when he was asked whether
Buddhism was firmly established in Lanka. Mahinda is reported
to have said that the religion was established, but that its roots
had not as yet gone deep. To the further question of the king,
'When will the roots go deep?' Mahinda replied: 'When a son
born in Ceylon of Ceylonese parents becomes a monk in Ceylon,
studies the Vinaya in Ceylon, and recites it in Ceylon, then the
roots of the Sasana are deep set.'

This statement throws light on what its fifth-century proponents in Ceylon thought of Buddhism. The remark attributed to Mahinda in the commentary is impregnated with strong nationalist sentiment. The sign of the permanence of the religion is given in the initiation of a religious order composed of the nationals of the country. To the writer of the commentary what was important, in this connection, was neither king nor people, but the hierarchy drawn from the 'native sons' of the country. The tests applied of the strength of a religion may have been unsatisfactory, or even invalid, but in fact the effectiveness of Buddhism in Ceylon was to be proved by the power of the *sangha*, recruited from the people, and performing the rites and ceremonies associated with the order, in the language of the country perhaps, for according to tradition Mahinda brought the sacred books of the Buddhists with him and had them translated into Sinhalese.

There is a distinction to be drawn between what Buddhism must have meant to a learned *bhikkhu* in the fifth century A.D. and the conditions requisite for its strong foundation in Ceylon. Of this the fifth-century commentator must have been aware. Even so, the impression left by this story is of a religion valued because of its identification with an institution like the *sangha* which had to have a national character. The general tendency of this story in the *Samantapasadika* is further clarified when it goes on to relate that the king's nephew, who was a minister of state, was selected for the task of reciting the Vinaya. It is unwise to read too much into this episode, but it would seem that the sign demanded was unmistakably provided.

Mahinda's answer to the king in the *Samantapasadika* story might be read as a clear indication of the stranger's desire to refuse any special rights for himself, or for any of those who had come with him as envoys of Buddhism to Ceylon. But at no stage in the *Mahavamsa* account had Mahinda been thought of as stranger. He was to Tissa the son of his dear friend, the emperor Asoka; to both king and people he was a man of great sanctity, almost a miracle worker. His statement, as a later age framed it for him, could scarcely have been due to a wish to prevent misunderstandings from arising, but to the commentator's clear understanding of the particular position of Buddhism in Ceylon at his own time. It should be read as an emotionally charged statement of what had perhaps become a political necessity by the fifth century A.D. What Mahinda's intentions may have been we can only guess. He had come as the evangel of a new religion in which the ruler of a kingdom in the island of Ceylon was to take refuge with his people. He did everything to propagate the religion he was commemorated as having preached there for the first time on the full moon day of June. The conditions requisite for its taking deep root in the island would have been easier for a later age to judge, so that whether the story of his insistence on the necessity for a native of the island to perform the duties of a *bhikkhu* was genuine or not, it does reflect the demands of an age when the early stages of missionary zeal and conversion were long past, when what was important was not a message which its hearer had to understand, but institutionalized religion which had left its mark on the history of the island for over seven hundred years.

The *Mahavamsa* story, the commentary's elaboration of one detail of it, may yield interpretations different from those suggested here. But to many Buddhists in contemporary Ceylon, whether they have considered either *Mahavamsa* or *Samanta-pasadika* comment on it, it would appear that the test of the *Sasana* in the country—however that word of multifarious meanings is glossed—is its official status as institution identified with the *sangha*, patronized by the state and patronizing it. The records of 1,500 years ago are not the dead hand of the past, they are the voice of the living present.

Where is the importance of the Buddhist connection with the Sinhalese kingdom to be sought? One might indeed ask where is it not to be found. Will it be discovered in the difference made by a system of thought and attitude to life to the thought and attitudes of the Sinhalese? Is there a specific Buddhist attitude to life—the result of professing acceptance of the religious system and even imperfect practice of its ethical code—which distinguishes the Buddhist in Ceylon from the adherents of other religions there, and from Buddhists elsewhere in South-East Asia? It would be only slightly less exacting to attempt to describe the attitude to life of Buddhists in Ceylon, as it has developed in the changes of over two millennia. Even this undertaking, much beyond the scope of this book, must be of questionable utility, for so many factors converge to produce the uncertain quantity of an attitude to life that it would be difficult to isolate one and pick out its connections. Besides there is a necessary distinction to be drawn between the attitude of Buddhists, which may not differ from that of Christians or Moslems, and a Buddhist attitude in whichever way this is to be computed. It would be better to leave this subject mined with traps for the unwary, and to consider what difference was made historically by Buddhism to the story of Ceylon.

It made no revolutionary change, because it absorbed and found a place for older attitudes to life already established. No new religion cuts itself off from contact with the older religion it replaces or absorbs, even with what might be abhorrent to it in the old. This is as great a platitude as the observation that organized religion can ingest whatever seems useful to its continuance, even what is antipathetic to its original ideas. There were already in Ceylon large areas of belief tilled by the practitioners of cults. These continued to be cultivated. A religion like Buddhism which valued the understanding individual's self-cultivation as the greatest good, would accept what the individual needed for his daily life, and would not interfere with what was in effect a less significant sphere than that of the understanding. Perhaps the tolerance of Buddhism was its most revolutionary feature.

According to Buddhist tradition, the old animistic gods of tree, river, rock, and the powerful spirits of the demon world whom the Buddha had quelled, accepted his domination and remained in submission to him. They were tolerated so much that they were allowed to retain some of their powers. Theirs, in popular belief, was an *imperium in imperio*. The Buddha himself emphatically rejected the practice of paying the old deities honour or of propitiating them with sacrifices. But as they persisted in countryside and town, the priests of the miscellaneous array of devils continued to exercise their functions. In time divided allegiance to the Buddha, the *sangha*, and to the denizens of the spirit world was established. There are sites in Ceylon today which testify to the transformation of ancient animistic belief by Buddhist legend—the most important being the peak now held sacred because the Buddha was held to have left his footprint on it. There are cults which took over a specious colouring of Buddhism in their jargon and in their reverent docility to the sacred texts. They existed side by side with Buddhism, and are still practised.

Against the inroads of spirits, powerful to harm human beings even though they were once subjugated by the Buddha, there is help offered not specifically by Buddhism, but by the various grades of shamans and exorcists who are Buddhist. This vast tribe, differentiated by their functions into exorcists, charmers, and dancers, has a definite place in the community which may know of the Buddha's opinion of them, but which is in need of their ministrations. It would be wrong to believe that the exorcist's 'skills' are valued only by the ignorant or the lower classes. His sway extends over practically all, Christians not excepted. Wirz, who studied exorcistic rites and practices in Ceylon not long ago, observed the strength of the belief in the physical reality of demons. 'This', he remarked, 'is the explanation of the unshakeable confidence of the natives (and also of some Europeans!) in the beneficial effects of the various ceremonies.' If it is true that even 'some Europeans' are susceptible to the age-old belief, then the potency of the old gods will be granted. The exorcist, though he is not socially estimable, has his own spheres of influence. It would be false to claim that he is as influential as the *bhikkhu* in the life of the Buddhist, but he certainly seems to touch the life of the community at more points than the *bhikkhu*.

Nor did Buddhism attack the institution of caste as it existed in Ceylon. The Buddha himself recognized no differences of caste and social occupation among his lay followers or in the *sangha*. More important to him than one's place in the existing social order was the need of the human being to strive through understanding to release himself from the bondage of birth and death and rebirth. It has been claimed—and denied, too—that the impulse behind the Buddha's teaching was the revolt of the Kshatriya against the power of the Brahmin. Whether this was so, or not, the tendency of Buddhism was to deny the special rights of any group to decide for the individual what only he himself could attain through the use of his own faculties and intelligence. As this was so, there could be no special place or rights attributed to caste in Buddhism. But in the same way as older beliefs were absorbed in the new, once they had been relegated to a subsidiary position, so too with caste. Though caste remained, the influence of Buddhism rendered it less rigid in its divisions and less conscious of itself. But it persisted nevertheless. It even crept into the *sangha*.

It should not be forgotten, finally, that the Theravada Buddhism of Ceylon has been little susceptible to development as a highly structured organization, which takes up in detail the lives of laymen and the religions, enforcing on them an obligatory code. The ease with which the robes of a *bhikkhu* can be donned, and then cast away, has often been commented upon by writers on Buddhism. Mendicancy, which distinguished the *bhikkhu*, was in the course of time given up for a settled life in an establishment resembling those of the Christian monastic orders, where his needs were looked after by lay patrons or administrators of the revenues of the *sangha*. Besides, the *bhikkhu* was not really monk, nor officiating priest. The traditional rules with their insistence on a simple code of conduct left to his devoutness how he should live a life contained within the framework of poverty, celibacy and meditation. Buddhism has hardly any ceremonial as such either for the *bhikkhu* or for the pious layman. On both were cast the sole duty of trying to free themselves from the chain of existence.

The first Sinhalese convert to Buddhism, according to the *Mahavamsa*, was the king, and he freely placed himself under the direction and control of the *sangha*, undertaking to protect and support it. The first *bhikkhu* to visit Ceylon was Mahinda, and he carried out his task of ensuring that Buddhism 'stood' in the land, satisfying the desire of the king that his capital city and himself should be included in the boundaries of the dwelling of the *bhikkhus*.

Apart from its political import, Buddhism placed the small communities of Ceylon and its Sinhala kingdom, through its establishment as the religion of the state, in the main stream of the Buddhist culture of India and of the kingdoms overseas to which the new religion went. For close upon a millennium after the time of Asoka two strong currents in Indian culture were those of Buddhist intellectual studies and the artistic tradition transformed by the demands of the religion for monuments and shrines. Without Buddhism there would have been no such development of architecture, of sculpture, of language and literature as distinguished these forms in Ceylon. Scholars who travelled about the Eastern world, spreading the knowledge of Buddhism and in search of it, schools of sectaries who disputed points of interpretation, artists and sculptors working for courts bent on honouring the relics of the Buddha and of venerable members of the order, the example of kings who were patrons of the teaching and memorable builders of monasteries and temples—all these were not without their effect on Ceylon. It may be said that, as the Sinhala kingdom developed, there was hardly anything in the lives and interests of its people which lay outside areas partially reclaimed from ancient superstition and resettled by Buddhism.

To the great mass of men and women in the Sinhala kingdom, unaware of the philosophy of the religion they professed, Buddhism brought the knowledge and example of a great teacher who was venerated. The stories of his previous births became part of the folk tradition, the recommendation of an ideal of austerity and the contemplative life, of the duties of giving to the *sangha*, and of tolerance must have been sensed, however imperfectly they were practised. Religion, whatever its articles of faith or its philosophical basis, is grasped by those who accept what it is believed to afford as a relief from the complications of life in a world which is too much for all of us. In this sense it is, as Marx described it, 'the sigh of the hard-pressed creature, the heart of a heartless world, the soul of soulless circumstances . . . the opiate of the people'. It was in Ceylon, no less than elsewhere, the medicament for the ills of the world offered by a Great Physician.

The religion had been established in the Sinhala kingdom, then synonymous with Ceylon. The next step was the provision of a national hero. As always gods give place to heroes, and from them it is an easy stage to the figures of history in whom the ancient god-like lineaments could be perceived. The three figures so far accorded heroic status in the *Mahavamsa* were conquerors in realms some distance away from the common-places of daily living. The Buddha and Mahinda were as persons so extraordinary and removed from the generality of men, that even those who knew of them as teachers could scarcely refrain from giving them the veneration reserved for the gods. As for Vijaya, he was conqueror too, but he inhabited a shadowy realm, and was important not on his own account but as the part of a larger design. The kingdom which came into existence to have its religion established had no national hero. This was soon to be supplied.

CHAPTER 3

History and Legend—Warrior King

The story of the introduction of Buddhism into Ceylon, it has been suggested, is the record of the establishment of the state religion of the Sinhalese. One strand of special significance in the net of miracles and wonders woven round the cutting of the branch of the *Bo* tree (*ficus religiosa*), its despatch to Ceylon and its reception there, is the *Mahavamsa* statement: 'The king of Lanka, worshipped it (the tree) by (bestowing on it) the kingship of Lanka.' Kings of Ceylon were to honour the *sangha* and the religion by bestowing on them the kingdom and lands. One king went so far as to bestow his queen on the *sangha*. These were symbolic gestures. Their prototype is here, in Devanampiya Tissa's bestowal of the kingdom on the tree which represented the religion.

A specific relationship was here instituted between religion and state. Whatever interpretation is placed upon this gift, there has existed in the mind of Buddhists since then the conviction vaguely defined, but none the less certain, of the identification of the state with the religion, and the maintenance of the latter as the most important factor of the strength and wellbeing of both. It is likely that the *Mahavamsa* brought into being what its own time wished to produce. It could be said therefore that what the fifth century A.D. demanded has been vouched for by more than 1,500 years of the recorded history of the Sinhalese as an emotional article of belief. It still remains the strongest reagent in the emotions of Sinhalese Buddhists.

The major subject in the account of the founding of the religion in the Sinhala kingdom is given its necessary development in the story of the warrior king to whom the identification of nation with religion was natural. There can be no misunderstanding of this: Dutugemunu, the national hero, is not a

55

mythical figure. He belongs to history, his existence as an historical figure is attested by much more than the chronicle provides. But he lives in the minds and hearts of the Sinhalese through the chronicle. Try to discover him outside it, and at best he is a shadowy reality. But in the reflected glory of the *Mahavamsa* he is a luminous personage. In it he is hero, the legendary warrior who gives to the land with its special myth of election as the stronghold of Buddhism its national hero.

In his story will be found two important elements: the arrival of the Sinhala kingdom of Ceylon at maturity—in the picturesque phrase 'the king raised his umbrella over the whole land'; and the dependence of this on the religion in whose name the hero conquered.

Before his story is taken up, it is necessary to try to recall in the broadest outlines the Ceylon of the third century B.C., in which the Sinhala kingdom of the northern and central plain —the region known as Rajarata—had become a Buddhist kingdom. From it Buddhism had spread to other parts of the island, where there were other kingdoms, Ruhuna in the south being the most important. That the years following upon the reign of Devanampiya Tissa were a period of comparative prosperity would be borne out by the edifices which accompanied the establishment of Buddhism as official religion—the building of viharas both at Anuradhapura and Mihintale. Another conspicuous sign of the economic well-being of the kingdom would be the beginnings of public works necessary to the life of expanding agricultural communities—the reservoirs (or tanks as they came to be called), from which the village cultivator drew water. The first of what was later to be a finely engineered system of irrigation works, the Tissavava, was begun by King Tissa himself. In the next century population had obviously grown, it had spread south and west from the regions originally colonized.

That there were connections with the kingdoms of the Indian mainland has already been made clear. Sinhala kings had sought brides from the South Indian kingdoms; Devanampiya Tissa bore a title which resembled that of the Mauryan emperor, Asoka, whose suzerainty he probably acknowledged. Trade along the coast kept Ceylon and India in close contact. What is more, new waves of soldiers and traders, from the south of India this time, were bringing into conflict the older settlers and the new.

So far in the *Mahavamsa* references to the Indian mainland are to the country adjacent to Ceylon. Various regions and their rulers are mentioned, but nowhere is the impression left of any difference between island and mainland except as areas distant one from the other. Indian towns such as Pataliputra and Supparaka are referred to in the chronicle as parts of the one world to which Ceylon belonged. The first reference to a group of peoples described as Dravidian through the word *Damilas* (Skt. Dravida), from which the present-day Sinhalese word for the Tamils is derived, is in connection with Sena and Guttika, the sons of 'a freighter who brought horses hither'. The *Mahavamsa* records that they conquered the Sinhala king and reigned (both together) 'twenty-two years justly'. A similar comment is made on the second Tamil ruler of the Sinhala kingdom Elara: 'A Damila, of noble descent, Elara, who came hither from the Cola-country to seize on the kingdom, ruled when he had overpowered King Asela (the Sinhala monarch), forty-four years, with even justice toward friend and foe, on occasions of disputes at law.' The word *Damila*, a generic term for any inhabitant of the South Indian kingdoms as distinct from the trans-Vindhyan Aryan country, soon becomes an epithet for the hereditary foes of the Sinhalese. To fact myth adds its emotive ingredients, and the idea of a Sinhalese nation is defined through the contrast with groups with which the Sinhala kingdom was linked, geographically, culturally and politically.

It was once claimed for the Tamils that theirs was the culture responsible for the civilization whose traces were excavated at Mohenjo-Daro and Harappa. Such claims are discounted now, but the historicity of the people who lived in the south of the Indian peninsula as a cultural unit different from their neighbours in Aryavarta, and their virility as a group of peoples, have never been denied. That inhabitants of their various kingdoms were known in Ceylon before the second century B.C. and had made settlements there, as colonists from Aryavarta had done, is not unlikely. But there are no records extant of their having been an important political force in Ceylon before that time. They were venturous seamen and traders. They are likely therefore to have sailed along the northern coasts of Ceylon and established trading posts. The recent *History of Ceylon* published by the University of Ceylon points out that 'the names of the first Dravidians mentioned in the chronicles as well as those whose names features in the Brahmi inscriptions of Ceylon are of persons who either came from a Dravidian pocket in Aryan country, or who had come under Aryan influence before they had moved south'. What is significant for the future development of the story of Ceylon is not where these Damilas came from, or whether they were in the island before the Sinhalas or arrived there after them, but the likelihood that both they and the Sinhalas had been living together in the island for some little time before the Tamils were cast for the role of hostile stranger against whom the national consciousness of the Sinhalese was whetted. The scholar, wary of the ground on which he treads, acknowledges that 'it thus seems not unlikely that the Tamils were not strangers to the Sinhalese before both encountered each other as friends or foes in this island'. The two groups of peoples who met either on the mainland or in Ceylon were bound with many ties to each other, but tradition and legend lent their creative powers to a history of warfare between them and dramatized the conflicts of small kingdoms as an antinomy. And those who have moulded history, or tried to, in the course of centuries have been only too ready to borrow from myth and legend in shaping their artifact.

By the fifth century A.D. the Sinhala kingdom, involved in the struggles of rival clans disputing for the throne, had been embroiled in the strife between South Indian kingdoms, mercenaries from there being enlisted to fight in the island. Episodes in history made the term *Damila* synonymous with the hereditary enemies of the Sinhalas. What was overlooked, but what must have been general in the seven hundred years between the establishment of Buddhism in the country and the writing of the *Mahavamsa*, was that over large tracts of the northern plain Tamil and Sinhalese must have been indistinguishable from each other. In these years there were Tamil rulers who had been patrons of Buddhism, then flourishing in South India. Brahmins were officials in the court of Sinhala kings, and the gods of the Hindu pantheon were respected by Hindu and Buddhist alike. The complicated history of the two millennia dealt with by the *Mahavamsa* and its continuation the *Culavamsa* up to the arrival

58

of the Portuguese in Ceylon in the sixteenth century A.D. apparently yields no clue to the vagaries of internecine warfare between Sinhalese and invaders from South India. The record is relieved from time to time by the reigns of kings in Ceylon powerful enough to secure unity at home and even to carry successful war across the strait to India. If the theme is the ancient epical motive of celebrating the small kingdom struggling to preserve its identity, then it would be difficult to see the Tamils (or any of the marauding bands who crossed from mainland to island) as anything but the irreconcilable opposite of the Sinhalese.

But this clue disregards the most familiar paths even if they are not traced in history or tradition. It places the observer so firmly in Ceylon that his gaze is directed away from the most obvious of happenings just around him. If he looked again, perhaps what is a tangle from his selected point of view or the foreshortened outlines of the foreground of the Pali chronicle, falls into place as a temporary phase in the history of Indian kingdoms, each belonging to the common culture they shared. One of them, however, geographically separated from the rest, is enabled to develop in some ways differently from the others, though all of them were devoted to what seems, at the present time, an uncharacteristic activity of South Indian peoples—aggressive warfare with each other. Legend made the temporary permanent, it assured it of that typical repetitiveness which is one of the catastrophes of history.

It would seem that the by-product of the turbulence of South Indian politics at times when the extraordinary vigour of its Dravidian peoples could not be contained within the framework of South India becomes the means by which the significance of Buddhist Ceylon is the more sharply differentiated. At these moments language, religion and race, unstressed at other times, seize the body politic and convulse it. It is an exaggeration to state that if the national enemy is not available to the myth-maker he is invented. The Dravidian was not invented. He was there. He could be felt either as intruder or as threat of future intrusion. South Indian armies ravaged the northern plain several times in the first two thousand years of Ceylon's history. It would seem that these fires have not as yet died down.

The story of Dutugemunu is an important part of the story of
Ceylon. Basically he is the first king through whom the *gloire* of
the Sinhalese nation is expressed. Vijaya as founder of the race,
and Devanampiya Tissa as saintlike figure who fulfilled its
Messianic prophecy establishing the *Dhamma* in Ceylon, have
none of the characteristics of epical heroism and martial prowess
which belong to Dutugemunu. Those sections of the *Mahavamsa*
which tell his story are epic.

Having praised the justice of Elara, the Tamil king, and
attributed it and his miraculous powers to his abstention from
walking in the path of evil in spite of his false beliefs, the
chronicle asks the rhetorical question: 'How should not then an
understanding man, established in pure belief, renounce here
the guilt of walking in the path of evil?' The statement that
Dutugemunu became king when he had slain Elara is ostentatiously interrupted, and there follows the saga of the Sinhalese
king—his ancestry, his birth, childhood, his triumphant war
against the *Damilas*, his slaying of Elara, and his devotion to
Buddhism.

The legendary accompaniments of this story of the king of
the second century B.C. are very well known to anyone at all
who has lived in Ceylon and has been interested in its peoples.
In it have been invested, quite naturally by the Sinhalese,
emotions of pride in the national hero and spirited self-satisfac-
tion and confidence in the regenerative powers of the race. In
addition to its interest as a story of dedicated adventure, with
its champions who assisted the young prince in his battle
against odds, it has the strong attraction of the tale of a young
man devoted to his mother and loved by her. He set himself up
against his father, and earned the reproach of being undutiful,
but none the less he triumphed, helped by his mother when his
father was dead and he came into his own. There is in the story
the perennial interest of the figure with whom the young man
can identify himself, much more strongly than in the story of
Vijaya, who likewise redeems a scapegrace youth by his eventual
success. This is the story of a young man whose lapse, if lapse it
was, was the consequence of his patriotism and was justified by it.

His mother, Vihara Maha Devi, was a princess from the kingdom of Kelaniya. She was set adrift in a boat in order to appease
the wrath of the sea-gods intent on punishing her father for an

offence done to an innocent *thera*. The golden boat carrying her came ashore on the southern coasts where she was found by the king who made her his queen. For many years the queen, who was a devout Buddhist, bore her husband no child as she wished to, until a novice whom she had tended during his last illness was persuaded by her to utter the pious wish that at his death he should be reborn as her son. (In Buddhist belief such wishes fervently uttered are realized.) The novice passed away, returning to life in the womb of the queen. So to the hero were given a mother miraculously preserved from the waters of the sea and, against its currents, brought to the shores of the southern kingdom, and a birth that partook of the miraculous too. The story of Dutugemunu is the story of both warrior and the incarnation of a Buddhist novice. The *sangha* at his birth prophesied for him the kingship of the whole of Lanka and the glorification of Buddhism in Ceylon.

A second son was born to the queen and her husband, but his birth was unmarked by any of the wonders attending that of his brother. When the ceremony of feeding the two children with their first meal of rice took place, the king submitted both to the test of being able to digest their meal only if they would uphold the doctrine of the Buddha. Later, when Gemunu, as his name was then, was twelve years old, the king placed three portions of rice before his sons, enjoining them to eat, swearing as they ate the first that they would never turn away from the *sangha*, and as they ate the second that they would live together in amity. This they did. The king then asked them to eat the third portion of rice, asking them as they ate it to swear that they would never fight against the *Damilas* (who ruled the north). Both boys refused, flinging the rice away. Gemunu went to his bed on which he curled himself up, hands and feet drawn in, because, as he explained to his mother who asked him why he did not stretch himself out and lie in comfort, on one side of him was the river which was the boundary of the Tamil country and on the other the great ocean.

When he was sixteen Gemunu had gathered a band of champions round him and was determined to attack the Tamils. His father, however, forbade him to do anything of the kind. In exasperation and with the intention of twitting his father with cowardice, Gemunu sent him a woman's ornament to wear.

For this unfilial act he was from that time known as Dutugemunu, Gemunu the wrathful, who was so enraged against
his father that he failed to respect him. The son fled to the hill
country to escape his father's anger, and emerged from hiding
only on his father's death. He had himself declared king, but
his brother Tissa, who had seized the queen and the state
elephant, refused to hand them back to Dutugemunu. War followed between the two brothers. Only the intervention of a
thera put an end to what might have become a fratricidal
struggle. Dutugemunu's words to the *thera* are illuminating. He
assured the priest that even though he was king he was still the
servant of the *sangha*, for which he expressed his great veneration in the remark that, if even a seven-year-old novice had
been sent to his brother and himself, there would never have
been enmity between them, and everything would have ended
without the loss of life. The *thera* acknowledged the guilt of the
sangha in not having made peace between the brothers, and
expiated for its guilt by acceding to Dutugemunu's request that
bhikkhus should accompany his army in its campaign against the
Tamils. In his message to the order Dutugemunu described the
war he had undertaken as one intended to bring 'glory to the
doctrine'. He had a relic of the Buddha let into his spear, so
that his was, as the *Mahavamsa* treats it, a holy war. Five hundred *bhikkhus* accompanied the army. His mother, too, shared
the rigours of the field, and on one occasion used her wiles to
outwit a *Damila* general.

The story of Dutugemunu's march from the south over the
Mahaveliganga until he defeated his enemies one by one, and
faced the Tamil king Elara in single combat, is an epical
episode which must have given the pious the serene joy of con-
templating the success which rewards the good man mindful of
his duty to the religion and to the *sangha*. Elara fell pierced by
his rival's dart, and Dutugemunu, the undutiful son who had
expiated his guilt, marched into Anuradhapura and united
Lanka under the one royal umbrella. He celebrated the funeral
rites of his defeated enemy, and decreed that no one, not even
princes of the land, should pass by the monument marking the
site of his cremation without doing honour to the Tamil king.
The chronicle noted that 'even to this day princes of Lanka,
when they draw near to this place, are wont to silence their

music because of this honour'. Though this has since been noted by almost every single writer on ancient Ceylon, time has dealt harshly with Elara's monument. It has disappeared, and perhaps the back garden of a government medical officer's residence now contains all that is left of it.

Is it fair to read between the lines of Dutugemunu's story the disquiet of a man who suffered from an excessive sense of his guilt for his aggression, of which his public derision of his father was only one symptom? Earlier he had, like his brother, refused to comply with his father's wishes to live in peace with the Tamils, and shortly after, as he lay in bed, he had been comforted by his mother. Since that time he had, after his father's death and breaking the oath he had sworn, been drawn into war with his younger brother, coming out of it with the feeling that all the bloodshed might have been spared if only the *sangha* had intervened. On that occasion it had accepted the role of the guilty party. Now after his victory and the conquest of the whole of Lanka in which thirty-two Tamil kings had been defeated and slain, the *Mahavamsa* pictures him as taking no joy in his victory, 'remembering that thereby was wrought the destruction of millions (of beings)'.

Once again religion was at hand to lighten the burden of guilt which pressed on the king. The passage is interesting as a record of the consciousness of the interdependence of 'church' and state: 'Sitting then on the terrace of the royal palace . . . he, looking back on his glorious victory, great though it was, knew no joy, remembering that thereby was wrought the destruction of millions (of beings). When the arahants in Piyangudipa knew his thought they sent eight arahants to comfort the king. And they, coming in the middle watch of the night, alighted at the palace-gate. Making known that they were come thither through the air they mounted to the terrace of the palace. The great king greeted them . . . he asked the reason of their coming. "We are sent by the brotherhood at Piyangudipa to comfort thee, O lord of men." And thereon the king said again to them: "How shall there be any comfort for me, O venerable sirs, since by me was caused the slaughter of a great host numbering millions?"

' "From this deed arises no hindrance in thy way to heaven. Only one and a half human beings have been slain here by

63

thee, O lord of men. The one had come unto the (three) refuges; the other had taken on himself the five precepts. Unbelievers and men of evil life were the rest, not more to be esteemed than beasts. But as for thee, thou wilt bring glory to the doctrine of the Buddha in manifold ways; therefore cast away care from thy heart, O ruler of men!'' Thus exhorted by them the great king took comfort.'

(An arahant is a being no longer subject to re-birth. In the numbers of those slain were only one person who happened to be a Buddhist (who 'had come unto the (three) refuges'), and another reckoned as being half-way on the path (who had 'taken on himself the five precepts'.)

If the political power was an instrument of religion, then if ever it needed justification, religion was at hand to provide it. The distance travelled between the teaching of the Buddha as it was recorded after his death and the justification of a holy war was great, but the point reached is a familiar outpost of all times.

The rest of the king's life was devoted to works of piety, the building of *stupas* and edifices for the *sangha*. One of his monuments, the Mirisavetti Dagaba, was built because of his remorse that he had not shared a dish of peppers he had eaten with the *sangha*. He died before the greatest of his *stupas* was completed. This was the Mahathupa or the Ruvanvelisaya (as it is known today), which marked the precincts of the Mahavihara, the home of the *bhikkhus* of the *Mahavamsa*.

Bhikkhu Rahula sees Dutugemunu's war as a 'great crusade to liberate Buddhism from foreign rule. His war-cry was "Not for kingdom but for Buddhism". The entire Sinhalese race was united under the banner of the young Gamini. This was the beginning of nationalism among the Sinhalese. It was a new race with healthy young blood, organized under the new order of Buddhism. A kind of religio-nationalism, which almost amounted to fanaticism, roused the whole Sinhalese people. A non-Buddhist was not regarded as a human being. Evidently all Sinhalese without exception were Buddhists.'

It is worth remembering this assessment of the career of Dutugemunu by a scholar who is himself a *bhikkhu*. Nationalism in the East has long been regarded as the twentieth-century acceptance of an outdated Western mode, the result of the heady intoxication which followed upon draughts of western European political thinkers. It would seem that it was known in Ceylon two thousand years ago. The myth which made religion expedient and sanctified politics becomes a fact of history.

Historically the Sinhala kingdom was saved from being drawn into the orbit of one of the South Indian kingdoms by its own exertions first of all, and then by the inability of these kingdoms to stand up against Islam and, later, the Portuguese. Nearly one thousand seven hundred years passed between the time of Dutugemunu and the arrival of the Portuguese in Eastern waters. Long before that time it was clear that South India could no more threaten the integrity of Ceylon. As for the Tamil kingdom of the north, it was one of the entities into which the political power of the old Sinhala kingdom had disintegrated. Continual fighting took place between these kingdoms, and we shall see how the rulers of one kingdom invoked foreign aid against their kinsmen of another. Against the kingdom of Jaffnapatam (as the kingdom of the north was known) and all those people of Dravidian origin over which it held sway, a special quality of hostility could be elicited.

That this attitude is still alive and nourishes strong emotions cannot be doubted. Myth and tradition have reinforced fact, and nothing has gainsaid its strength. Could anything have prevailed against this subtle combination of fact and legend? There are in Sinhalese and Pali literature epics similar to the *Mahavamsa*, stories celebrating lines of kings, the fortunes of a relic and the annals of the island. But there are no tragedies in either literature. Even if this dramatic form had been known to the ancient Sinhalese, there are no extant examples. Had it been known, would things have been different? Would the myth derived from an epic have lost some of its intensity, if the same material had been taken up in a form like tragedy, which sees the human being pitted against either the limits of his own humanity or what the gods had assigned him as his proper field of activity? Tragedy, much more readily than epic, would have admitted another point of view, an attitude even faintly critical of epic's tendency to accept and to glorify. It would certainly have allowed opposition to orthodoxy of opinion to have expressed itself. In seeking some understanding or resolution between the consciousness of human energies and the inadequa-

E   65

cies of humanity, it would have forced the simplicities of epic's raw division of men into heroes and beings not fit to be thought of as human into more reasonable shapes. Tragedy sometimes evades the conclusion it seems to be drawing. It has often plumped for justifications as crude as that offered to Dutuge-munu by the eight *arahants* from Piyangudipa. But through the free play it gives to the spirit of questioning and to criticism of the accepted values of the audience, it prevents dogma from settling like a blight on the imagination. The reality of ancient Ceylon owes most to literature. Whatever the reality may have been, the one picture provided has been that of epic. Impressive though that picture may be, its lack of shading and the hard masses of its two tones are sometimes wearying.

In actual fact there were as many schisms and breaks between Church and State in medieval Europe as between *sangha* and the rulers of the Sinhala kingdom. Some kings upheld heterodox views and regarded themselves as gods. Sectarian *bhikkhus* persecuted the orthodox and were persecuted by them with a vigour which recalls the Inquisition, and among the laity there were followers of rival schools involved in the strife of their betters. But the form in which the chronicle of the Sinhalese kings and the religion is composed, admitted these things only on its own terms, denying them the importance which other evidence gives them. They are mentioned only to be dismissed as doctrinal error, never is a case for them imagined possible. With mind made up the chronicle records the distresses of the orthodox and their final vindication. As a result an important part of the life and belief of the times fails to appear. A sophisticated dramatic form like tragedy may have included it. If it could have done that, the epic would not have had the power, as it seems to have, to inhibit thinking and to hold fast in the moulds of several centuries ago the attitudes of many people living today.

CHAPTER 4

The Shaping of History

By the fifth century A.D. the form and pressure of the age
had left its mark on the chronicler's story of Ceylon. Both
kingly power and the *sangha* in their relation of mutual
dependence had passed through certain vicissitudes. There had
been dissensions in the *sangha*, and recent kings had swerved
from their loyalty and support to the Mahavihara and Theravada Buddhism. The final chapter of the *Mahavamsa* describes
the reign of Mahasena, heretically inclined and consecrated by
the implacable foe of the Mahavihara who 'won the king to
himself with the words: "The dwellers in the Mahavihara do
not teach the (true) Vinaya, we are those who teach the (true)
Vinaya, O king", and he established a royal penalty: "Whosoever gives food to a bhikkhu dwelling in the Mahavihara is
liable to a fine of a hundred (pieces of money)".' The short
chapter on Mahasena's reign which could not exclude mention
of the temples and tanks he had built, for he was responsible for
Minneriya tank where there is a shrine built to him, ends with
the words: 'Thus did he gather to himself much merit and much
guilt. The Mahavamsa is ended.'

Its thirty-seven chapters arranged its own highly subjective
record of the past so decisively that later history was influenced
by it. The clearest outlines of its own reconstruction of its events
were: the identification of religion with state; the dependence
of the stability of the country on this; the development of a
strong sense of Sinhalese nationalism out of opposition to the
Tamils. What was left out by the chronicler, what was slurred
over, what was added and amplified, seem to have sprung from
the need to mould the traditional material in his own way.

If the shape given to the past depended on the relation between religion and state, never completely and finally settled or

67

even tentatively recorded, it could be claimed that its very uncertainty and nebulousness were an advantage. Like Proteus it
was difficult to pin down, and it could transform itself hundred-
fold to meet extreme situations. Bhikkhu Rahula writes that by
the tenth century A.D. the belief that only a Buddhist had a
legitimate right to be king of Ceylon 'had become so strong that
the king of Ceylon had not only to be a Buddhist but also a
Bodhisattva. The Jetavanarama slab inscription of Mahinda IV
(956–972) proclaims that "none but the Bodhisattvas would
become kings of Sri Lanka", and that they "received this
assurance from the omniscient Buddha".' The rights kings
arrogated to themselves smacked more and more of Mahayan-
ist heterodoxy rather than any extension of Theravada belief.
Increasing wealth—through the twin sources of the cultivation
of rice-fields and the royal control of trade—enabled them to
fish in the troubled waters of South Indian politics, sometimes
at considerable strain to the resources of the kingdom. The religion—its status, its rights and its properties guaranteed by the
state—absorbed more and more from Brahmanic forms. It was
clear that the monarch had the right, which he exercised, to
discipline the *sangha*, generally with its approval. But it was
the *sangha*, as both religious body and political force, which
kept the national consciousness alive in spite of the deficiencies
of kings and the misadventures of the state. The king interfered
at times in matters of religion, and *bhikkhus* who were never
expected to be civil servants or politicians, did interfere in
affairs of state.

In the 1,200 years between the last of the *Mahavamsa* kings—
Mahasena (A.D. 276–303)—and the arrival of the Portuguese in
Ceylon one constant feature in the pattern of events is to be
noted. This is a politico-religious nationalism made use of by
monarchs strong enough to have overridden their rivals in
palace politics and then to have attempted to assert their rule
over the whole island. Much more than this was indeed needed
for their ultimate success, but in the convergence of various
factors leading to the consolidation of their rule over the whole
island, it must not be overlooked. Politically king and *sangha*
depended on each other, but economically the *sangha* could not
stand out against a withdrawal of royal support, nor could a
king disregard the ill-will of the *sangha*. Only so long as the

sangha was not weakened economically and spiritually beyond a certain level could it respond to the political needs of the kingdom. When this happened because kings had failed to provide for it, or when through civil war, invasion and its consequences, abuses crept into it, then the *sangha* could not be relied on to save the kingdom from the deficiencies of its kings.

By the fifth century A.D. Dravidian rulers had for a time established themselves in the north of Ceylon. Though they had been repulsed by Dutugemunu and the island freed from their overlordship, before very long the ruler of Ceylon was in hiding from successful invaders from South India. The Ceylon ruler, following the dictates of the military strategy advocated at the time, allied himself with Indian kingdoms to the north of his immediate enemies, so providing himself with a supporter who would harry them on another flank. Before long mercenery soldiers from the Continent, at the request of the Sinhalese king, had begun to intervene in the feuds between rival claimants to the throne. Even if Ceylon had been able to exist as an island in prudent isolation from the private wars of the South Indian kingdoms and their attempts to control the trade of the Bay of Bengal, a stage would have been reached when the island could not have escaped being drawn in. For it was itself an important entrepôt for traders from the Malay peninsula and farther east and from the shores of Arabia and the Persian Gulf.

The story of Ceylon for the best part of one thousand two hundred years is a record of stability then decline, relieved by three or four heroic episodes. It is the story of an island torn by dynastic rivalries and civil strife. If only the story of its kings is looked at, the record would seem to illustrate the hoary adage that a kingdom divided against itself cannot stand. It was brought to its knees quite as much by internal dissensions as by pressure from abroad. Rival clans contested the kingship, provinces lying outside the old Rajarata were only insecurely held except for short periods of strong rule; court and army intrigues shortened the lives of kings and commanders; claimants to the throne habitually invoked the aid of their South Indian allies. All these complicate the threads of a story in a seemingly hopeless tangle. But the strong ruler does on occasion emerge—the man who after the vicissitudes of defeat and temporary success is at last able to unite the land 'under the one umbrella'. Under pressure from hostile South Indian armies the capital of the ancient kingdom moved south-east, farther away from the threat of the invader who had established himself in the north, and closer to the Mahaveliganga, the river which gave strategic control of the southern principality, the nurse of rebellious claimants to the throne and of refugees from Dravidian rule.

The graph of movement of the capital indicates the gradual decline of the Sinhalese kingdom. Its course was like that of other South Indian kingdoms which reached their heyday and yielded to stronger and more successful rivals. The history of ancient Ceylon has for convenience been divided into various periods named after the capital from which the kings of the Sinhala kingdom ruled. The Anuradhapura period covers nearly one thousand three hundred years—from the time of Devanampiya Tissa (250–210 B.C.) to A.D. 1029. The last of the *Mahavamsa* kings was Mahasena (A.D. 276–303). His successors ruled over the country with varying fortunes until the fifth century A.D. when control of the kingdom passed into the hands of South Indian invaders. The head of a rival Sinhalese clan was able to wrest control of the island from the Tamils in A.D. 463. A period of 'dynastic instability' followed the failure of the line of this king to maintain itself in power, until Manavamma with an army given him by the South Indian Pallava ruler, having failed at his first attempt to establish himself, succeeded at his second attempt in A.D. 684.

His successors ruled for two hundred years—a period of comparative peace, though there were always threats of invasion from India. In the ninth century Ceylon was invaded by the Pandyans who were content to plunder the country and leave, having forced a humiliating treaty on the Sinhalese king. In revenge the next king of Ceylon, allying himself with the Pallavas, invaded the Pandyan country, and placed his nominee on the Pandyan throne. Invasions from India and counter-invasions followed, until the country was in ruin. The *Culavamsa* recorded the difficulties of the king Mahinda V (A.D. 982–1029) in paying his South Indian mercenaries, and the confusion in the kingdom where 'Keralas, Sinhalas and Kannatas carried on the government as they pleased'. The kingdom was ripe for its

fall. In A.D. 992 Anuradhapura was abandoned by the king as
his capital. Anarchy was succeeded by foreign invasion, and
soon the Colas, the paramount power in South India, ruled
over Rajarata, having despoiled the country. On this the *Culavamsa* has the following philosophic comment: 'Thus fortune's
goods if they were gained by one smitten by indolence, are not
abiding. Therefore should the prudent man, who strives after
his salvation, ever display ceaseless endeavour'—admirable
sentiments which any culture would have approved as good
counsel for kings and ordinary men.

Vijayabahu (1055–1110) was able, in the intervals of a very
troubled reign, to take advantage of the difficulties of the Colas
in South India to free Rajarata, and have himself consecrated
in Anuradhapura. But for reasons of security his capital was
Polonnaruva. The hundred and fifty years which followed
(1111–1215) are known as the Polonnaruva period. Among
its kings was Parakrama Bahu I (1153–86), the latter-day
counterpart of the early national hero, Dutugemunu. Warrior,
statesman, builder of tanks, palaces and temples, he is the figure
selected by the *Culavamsa* for epical treatment. Yet his reign
was not without its disorders, even after he had with a combination of statecraft and wisdom eliminated his rivals and controlled the whole island. In the chronicle accounts Parakrama
Bahu is, by comparison with Dutugemunu and even with
Vijaya Bahu, a much less attractive figure.

But he should be remembered, for besides glorifying his
capital Polonnaruva with splendid buildings, he understood
that the foundations of the strength of the Sinhala kingdom of
Rajarata were based on the control of water and not on land.
It is of him that the *Culavamsa* tells the oft-quoted story that
before he launched his campaign against his rivals for the kingship, he consolidated his base in the western regions with a
series of irrigation schemes designed to ensure the productivity
of his principality: 'From the Samantakuta mountain (Adam's
Peak) to the port at the sea he divided his army along the
frontier of the kingdom into various camps, and reflecting that
in the first place, in every possible way grain must be stored in
mass, he spake thus to his henchmen: "In the realm that is subject to me there are, apart from many strips of country where
the harvest flourishes mainly by rain water, but few fields

which are dependent on rivers with permanent flow or on great reservoirs. Also by many mountains, by thick jungle, and by widespread swamps my kingdom is much straitened. Truly in such a country not even a little water that comes from the rain must flow into the ocean without being made useful to man." '

With exceptional economic insight he secured the success against his rivals and the invader. When he ruled over the whole island, he built such a number of tanks and irrigation channels that his own energies and those of the people he commanded seem now to be fabulous. As a ruler of a kingdom he could be placed beside monarchs like Peter the Great of Russia and Frederick the Great of Prussia, for besides being warrior and statesman like them he perceived the sources of power. Like them, too, he must have had a somewhat calculating and sinister side to his character. The reputation of this twelfth-century ruler of Ceylon has been so impressive that a statue on a little knoll not far from one of his gigantic irrigation projects, still called, as it was first named, the Sea of Parakrama, has been supposed to be his likeness. Whosoever the statue may be, the fame of this ruler as the last great king of the Sinhala kingdom is in need of no such monument.

The Polonnaruva kingdom came to an end in 1215, when a South Indian potentate of a family connected with the Sinhala royal family invaded Ceylon and liquidated the kingdom. From this period onwards the capital changed several times, local leaders making a stand where they could rally their forces, the island gradually slipping into a state of division into which it finally settled by the end of the fifteenth century. A dynasty of kings ruled at Dambadeniya (1232–1326). The capital moved to Kurunegala. In the interim the rock of Yapahuva had been fortified and was the capital of one king (1272–84). The capital moved again to Gampola in the hills in the reign of Bhuvanaika Bahu IV (1341–51), away from Rajarata which had been given up to the jungle and the remnants of the population of a region in decline. The island, falling apart into provinces and kingdoms held by warring chieftains, subsided into three distinct entities; Udarata or the Kandyan kingdom which comprised an extent of territory stretching towards Batticoloa and the sea; the kingdom of Kotte, close to the port of Colombo; and a northern area ruled by a king of Jaffna In addition army leaders exercised authority over districts where no one's writ but their own ran. In South India in the meanwhile the sands of time had been running out for most of the vigorous small kingdoms which had exhausted themselves in their struggles with each other. Only the empire of the Vijaya-nagara kings was able to survive the long wars of the Dravidian kingdoms and the thrust of Islam into the south.

In 1411 a Chinese expedition invaded the western coast of Ceylon and carried off the ruler of the Rayigama kingdom. The last king able rightfully to call himself ruler of the whole of Ceylon was Parakrama Bahu VI (1412–67), the king of Kotte, according to the latest evidence instituted as king by the Chinese emperor. His was a long reign, rendered illustrious more by the peace which prevailed during its fifty-five years than by the literature of the period and the stores of legend and panegyric belauding his greatness. On his abdication and death the succession was again disputed. His kingdom broke up into various parts. Besides the two kings of Udarata and Kotte, there were rival princes in control of small areas.

In the formidable array of kings of the Sinhala kingdom is a great range of persons besides the few mentioned above. Among those still remembered by the mass of people are Valagam Ba of the second century A.D., who recovered his kingdom from the Tamils; Sirisangabo (247–9) who readily gave his head (on which a price had been placed by his rival) to benefit a peasant; a queen Anula of infamous memory; Subha, supposed to have been the palace guard who seized power because the king whom he resembled in feature once too often played the practical joke of changing places with him; Kirtisrimeghavanna, in whose reign the Tooth Relic was brought to Ceylon; Kasyapa I who killed his father Dhatusena and then built himself a palace on the rock of Sigiriya which was his capital for eighteen years. There were kings famous for their medical skill, for their artistic and literary abilities, and one king Nissanka Malla (1187–96) was a great builder at Polonnaruva and a self-conscious publicizer of his own greatness.

In the reign of Parakrama Bahu VIII of Kotte (1484–1508) occurred an event unnoticed by the *Culavamsa*—the baxels of the Portuguese landed on the shores of Colombo. The king, according to the Portuguese account, agreed to pay tribute to

73

the king of Portugal in return for protection. Europeans had visited Ceylon before 1505, as ambassadors, as traders, travellers and seamen. But for the first time now a king of Ceylon accepts the overlordship of a European monarch. Except for the race of the monarch such an event was another item in a prolonged series of wars, successes and reversals. Even at the time this part of the *Culavamsa* was written, in spite of the elimination of the kingdom of Kotte, a Sinhala kingdom still stood—the Udarata kingdom—and the chronicler understandably gave the arrival of the Portuguese flotilla no importance.

Though the Sinhala kingdom declined and its kings were limited to narrower domains, the more splendid grew the religious cults with which kingdom and king were associated. The development of the cult of the Tooth Relic of the Buddha between the twelfth and the sixteenth centuries, the magnificence of its rituals, the belief in its miraculous powers, the particular veneration in which it was held as an object of worship as well as guaranteeing the king his right to the kingdom, must have derived some of their fervour from desperation as well as from hope, even in periods of defeat, that magically the possession of the relic would assure the ultimate triumph of the kingdom.

Parakrama Bahu I fought a war to gain possession of the relic without which he could not establish his right to the throne. A special bodyguard was assigned to it, magnificent temples were built in its honour, and its exposition was the occasion of spectacular ceremonial. Over the other relics of the Buddha, acquired in the course of time, there had been temples built, and festivals instituted in their honour. But none of them, not even the branch of the *Bo* tree brought, according to the story, by the *theri* Sanghamitta from India, has been able to conjure so much popular emotion as the celebrated Tooth Relic. It moved with the kings who set up new capitals, for without it there could be neither kingdom nor king. For a short while during the first half-century of British colonial rule in the island, the colonial government was responsible for its security and the annual Perahera or procession in its honour. It is enthroned now in a temple of no aesthetic distinction in Kandy, and though there are no kings in Ceylon, to the devout Buddhist it is a guarantee of the future of the race and the religion. When ministers of a government, elected to a parliament insti-

74

tuted on western European democratic lines, make a journey to
Kandy to the Temple of the Tooth to dedicate themselves to
their task, it is clear that the tradition of the past is being
invoked.

Recorded history by and large adds up to little more than the
tale of the iniquity of the great and the stupidities of the mass of
men who have been content to accept too long what they have
later thrown off in exasperation or sunk under in supporting.
Except for this tepid generalization there seems to be no single
clue to the maze of the story of Ceylon in its first one thousand
seven hundred and fifty years of recorded history, however it is
viewed—whether in the context of the struggles of the South
Indian kingdom or in isolation. Seen in the perspective of South
India much more comes to life and has meaning. But to the
mind of the average reader straying uncomprehending through
the lists of kings and their acts, it must seem a monstrous jungle
left to thrive by human wilfulness. Yet it is not without its
strange blooms, and its clearings where bearings can be taken
and the traveller set out refreshed. The only valid generalization, other than the cold comfort of wisdom after the event,
seems to arise out of the conviction that the clue to its incom-
prehensible vagaries is bound up with the toughness of a social
and economic structure which could have enabled so many to
withstand what had been done to them by so few for so long.
But even this verges on platitudes applicable to other cultures
and most histories, for it would seem that, as ever, the peasant
or hired labourer on the land toiled in the fields, supporting
himself and his dependants, knowing little of the acts of the
great, until he was engulfed in their consequences. Perhaps this
went on though dynasties passed, until the land was impoverished and the jungle submerged tanks, villages and fields and
there were no people left on whose labours the great ones could
float themselves, their conspiracies and their wars.

It has often been observed that only the exceptionally
healthy could afford to be afflicted by a variety of diseases. The
man who is often ill can be thought of as possessing a constitution strong enough to stand his ill health. On the same analogy
only a strong country could have supported such vicissitudes as
were the lot of Ceylon. What then was the source of its strength
which enabled it to bear the travails of its recorded history?

The kingdom, like other autocracies, depended first of all on the productivity of its fields, from which most of its revenues were derived. As long as the supply of water was assured—kings in early times in Ceylon too were regarded as rainmakers—the rule of custom and caste, through which a quasi-feudal economy functioned, was assured. As population increased, more productivity was required of the rice-fields and a larger army of officials was needed to keep the network of new and larger irrigation schemes in order. Rajarata did support a larger population, but much more than the planning and work of small village communities were needed if the whole was to survive. This apparently was achieved by increased centralization. But it threw greater burdens on the community, and demanded in turn increased productivity if progress was to continue. But war, the exactions of officialdom, and one consequence of centralization—the supersession of the local man who knew and could act in an emergency by control from the capital—cut down production, and eventually led to the stagnation of the economy.

The king held a royal monopoly of pearls and gems. These and elephants were the most valuable articles of export from Ceylon. But trade, it would seem, was entirely in the hands of foreigners—Arab traders who by the eighth century A.D. had established themselves on the chief ports of the Indian Ocean and controlled its carrying trade. Chinese junks traded with Ceylon which was a half-way house between East and the Mediterranean West. In the communities of merchants settled at the capital and at larger towns the majority were foreigners again. The chief beneficiaries of commerce, besides the merchants who handled it, were the king and his officials. What part of the revenue was spent on increasing productivity is not known.

Both rice-field and the merchant's warehouse needed protection and peace, and both as sources of wealth were attractive prizes. Figures in the chronicles are often symbolic and should not be thought of as accurate representations of number. According to the old saying, 'A little more or less does not affect the principal number'. It is not possible therefore to credit the legends still current about the size of the population concentrated in Rajarata and Ruhuna, or the story that Ceylon was

'the granary of the East'. Undoubtedly there were large populations living in areas now covered by scrub jungle, and the
references in chronicles to tanks still identifiable show how increasing population demanded more numerous courses of
water-supply. As there was nothing on the same scale as these
irrigation works of ancient Ceylon on the Indian mainland, it is
not difficult to conjecture that the settled prosperity of the
northern and central plains of Ceylon must have been attractive to the warlike peoples of South India.

The kingdom's prosperity was based on the productivity of
its rice-fields, but there is a dynamic in the processes of agriculture which requires newer skills and the development of techniques if sclerosis first of all and then decline are going to be
arrested. These need not only peace, but the spirit of discovery
and invention if the impetus to the solution of the problem set
the first people who colonized the land is not only to be maintained but transformed. In the nature of things this transformation is sometimes achieved through technological means. The
rice-field needs an assured supply of water and efficient cultivation. With regard to the first of the requirements, the degree
of engineering skill and trigonometrical knowledge possessed by
the early builders of tanks was considerable. Ever since the
irrigation schemes of ancient Ceylon have been studied by
mechanical engineers of our time, there has been nothing but
praise for the scientific knowledge and the ingenuity of technical skill on which they were based. Nothing could be more
forthright than the comments of recent authority: 'This
achievement (in irrigation works), accomplished by the seventh
century, reveals the extraordinarily high technical ability of the
Sinhalese engineers of ancient times who were responsible for
the planning, design and construction of these works. Several of
these projects, if put in hand today, would still be regarded as
major undertakings. Nothing is known today of how these engineers of old and the technicians under them set about their
work, what preliminary surveys and gaugings they made, what
mathematical formulae they employed in their calculations and
what instruments they used; all this information must have been
contained in textbooks because it could not have been imparted
orally. Surveys made in modern times for the restoration of
ancient works have disclosed that the instruments they used

77

were capable of the same precision as modern instruments. Their contour levelling was exceptionally accurate because the fall in the ancient canals was generally one foot in a mile, though in some sections it was as small as six inches in a mile.'

Why did this achievement already reached by the seventh century lead to nothing more in the centuries which followed? Even if technologically no development in irrigation was possible except for mechanical handling in building, dependent on new sources of power to be discovered only in the last hundred years, what became of the corpus of scientific knowledge possessed by the old planners and engineers? Why did new stimuli, in the course of years when it must have been applied to satisfy other needs and perhaps to solve new problems, produce no new results?

As for the other element in the prosperity of the rice-field—its mode of cultivation—why did the empirical knowledge of the cultivator not proceed to meet, through newer methods, the new demands put upon him as producer? The belief that the Sinhala kingdom failed because the fields were impoverished by the cultivation of the one crop, rice, over countless centuries has been discounted. What then stood in the way of the discovery of new techniques in cultivation? War and civil strife explain a great deal. Here is an extract from the chronicle with a picture of conditions in the twelfth century: 'The officers belonging to the retinue of the monarchs on both sides who were established on the frontiers, fought with each other continually. By setting fire to many flourishing villages and market towns, by piercing tanks filled with water, by destroying everywhere the weirs on all the canals and by hewing down all useful trees like the coconut palm and others, they in fighting each other, so devastated the kingdom that it was impossible to trace even the sites of the old villages. And even the rulers did evil to the people letting their retainers plunder the towns and commit highway robbery.'

The best-integrated communities would have been hard put to it to survive such catastrophes. Actually the particular disasters referred to above were surmounted by the Sinhala kingdom for within three decades the troubles of these years were redeemed by the reign of Parakrama Bahu I. He unified the kingdom, restored tanks, built new ones, expelled the invader and despatched expeditions overseas. But both the state of

78

civil disorder in Ceylon in the years preceding his birth, and the strain put upon the kingdom by his reorganization and his foreign wars, suggest that not only the pressure of invaders and anarchy at home put an end to the kingdom, but that something else was wanting at this stage, wanting in the social and economic structure perhaps which inhibited development and made decline inevitable.

Karl August Wittfogel in his highly generalized study of what he termed 'hydraulic civilizations'—those of culture depending on a rice-crop needing large irrigation works—showed how a complicated bureaucratic system was necessary for their maintenance. In the twelfth century in Ceylon a stage had been reached when a centralized bureaucracy was superimposed on the old structure dependent ultimately, according to Dr. Paranavitane, on the efficiency and authority of the local chieftains. The destruction of this class of official by the invader has been sought as the reason for the end of the culture of Rajarata. From all the evidence presented in Dr. Paranavitane's valuable studies of Sinhala civilization, it would seem that a quasi-feudal culture, in which the king was the head of an agricultural community, had developed into a state in which the king, a much grander figure now, put upon the community, which economically had scarcely changed in its modes of production, the onus of maintaining two establishments—those of the state and the religion—both with ever-widening demands and with no new sources of productivity. Increased productivity was achieved temporarily only at the cost of centralization which upset the balance of the feudal structure already disturbed by political instability. The maintenance of an elaborate court invariably made further drains on the economy, stanched by such dubious procedures as debasement of the coinage and a change in taxation, which put the burden of payment in money on a peasantry beggared by the exactions of officials and the multiplication of dues owed to both state and religious establishments.

The old structure of society and the economy on which it depended were the basis of the strength of the kingdom up to the fifth century A.D. By the twelfth century it was already breaking up. What is interesting in the comment of the *Culavamsa* on the period of civil war at this time is not that the officials 'in their insatiability and money lust squeezed out the whole people as sugar in the sugar mill', for conduct of this kind is not surprising in the favourites of princes, but the statement, twice repeated, that people of good family were slighted and their possessions seized. In other words custom and the old order of society were subverted. They were distorted into an instrument of autocratic power. Kings relied more on their bodyguard of foreign mercenaries than on the natural loyalty of their people. When Dr. Paranavitane, with the dry humour which sometimes crackles under the pot of his learning, comments on the Polonnaruva period—the most magnificent in the annals of Ceylon's ancient history—that 'with regard to the tillers of the soil, on whom rested the burden of supporting everyone else, divine as well as human, in addition to themselves, we have less information during this period than for the earlier centuries', it is hard not to infer that the peasant staggering under a load too much for him symbolized the fortunes of the Sinhala kingdom.

Its magnificent achievement was obviously the efflorescence of a quasi-feudal society, dependent on a nice balance of custom by which the ruling class provided the conditions for the maintenance of an agricultural economy on which all depended. As it was a society regulated by caste and controlled at the top by both the temporal and the religious authorities, nothing irreconcilable to either was allowed into it. The great cohesive force in the kingdom was, as has been pointed out, Buddhism. But as this turned its face away from the world of material objects, which it regarded as illusory, it could hardly help, except as a rallying point for the recovery of the old. If conditions had so far changed that to save anything at all the new was required, then it could not help. As it was identified with the state which was the king, if the latter failed, then the religion failed with it. It could not resuscitate what was too far gone to survive. A changed situation in power politics in South-East Asia finally brought the kingdom to its end at the close of the eighteenth century. The enfeebled *sangha* still remained, its face firmly turned towards the past.

CHAPTER 5

The Best of Ancient Ceylon

I s it possible to draw closer to the one thousand eight hundred years of history to which the label 'ancient Ceylon' has been attached? Can we understand better the procession of the great ones of the past—deities, kings, *bhikkhus*, warriors with whose names the records of history have familiarized us? Or are they like large areas of the past, irreclaimable? The men and women whose lives were the stuff of human history are beyond our reach. But some part of the objects they created—their poems, their statues, their everyday objects of use—are still available to us. These surely are the best part of the record of the past. They are there for all to see, they may even be handled. There is perhaps more of fact in them as they stand than in the most brilliant reconstitutions of the past by the scholar today.

Yet to recreate the past through them is a perilous undertaking too, for the still objects, like the Chinese jar of Wallace Stevens, move and it is difficult to grasp them. As the past comes to live through them, awkward shapes from the present intrude. Between the past and the work of art intervene our own desires and predilections.

The work of art is, however, the most lasting record of any civilization. In the story of Ceylon they are perhaps the most impressive evidence of nearly two thousand years of its political and economic structure and the way the people lived. If the story of ancient Ceylon means anything at all to the veriest stranger in the land, the beginnings of understanding could come through these memorials of the past: a temple, a fresco, the scribbling on a wall, an old dance form.

Practically everything which survives owed its existence to the initiative of the great ones—kings, *bhikkhus*, Brahmins. But

F
81

these things have come into being through the work and the faith of common people, and as they now affect the sensibilities of those still open to their influences, they can exist and have meaning apart from specialist knowledge or interest in the kings or erudition in the religion the artist served.

Mansfield Forbes used to show his classes at Cambridge (in a course of lectures entitled 'From Blake to Hardy') a reproduction of the statue carved in the rock near the Potgul Vehera at Polonnaruva. To him it was a perfect expression of the moment of tranquillity or serenity created by the artist. It was known to be the work of a twelfth-century sculptor in Ceylon, but that its subject was (and still is) disputed scarcely affected the lecturer's response to the statue.

So it will be with the multitude faced with the art of the past. The special skill of archaeologist or Indologist could claim this piece of sculpture, and everything else in the field of the ancient art of Ceylon, as its own particular province. But after all its possibilities have been examined and patiently explored, the work of art returns from the study to where it properly belongs —the scrutiny of those to whom its subject or provenance can be perhaps irrelevant.

Two characteristics of the arts of Ceylon are surely incontestable. First of all they are part of the cultural diversity of India. Neither seventeen centuries of the political history of Ceylon, nor all the manifold differences in social and economic detail from the Indian pattern, can obscure that. Secondly, in their own uniqueness, or regionalism, there is a difference to be observed between the products of a classical past out of reach now and those of a folk tradition still surviving. To think of the artistic heritage of Ceylon is to remember its Indian background, in which and in reaction against which it developed. The Indian is part of an Asian which influenced and was influenced by the Mediterranean and the European. While the expert will have to disentangle the threads of the one from the other, the common man can, with good reason, see in the Indian or Asian a particularity which is to him the work of Ceylon, from whatever part of the world the artists and craftsmen responsible for it came. We know that the skills of workmen and specialists from the Indian mainland must have been used in the construction of temple and shrine in Ceylon. In the cul-

82

tural unit which was both India and Ceylon Buddhaghosa, a Brahmin from Buddhagaya, becomes in Ceylon the greatest commentator on the Buddhist canon; and in Nagarjunikonda *bhikkhus* from Ceylon probably first designed the decorative motif of the 'moonstone'.

Practically all the art of ancient and medieval times is anonymous. So it is with the ancient arts of Ceylon. Practically all of it which survives is religious and aristocratic—the temples of kings and generals, the epic poems and commentaries of the learned. It is the same with the art of medieval Europe. The common man, if we think of that peculiarly modern entity, hardly appears. He seems in both cultures to have been perfectly contented with the religious and the aristocratic art which he had helped to bring into being. Surely there were great differences between king and peasant in medieval Europe and in ancient Ceylon, but both belonged to worlds in which the same noble truths were cherished. So though the sculpture, the architecture, the painting and the poetry which survive seem to recall only the great, the insignificant are there too. They were the workers of brick and the builders; they were the audience edified and delighted by the poetry, the statue and the painting.

They are sometimes there in the records of the great, and they should not be overlooked. Out of epic poem came the themes of folk song, so whether they are referred to or not they should be remembered. We do not know for certain who composed the *Mahavamsa*, nor who built the *dagabas*. But we are told of master-builders who were designers. In the story of the building of the relic chamber of the Mahathupa in the reign of Dutugemunu there was a master-builder who in a moment of inspiration—he was possessed by the god of skill—solved an architectural problem: 'Thereupon commanding that the drums be beaten he (the king) called the master-builders together with all speed; in number they were five hundred. And one of them answered the king on his asking: "How wilt thou make (the thupas)?" "Taking a hundred workmen I will use one wagonload of sand in one day." The king rejected him. Thereon they offered to (work with) one half less and yet one half less again, and (at last with) two ammanas of sand. These four master-builders also did the king reject. Then an experienced and

83

shrewd master-builder said to the king: "I shall pound (the sand) in a mortar, and then, when it is sifted, have it crushed in a mill and (thus will use) one ammana (only) of sand." And on these words the lord of the land, whose courage was like to Indra's, consented, with the thought: "There will be no grass nor any such thing on our cetiya," and he questioned him saying: "In what form wilt thou make the cetiya?" At that moment Vissakamma (the god of skill) entered into (and possessed him). When the master-builder had a golden bowl filled with water he took water in his hand and let it fall on the surface of the water. A great bubble rose up like unto a half-globe of crystal. He said: "Thus will I make it." And well pleased the king bestowed on him a pair of garments worth a thousand (pieces of money) and ornamented shoes and twelve thousand kahapannas' (silver coins).

The same story of the king at whose command the great *stupa* was built in the second century B.C. brings in the workers labouring at it. Knowing that the forced levy which went into the work must have been burdensome, the king declared that the worker would be paid for the work he did. 'How shall I have the bricks transported without laying burdens on the people?' the king pondered. As the story goes on: 'When the gods were aware of this they brought night after night bricks to the four gates of the *cetiya* and laid them down there, always as many as sufficed for one day. When the king heard this, glad at heart, he began work on the thupa. And he made it known: "Work shall not be done here without wage." ' Not even the intervention of the deities could make the king overlook persons no less important than master-builders and supernatural beings in the execution of his act of devotion—his workers.

To undertake even the most cursory examination of the arts of Ceylon is impertinent for in its extensive field not even the expert could claim benefit of clergy. But the task has to be attempted for they are the most easily accessible by-products of the story of Ceylon. They are also among the most influential records of the past. A story of recent years, connected with the Soulbury Commission which visited Ceylon in 1945, will show how influential they are. The three Commissioners, it is said, were so impressed by the artistic excellence of Polonnaruva, even in its ruins, that they felt that the people who could eight centuries previously produce such work were fit to rule themselves in the twentieth century. Whether the story is an exaggeration or invention, the moral is obvious. By the most exacting test of modern times—that of political effectiveness—the arts of Ceylon have to be reckoned with.

With the literature of ancient Ceylon it is impossible to deal, for it must remain a closed book to those ignorant of Pali, Sanskrit or Sinhalese, until adequate translations into modern European languages are provided. To read extant translations of such classics as the *Mahavamsa* is to doubt whether the original could have afforded any joy at all. No recent edition of this text in English has attempted to capture some of the pleasure it must have given its hearer over and above the serene satisfaction gained from the information it conveyed. Where this has been attempted—in a single short extract by Professor Basham —the exhilaration of the artist could at once be felt. The store of verse in the literary tradition is similarly difficult to assess. It appears to have exerted an inhibiting effect on the development of poetry, because it was not a living tradition native to the writer. It tended to insulate the poet from both the language and the life of his times. Dr. Sarathchandra, in his Introduction to Martin Wickremasinghe's *Sinhalese Literature*, complains of 'the rift between the learned men and the common folk, a condition obtaining from the earliest times, (which) has made our literature, at best, a second-hand product. The poet and the pundit were one and the same. The creations of the folk-poet, who attempted to communicate his own experiences, whatever they were, were ignored in preference to learned translations of other peoples' experiences. This tradition of pundit-poetry was not abandoned till about the time of the Kotte period in the fifteenth century, when, for the first time, writers began to place their work against the background of life in Ceylon, instead of describing in meticulous detail things they had never seen or felt about.'

The vitality of the folk tradition in Sinhalese poetry could at once be guessed at by the visitor to Ceylon who has ever heard an itinerant vendor of medicines and herbs proclaim their efficacy, and noted how natural it is, on formal occasions, for the most unlikely people to recite their own verse compositions. These may be formal and demanded by the formality of the occasion, but that poetry is demanded proves that it is at least thought to be freely available. It seems spontaneously produced and naturally enjoyed, there being no shamefacedness or false modesty in the poets. It would seem that verse writing is still a common part of the abilities of a number of people. What is remarkable in this verse, quite apart from its usualness when contrasted with its complete absence in industrial communities, is both the assumption of quite humble folk that the skills of the poet are within their range and the pleasure taken in their exercise, both by the poet and his audience.

It has been well observed by Dr. Godakumbura that 'by temperament the Sinhalese is a poet. He speaks in poetry. The Sinhalese language lends itself easily to versification, or composition in metre, and very often prose itself turns into a sort of metrical language. It is flexible, it is varied, and it has a rich vocabulary, able to convey every subtle and diverse shade of meaning, to make vivid to the imagination any picture the poet wishes to conjure up. Sinhalese, with its large number of synonyms, made it possible for the poet to use any metre or rhyme he chose, and its homonyms with a multiplicity of meanings made it easy for the versifier to indulge in all sorts of verbal gymnastics'. Whether verse composition is a less formidable task in Sinhalese than in other languages is for the expert to decide, but it was, and is, popular.

That the popular tradition was long continued has been shown by Dr. Paranavitane in his work on the graffiti found on the Mirror Wall at Sigiriya. With only the slightest rearrangement of the literally Englished text—as W. G. Archer has shown—these samples of occasional verse of the eighth, ninth and tenth centuries A.D. give as delicate and memorable examples of man's sensitiveness to art as could be found in any literature. Of course most of the verses scribbled on the wall are by kings, nobles and learned clerics. The forms and metres they used would show affinities with a sophisticated literary tradition. But other writers are represented too. Though most of the signed verse is by the aristocratic and the learned, some of it belongs to the worker, the merchant, to people who could be reckoned among the common men of their times. They should not be thought of as being possessed with the unusual wish to be poets, but as enabled to write as poets wrote, even though they may never have written great poetry, because they were at home in a tradition they knew and composed their verses without fuss.

The subjects of most of the verses are the paintings of women, identified as cloud-maidens, which have survived only in a rock-pocket. It is likely that in the fifth century, when the palace of the king was built on the rock, there were on the rock-face numerous paintings. Only twenty-one remain. The upper part of the women is shown, formalized cloud cutting off the lower parts of their bodies. The painter apparently differentiated between two kinds of women according to the colour he used. Those to whom he gave a golden hue appear to be attended by others of a darker olive-green complexion. Flowers are held in the hands of the golden-hued women, or drop from them; while those in olive-green seem to be carrying trays of flowers for the others.

The former are the recipients of most of the verses incised on the Mirror Wall, which gets its name from the high polish of the plaster. The poems are short compositions recording the emotions of the writers on seeing these beauties on a desolate memorial of royal grandeur, for the site had been abandoned for more than a century. There is a great range of content in the reactions of the writers. Most of them confess their passion for the women, who in the classic convention of many literatures are referred to as being cold and stony-hearted—like the rock on which they stand. Undoubtedly much of the quality of the verse would reside in the executant's skill in the form he chose. But metrics apart, the best of them give the surprise of poetry which succeeds in expressing clearly and memorably the feeling of the writer.

One of the longest, by an anonymous writer, has been re-set by Mr. Archer thus:

> *Your beauty charmed the heart.*
> *My eyes lingered and were lost.*
> *You took them to yourself.*
> *If you had not accepted me as your lover,*
> *I would have known you had never been in love.*
> *You have repulsed a king and taken a hard rock as your lover.*
> *Travellers come and go.*
> *Stay where you are, watching them with your cold gaze.*

A novice who had climbed the rock to see what he had heard spoken of so often, sets 'wakefulness of mind' on guard to prevent temptation assailing him through his ears. But seeing the paintings his mind 'trembles exceedingly'. There is a beautiful verse by a metal-worker, ironically aware of his infatuation and his unworthiness. He pulls himself back to reality remembering the gold of the complexion of the girl (in contrast perhaps with the metal he works in) and asks for his words to be reported to her. The term he uses to address the figure in the fresco has been rendered by Dr. Paranavitane as 'little honey-heart'—a colloquial term of endearment found nowhere else. The verse might be arranged as follows:

> *Hail! I speak, a worker in iron:*
> *'Little honey-heart,*
> *Golden girl.*
> *All you asked of me,*
> *Passionately, senselessly,*
> *I myself have done.'*
> *Pray tell the gold-hued one*
> *What I have spoken.*

The shiny beige wall and the frescoes in the pocket of the rock could be regarded as emblematic of the arts of Ceylon. Here on rock and wall, close to each other but yet apart, are the sign manuals of two dominant traditions: the muffled echo of the Indian, and the virile indigenous. It is not possible to divide the two into mutually exclusive spheres, for there must have been—it could not have been otherwise—some interaction between them in the earliest times. The frescoes in Sigiriya have been linked with the murals at Ajanta. The painter in Ceylon does not repeat the Indian in form, composition or colour; he uses the same mode but with a difference. This is to be felt in the contrast between the distance placed between painter and picture in Sigiriya and the involvement of the Ajanta artist in his own luxuriance. The stylized women in Sigiriya seem restrained and hieratic. The very sensuousness of their figure appears to be held in check by the touch of hardness in the definition of the curve, and given a dimension different from that of physical representation. The women, as the writers of the poems often observe, appear to be both living and without

88

1. Sigiriya: Palace and rock-fortress, fifth century A.D.

Batecotte

The House belonging to ye Church

The Church

2. Dutch Church and Mission House: Vaddukoddai, eighteenth century A.D.

life. The painter's hard curved line and the flatness of the colour give them their characteristic poise of superiority to the touch of earthly years.

The folk tradition in verse appears to have its own simplicities and directness. Could it be said of this tradition—in poetry, painting and the plastic arts—as it survived the collapse of the power of the ruling classes, that its strength lay in its freedom from the restraints laid upon the arts by the learned tradition? Religious orthodoxy at times bade the sternest good night to such arts as poetry and painting in which clerics were proficient. They were 'low arts'. As for dancing in the social system of both Sinhalese and Tamils, it was the preserve of those low in the social scale. But the dancer, like any other artificer, was made much of and rewarded for his skill by his upper-class patron. Such arts were free from the frigid touch of literary conventionality, they were free to develop, creating a tradition of their own. There is in the dancing of Ceylon a strong mixture of folk vitality and some formal sophistication. Like all other survivals from ancient Ceylon its present unhappy condition must be put down to the disintegration of the social structure in which it had its place, and the impoverishment of the peasantry. It looks as if in the break-up of ancient Ceylon—a process which set in before the territorial ambitions of the Portuguese applied fresh pressures to the damaged fabric—some parts of the old structure; the dancing and the painting for instance, remained relatively strong. Both were needed in magical rite and at temple festival. The dancing in particular remained the most vigorous of the community arts. As medical prescription it had to be exactly dispensed, with every scruple of material carefully weighed. As it survives today in cults and exorcistic rites it is formal and part of a popular tradition. In ancient times it was presumably more ceremonious than it can be today, nor can this quality of pageantry ever be recovered. It was the product of a society which believed in the efficacy of magical rites. Processions, exorcistic rites are still known, but except for a continuation of the very much later *perahera* (procession) in honour of the Tooth Relic of the Buddha in Kandy in the full moon of July-August, they lack the universal significance they once had. They are as unlikely to resume the place they once held in the community as the medieval miracle play is likely to be resusci-

89

tated by urban or borough councils in England. Some of the dance rituals, like the *Kohomba Kankariya*—a combination of dance, song and mimed episodes presented by a village to propitiate the powerful deity Kohomba—have all but vanished. Miss de Zoete, whose *Dance and Magic Drama in Ceylon* is an artist's quest for a *Kohomba Kankariya*, had to report in the end that she could not see it performed.

The dance of the exorcist, performed for the utilitarian purpose of working the cure of the patient, has survived in a form closest to its ancient originals. Changed habits and modern medicine have eaten their way into that too, but the tradition is still handed down, and reveals the bravura acrobatic skill of the dancer. The prodigious feats of which he is capable at a *bali* ceremony are possible only because of the sublimating power of the craftsman's inspiration. Like the rhapsodist, whom Plato distrusted, the dancer is a sophisticated and highly trained creature with power to move men. Though performers at exorcistic ceremonies belong to castes held to be inferior, their art enables them to transcend this social disadvantage. The dance therefore benefits both patient and physician, and has a twofold therapeutic effect.

The traditional Kandyan dancer of today in full panoply looks a prince and bears himself like one. He is resplendent from the finely carved and lacquered head-dress to his silver anklets. The costume is traditional, except for the tights, and accentuates the lordliness of the conventional posture of knees splayed outward and torso thrust forward. It is in keeping with the masculinity of the dancer's figure and position. It would be a mistake, however, to think of Kandyan dancing as being rigid or formal. It is full of fluency, of a great range of variety with conventional patterns, and accompanied as it always is by the drum with its spectrum of seemingly infinite shades of tones, it is perpetually exciting. It is a masculine dance *par excellence*— the muscular agility of the dancer, the great physical endurance manifested throughout hours of singing and dancing, the control of every finesse of movement of the body, the superb walk between a change of modes in the accompanying music, are all evidence of the virility of this act of artistic creation. Ignorance of the meaning of the words sung by the dancer, or of the significance of the gesture, hardly lessens the force of its impact on the uninstructed. It is pure dance with its own universal language.

The most considerable achievement (in every sense of the word) of ancient Ceylon are the tanks. Their size, the scope of their conception, the magnitude of the task, the weight of energy which went into their upkeep, their integration with the landscape which has assumed beauty through their presence, all entitle them to special notice and distinction. They are beautiful in their adjustment of means to end. Even tanks now in ruin, where only the bare bones of the grand design remain, are beautiful. The expanse of water bounded by man-made banks must always appeal to that side of our natures which rejoices in fresh evidence of man's assertion of himself, his conquest of nature. We are given the complementary feeling, too, that these are not the works of men at all, and that beside natural lakes which break up the monotony of the plain, men seem meaningless. If neither feeling comes to mind, the quiet water, the grass, the stream issuing from the sluice must refresh the mind with the feeling that here are the sources of life. The satisfaction the tanks give resides ultimately in their harmonious blending with the landscape, whether they are close to the valley across which the dam was thrown as in Giritale, or whether two depressions and a stream brought a tank together as in Kalavava, or the tank in its rocky solitude, as at Rufuskulam, appears to exist in complete isolation.

Kings were responsible for their building, and by the banks of one of them is a shrine to the king who planned it and is now deified. Another king shortly before he knew he would be put to death, asked to be allowed to go to the tank he had built. 'This is my treasure', he explained to the guards who had brought him there in anticipation that the hiding-place of the royal hoard would now be revealed. These tanks are the greatest achievement of the common folk of Ceylon, from whomever they acquired the skill which went into their construction. They are a distinctive feature of the culture of ancient Ceylon. India has nothing like them.

Not one of the ancient *stupas*—the dome-like structures built over some relic—survives today in its original form. Their immensity is impressive because of the basic simplicity of their form. What they must have looked like in the heyday of Anuradhapura we can guess from Fa Hsien's fifth-century A.D. account of his stay in Ceylon. Their attraction and splendour then must have depended much more on their external ornament. Now in ruin they are perhaps more eloquent in the simplicity of their line—the curve slightly flattened on top, the greying plaster of the rounded surface or the exposed brick contrasting with the green of the vegetation. Even in the poor and clumsy imitations built at the present time, something of the ancient proportions occasionally flashes out from these characteristic landmarks of Buddhist Ceylon.

The loss of the original character of these *stupas* has been offset by their new accord with their surroundings which have altered too. Fa Hsien saw the Abhayagiri as 'a great dagoba . . . four hundred feet in height and decorated with gold and silver and all kinds of precious substances combined'. Ruined and overgrown now, it still has the beauty of its composition to flaunt—the generous curve and the line which takes the eye away from the solid circular base but none the less anchors it the more securely there.

The sculpture of Ceylon has marked differences to show even in what was shared with the Indian. These must spring from the difference in intention and attitude of the artist and in his skill with his instrument. The Buddha images of this time, as befitting the severer nature of the doctrine in Ceylon and the less brilliant execution of the sculptor, are plainer and simpler. But the genius of the artist, early and late, is seen in the sweep of his design, in the way in which he wrests from the limestone or gneiss on which he is working a finely balanced group, or a single figure which has both power and humanity, so fine is the moulding of the rock. Of both these qualities the twelfth-century A.D. Gal Vihara at Polonnaruva is the best example. In its fulfilment of every demand made by the convention it is the classic example of the rock-cut Buddhas of Ceylon. The figure of the recumbent Buddha must always take the spectator by surprise, so exquisitely is the detail subordinated to the excellence of the whole.

'Moonstone'—the term used to describe the semicircular carved stone which forms one part of the complex of steps, balustrade and landing leading to the shrine housing the Buddha image—is, like the tank, a characteristic product of

Ceylon. Its shape was fixed, and only within the mathematical figure of the semicircle made up of concentric bands round the half-lotus centre was variation possible. Like the tank its original purpose seems to have been utilitarian: through its symbolism of the series of sculpted figures, the 'moonstone' directed the attention of the devotee to the stages in the Buddha's attainment of enlightenment. There is a highly sophisticated art to be observed in them—the bands of animals and the creeper design are conventionalized, but offer scope to the sculptor. They are an index of a developed art which aids refinement of worship. The 'moonstones' at the circular shrine at Polonnaruva—the Vatadage—are perhaps examples of an advanced stage of this development, for they are baroque in their detail. .

Temples and shrines betray a Hindu influence never far away. The ancient kings had Brahmin *purohitas* or chaplains to perform 'numerous rites prescribed for royalty at various stages and occurrences in life'. Buddhism did not reject Hinduism. If the Buddhist was intolerant, it was of divergence from Buddhist orthodoxy. Like all sectarians he was more unrelenting in his hostility to deviations among Buddhists than to the adherents of other faiths. Sculpture and architecture in the Anuradhapura and Polonnaruva periods are as indebted to the Indian tradition as they ever were. As Buddhism gradually lost its hold over its Indian homeland and new Hindu cults flourished, traces of these might be found in Ceylon too.

It is ironical that the most impressive survival of ancient Ceylon should be the palace and fortified capital of a parricide king to whom the *Mahavamsa* paid scant attention. Priestly orthodoxy condemned him both on account of his crime and his arrogation to himself of divine status. Sigiriya, already referred to in connection with the frescoes on the rock, was for eighteen years the capital of the fifth-century A.D. monarch Kasyapa. He must have been an efficient tyrant or have enjoyed the support of his people, for in those years they turned the rock into a palace which emulated the fabled abode of the god Kuvera in the Himalayan Kailas. For nearly a millennium the site was shunned by the visitor and an evil reputation grew round it. When H. C. P. Bell began excavating it in the late nineteenth century, many of his workmen at first refused to have anything to do with such an ill-omened place. Bell's pioneer work was extended to new and surprising levels by the last Archaeological Commissioner, Dr. Paranavitane. It is one of the most beautifully conserved of all the ancient sites of Ceylon. Neither the brashness of a modern provincial town as at Anuradhapura, nor the unsightliness of the market-place of a peasant colonization scheme as at Polonnaruva, detract from its setting.

The ruins at Sigiriya are the most interesting of the ancient monuments of Ceylon. First of all, if proof were needed, they reveal the stability of the old kingdom, which even in its episodes of dynastic struggle could afford such a splendid testimonial of itself. These struggles between royal princes seem to fall into clearer focus. Wars, if they could be so called, were but a ripple on the surface of deep water. There are ruins of other ancient palaces in Ceylon, notably in Polonnaruva, but glowingly described as the original structures are in the *Culavamsa*, they are now no more than cemeteries of stone. Sigiriya forces the attention, it jolts one into awareness of the grandeur of its conception.

As attestation of the genius of the engineers and the artists connected with it, Sigiriya is both affirmation of the tradition and a variation of it. Those responsible for the Lion Gateway and the frescoes were sustained by a living tradition. So were the engineers, for the builders of tanks must have been skilled engineers. The accumulated heritage of the religious and the secular traditions are at Sigiriya made over, as they must have been elsewhere too, to ends which vary the usual, for what is noteworthy there is the intent of the king who raised this monument to himself. It is on this account unusual. Our appreciation of the culture of ancient Ceylon would be limited without Sigiriya.

We neither see the monuments of the past as they were nor with the state of mind of those for whom they were intended. It is possible that we can derive a new and original satisfaction precisely from this difference in our attitude or their state. In their present bareness, stripped by the action of time (and of human agents) of all the colour, ornament and wealth which decked them, they can acquire a new quality. In their ancient splendour they may, to some tastes now, have seemed chryselephantine. It is arguable that the appeal of the statue of the

Buddha at present on the North Circular Road at Anuradhapura is due to its austerity and its freedom from the in-
essentials of its adornment with gold and precious stones. We
see it in the uniqueness of the weathered stone, and respond to
it as we do to the magnificent statue of the charioteer of the
tyrant of Gela at Olympia without the colour and the silver
once lavished on it. But the weathered stone has its dangers too.
It may cheat the eye into believing that more is there than what
was ever intended. This is the price we have to pay when we
confront the masterpieces of another age. If we feel that they
are memorable, then we are at the first stages of understanding.

Old Ceylon

CHAPTER 6

Agents of Change—Fidalgo

The story of the Portuguese in Ceylon is that of a small group of Iberian people in the early sixteenth century, to whose superior armament at sea and desperate soldiering on land a large empire fell. For the better part of this century Portuguese ships were the hardiest and most numerous in Eastern waters, and their soldiers were engaged in slicing off for themselves portions of Africa and the East as long as sea power was theirs. Their difficulties in maintaining what they had taken possession of were tripled by their own shortage of man-power, their restrictive social system which considered only persons of gentle birth (*fidalgos*) for rank in the army or the civil administration, and their own domestic troubles during the period (1581–1640) when Portugal ceased to be independent and became part of the dual monarchy of Spain and Portugal.

Their largest possession in Asia, to which their writers generally referred as India, was their holding in Ceylon, an island to which with little show of legal justification they laid claim after 1580, when Don Juan Dharmapala, the king of Kotte, made the Portuguese king his heir. Since Don Juan never had been in possession of the island himself, his disposition of it to the latter could only be regarded as a polite gesture. Between 1505, when Portuguese caravels first appeared in the coastal waters of Ceylon, and 1658, when with the fall of the fort of Jaffna the last Portuguese troops left Ceylon, they had extended their holding in Ceylon from the trading station they were allowed to build in Colombo in the kingdom of Kotte to that kingdom itself, the kingdom of Jaffna, as well as a fair portion of the territories belonging to the one-time kingdom of Sitavaka.

Ceylon was important to the Portuguese on several scores.

First of all, it was the producer of cinnamon, the source of most of their profits in the early days of their control of the maritime provinces of the western seaboard. Secondly, it was strategically important in the grand design of Portuguese empire in the Indian Ocean. Finally, as an island, and a fruitful island with a climate far superior to any of their other Eastern possessions, with the possible exception of Malacca, it could have been the centre of their naval and commercial power. They lost it, as they lost practically all their positions on the mainland of Asia with the exceptions of Diu, Goa and Macao, because naval power slipped from their grasp.

Ribeiro, one of their soldiers in Ceylon, who served in the campaigns and sieges of the last years of their rule there, described his experiences in a book entitled *Fatalidade Historica da Ilha de Ceilao*. His *Historical Tragedy of the Island of Ceylon*, as it has been translated into English, could well be thought of as presenting his countrymen with an account of the 'fatality'— the sombre working out of a fatal destiny—of Portuguese rule in their possessions in Ceylon. Looking back over their one hundred and fifty years there we can hardly avoid noticing one of the ingredients of tragedy—the inexorable logic of a type of neo-classic tragedy—in the development of its action: the 'hamartia' of the *fidalgo*, the eminent man, neither wholly good nor wholly bad by the standards of the time, whose 'greed'— the moral sin of Avaritia—involved not only himself but his people (the people they ruled over in Ceylon) in ruin. But it is doubtful whether a genuine tragic emotion could be derived from the survey of such a spectacle. If the story of the Portuguese in Ceylon evokes the memory of any particular literary form, then the medieval sermon with its *exemplum*, in this case the Vergilian text of

Quid non mortalia pectora cogis
Auri sacra fames!

and moral disquisition thereon, is more likely to come to mind than tragedy.

Queyroz, whose *Spiritual Conquest of Ceylon* was written after its last scenes were played, regarded the story of his countrymen in Ceylon as that of God's judgements on the transgressor. Very much the gloomy and narrow-minded Jesuit, he had his

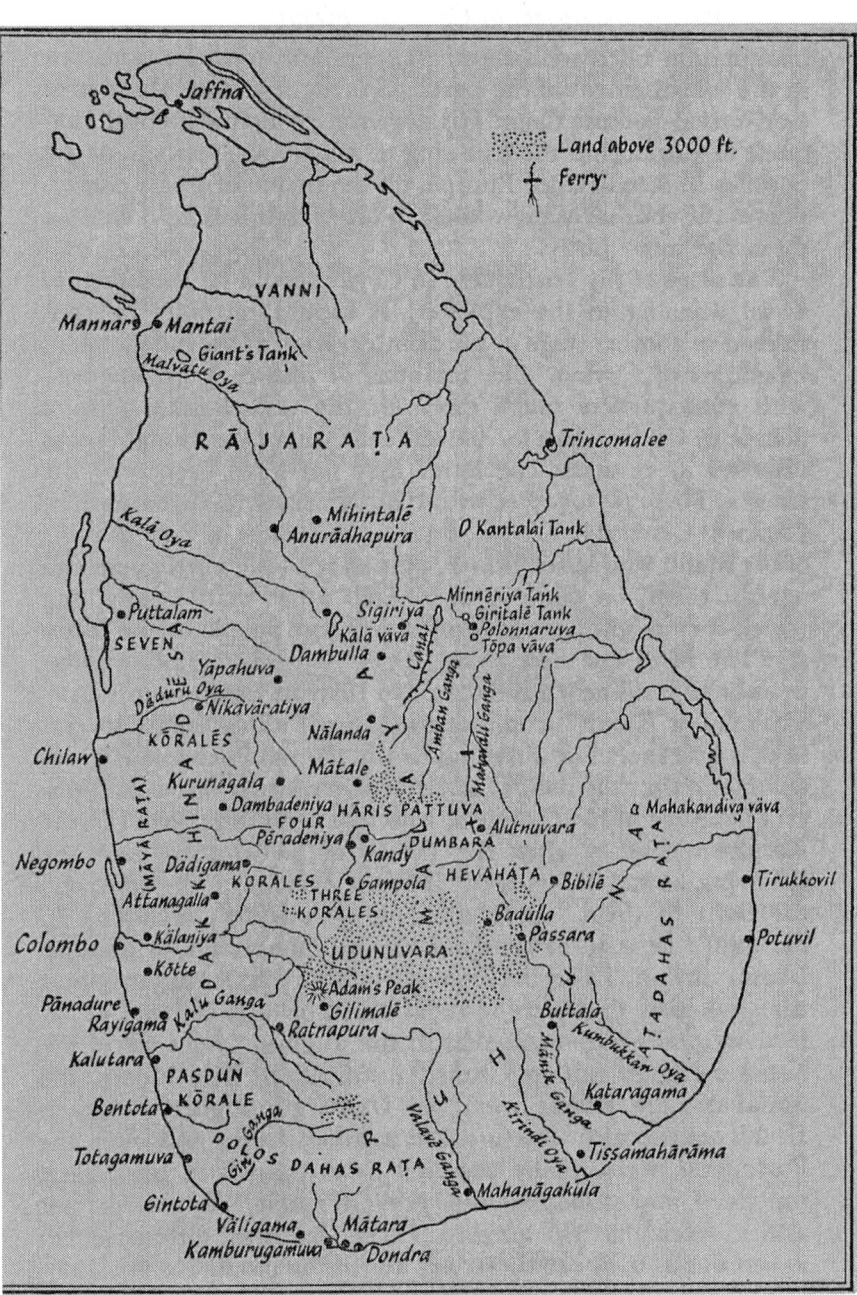

Land above 3000 ft.
Ferry

Jaffna

VANNI

Mannar • Mantai
Giant's Tank
Malvatu Oya

RĀJARAṬA

Trincomalee

Mihintalē
Anurādhapura

O Kantalai Tank

Kalā Oya

Puttalam

Sigiriya
Kalā vāva
Dambulla

Minnēriya Tank
Giritalē Tank
Polonnaruva
Tōpa vāva

Canal

SEVEN
Yāpahuva
Dāduru Oya
Nikāvāratiya

KŌRALĒS

Nālanda

Ambam Ganga

Mahaväli Ganga

Chilaw

Kurunagala
Dambadeniya
FOUR
Pēradeniya

HĀRIS PATTUVA
DUMBARA
Alutnuvara

a Mahakandiva väva

Mātale

Negombo
Dādigama
KŌRALĒS
Attanagalla
THREE
KŌRALĒS

Kandy
Gampola

HEVĀHĀTA
Badulla
Passara

Bibilē

Tirukkovil

Potuvil

Colombo
Kālaniya
Kōtte

UDUNUVARA

Pānadure
Rayigama
Ratnapura

Kalu Ganga
Adam's Peak
Gilimalē

Buttala
Kumbukkan Oya
Kataragama

Kalutara
PASDUN
KŌRALĒ

Bentota

Totagamuva

DOLOS DAHAS RAṬA
Gin Ganga

Vāligama
Kamburugamuva

Gintota

Mātara
Dondra

Mahanāgakula

Välavē Ganga
Kirindi Oya
Manik Ganga

Tissamahārāma

MEDIEVAL CEYLON

imagination filled with signs, wonders and miracles, and saw in the 'chastisement of the Eastern Portuguese state' the arm of God raised against them. His account of their temporal conquest of Ceylon has the true ring of a medieval sermon, as yet popular in Renaissance Europe, on the theme of God's perversion of the counsel of the wicked in order that he might chasten them the more justly.

The story of the Portuguese in Ceylon could be read then as awful warning to the exploiter. It should certainly be considered as another stage in the disintegration of the independent kingdoms of Ceylon. The fatalities of history were involved with consequences much direr for the unfortunate mass of people in Ceylon than for the eminent whom the almighty was disposed to chasten. The latter may not have been only the kings of Portugal together with their Viceroys in Goa and their Captains General in Ceylon, but also the rulers of various parts of the island who seized power, plotted with the Portuguese and against them, no more loyal to each other than to anything which they might have identified with the people or the country. The record of these years—1505–1658—is one of disunity, perfidy and military adventure. No ruler in Ceylon—in Kotte, Sitavaka or Kandy—could assure himself of legitimate succession, a quiet reign or a natural death. To the Portuguese it was axiomatic that the natives of Ceylon were treacherous and unreliable. One of their soldiers, who had been imprisoned in the Kandyan country after the defeat of Sa in 1630, says the following about the natives: 'It is the custom of all those who are born in them (i.e. islands) to be traitors', including in St. Paul's censure of the Cretans the inhabitants of another island, Ceylon. To all the Sinhalese military adventurers of that time, whether they were of royal blood or only claimed to be, it was equally axiomatic that in the attempt to get rid of the hated foreigner nothing lacked justification. The Moors, the Malabars, the Dutch, even the Danes (through a renegade Dutch sea captain) were invoked as allies. In the end when the Portuguese were finally expelled from the island the Dutch remained, and as the Sinhalese proverb had it, 'We gave pepper and in exchange got ginger.' There was little difference between them, both eaten raw are hot in the mouth.

The annalist of the *Rajavaliya* seized on the main reason for the success of the Portuguese in Eastern waters when he reported that 'the report of their cannon is louder than thunder when it bursts upon the rock Yugandhara. Their cannon balls fly many a *gauva* (a distance of one to four miles) and shatter fortresses of granite.' The superiority of their guns gave them their control of the Indian Ocean, until others had profited from the lessons they had taught. Artillery was known in the East before the Portuguese arrived there, but the Moors who had guns hardly used them. They had no occasion to. But when they met the armed Portuguese ships, they could not stand their gunfire. Varthema, the apostate Roman Catholic who was also an apostate Moslem, describing the engagement off Cananore between the Portuguese and a Moorish fleet, during which he was on one of the Portuguese vessels, writes: 'In the meantime the immense fleet of the Moors came towards us to pass by. On the same day, our captain departed with two ships, and went towards the Moors, and passed between two ships, which were the largest in the Moorish fleet. And when he passed between the said ships, he saluted both of them with very great discharges of artillery; and this our captain did in order to know these two ships, and how they behaved; for they carried very great ensigns, and were captains of the fleet. Nothing more was done that day. Early on the following morning, the Moors began all to make sail and come towards the city of Cananor, and sent to our captain to say that he should let them pass and go on their voyage, for they did not wish to fight with Christians.' Portuguese artillery had decided the day.

In November 1505 Don Lourenço de Almeida was blown off his course to the Maldive Islands. His navigational instruments failed to put him back on the right course and he found himself near Ceylon. His nine Baxels or buggalows anchored off Colombo. The king of Kotte, Dharma Parakrama Bahu VIII, sent a message to the Portuguese, whose reputation had already preceded them in Ceylon, with offers of peace and tribute to their king.

Out of a situation which practically compelled the king of Kotte, surrounded by enemies and princely claimants to power, to offer the Portuguese what was not asked—tribute and vassalage—his emissaries derived what innocent satisfaction they could by elaborately conducting the Europeans from Colombo to Kotte, five miles away, by a circuitous route requiring three days on the road. A proverb still extant in Sinhalese testifies to the extraordinary pleasure derived by them in this manœuvre, but the difference between the attitudes of the two peoples might well be illustrated by this episode: the Sinhalese childishly delighted by what they imagined to be a successful ruse; the Portuguese consenting to the make-believe, but with foresight checking on the actual distance from their ships which had been ordered to fire a gun at every turn of the hourglass. The first stage of the meeting of the two races showed that really to outwit the Portuguese the Sinhalese would have to learn ruses that spoke the language of guns.

The king, with the consent of his ministers, made a treaty with the Portuguese promising to pay the king of Portugal 400 *bahars* of cinnamon annually, in return for the 'protection' they afforded to the ports of Ceylon. Before they left Colombo they built a factory and a chapel for those they left behind. Whatever was in their minds with regard to Ceylon at that stage, it was obvious that here was the possibility of enormous gain. Queyroz notes that the Viceroy (the title given to the Portuguese commander of Goa) Don Francisco de Almeida 'confirmed the agreement forming such an idea of the advantages of Ceylon, that he wrote to the king, D. Manoel, persuading him that a part of the fleet setting out from the Kingdom should be directed to Ceylon, where, after subjecting that island, a new government could be created independent of the one already begun'. Though years were to elapse before such advice could be taken, the prospect of the conquest of Ceylon was being dangled before the imaginations of the Portuguese very early indeed.

They were in fact too busy with the extent of the seas and territories opened to them by their incursion into Eastern waters to be able to deal practically with Ceylon. From Sofala on the East African coast, through the Arabian Sea and the Persian Gulf to the Malabar coast and the Malay peninsula, they were engaged in reducing their maritime rivals to impotence and for the time being Ceylon had to wait. The Viceroyalty of Alfonso d'Albuquerque made it plain that the Portuguese had resolved to entrench themselves in the ocean their ships had more or less cleared for them. Goa was captured in

1510, Malacca in 1511, and Diu and Ormuz were already in their hands. Albuquerque first saw the possibilities of Portuguese empire and the colonization of strategically important positions in the East as the surest method of guaranteeing their control of its valuable trade. The Moors who controlled it were merely merchant shippers; they were neither colonists nor did they deny to others the freedom of the seas. Like the Dutch and the English after them the Portuguese learned that, though their main interest was the monopoly of trade, ships, soldiers and bases were needed to ensure its maintenance.

To enter into the anarchic events of the one hundred and fifty years of the story of the Portuguese in Ceylon is to gain little but an understanding of the chaos into which the old Sinhala kingdom had slipped. Even in the fastnesses of the Kandyan kingdom or in the Vanni—the forest regions, part of Rajarata—now ruled by chieftains tributary to the king of Jaffna or of Kandy, where an attenuated stream of life still trickled, wars, rebellions, the rumours of wars and the isolation of those parts changed the tenor of life of their inhabitants. Ceylon was passing through a phase reminiscent of that of the German states during the Thirty Years' War. Things were falling apart, but the Portuguese could not provide a centre which would hold, for they themselves were nothing but soldiers and sailors inadequately controlled by their officers or their priests, between whom there was more likely to be discord than any agreed policy. Had they possessed more men, control of the whole of Ceylon which continued to elude them might have been theirs. But each was a law unto himself and what marked their exploitation of Eastern trade was the philosophy of each for himself and devil take the hindmost, typical of the first stage of the contact of European nations with the East in tropical latitudes, when the adventurer took what he could lay hands upon.

To the complicated internecine struggles of the Sinhalese in these years a further complicating factor was added, that of the presence in the island of an alien race backed up by sea power and waging a mode of warfare, based on fortified positions manned by cannon, in which they were at a disadvantage. Until 1540 the Portuguese, occupied with securing their position in the Indian Ocean, did not apparently give much thought to

Ceylon, or Colombo. In 1524 the fort at Colombo was dismantled as the Viceroy, the old Vasco da Gama, did not think it worth maintaining.

But in 1540 Bhuvanaika Bahu VII, the king of Kotte, sent an embassy to Lisbon asking the king of Portugal to 'confirm Dharma Pala Astana (his grandson) in his empire, so that when he himself is no more, his spirit may survive in him, and with your support, triumph over those who seek his overthrow'. The ambassadors who presented this message to King Joao III described themselves as coming from 'the compassionate, wise, righteous, holy, admirable and victorious Boneca Bau, your vassal, Emperor of Taprobane'. A golden figure of the young prince accompanied the ambassadors and this was 'crowned with great solemnity'.

Joao III's solemn pledge of support of Dharmapala as king of Ceylon on the death of his grandfather was formally ratified in 1541 and promulgated through 'all the parts of India'. Notwithstanding these express legalistic statements, which are in interesting contrast to the 'elegance of Asian rhetoric' of Bhuvanaika Bahu's embassage, in 1551 the latter was shot dead, probably at the instigation of the Viceroy. The first experience of Portuguese support for his succession the unfortunate Dharmapala underwent was the sacking of the royal palace of Kotte by the Viceroy and his troops, who, disappointed in their booty, tortured a number of people in the hopes of finding more treasure and ended by terrorizing the inhabitants of the capital, 'robbing houses, violating women with great insolence and high-handedness'. Queyroz's comments on these reports of the behaviour of the Portuguese are instructive: 'At sight of this, the Chingalaz (Sinhalese) began to realize the evils which ensue from communication with ill-conducted foreigners, on account of the scanty military discipline that was almost habitual in India, for far different were the injuries which we received from the native enemies, who, if they did not spare property and sometimes even life, are not wont to break out against the honour of women. A great disgrace to Christians that Pagans should be more moderate in this!'

In 1557 Dharmapala, who had been educated by the Superior of the Franciscans, was baptized as Don Juan Dharmapala. He was little more than a puppet in the hands of the

Portuguese. As a Christian he could count no longer on the support of his subjects. Even before his baptism his forces were unable to check those of his warring kinsmen—Mayadunne, his grand-uncle, and his son Rajasinha I who lorded it over the better part of the kingdom of Kotte. Their successes in the field made the position of Kotte precarious.

In 1565 on the instructions of the Viceroy Kotte was abandoned. Its walls and fortifications were razed to the ground and Dharmapala took up his residence in Colombo. An attempt by poison on his life by Mayadunne left him toothless and a physical wreck. Whether the Captain General in Colombo, Diogo de Melo Coutinho, was privy to the attempt is doubtful; it was, however, one of the charges laid against him at the termination of his period of office in 1578.

In the meantime whenever the Portuguese had the available forces they made forays into the country. They had captured and sacked Mayadunne's capital of Sitavaka, had invaded the Jaffna peninsula, and had sacked and destroyed the temples and shrines at Dondra in the southernmost part of the island. Their foes retreated but were soon back again in the field, harrying them and even besieging Colombo, which could never be taken as long as reinforcements could relieve it by sea from Cochin or Goa.

In 1580 Rajasinha I, the son of Mayadunne, occupied Kandy, and expelled its ruler who took refuge with the Portuguese. In this same year Don Juan Dharmapala ceded his throne to the Portuguese king Dom Henrique. In 1583, since Portugal and Spain were united he ratified this gift, making over his rights to the whole of Ceylon to Philip II of Spain and I of Portugal.

In 1591 a protégé of the Portuguese, Konappu Bandara, who was a baptized Christian, turned tables on them in Kandy whither he had been sent with an army to install the son of the king deposed by Rajasinha I. He made himself king and assumed the name of Vimala Dharma Suriya I—'the apostate of Candea' as Queyroz called him.

Rajasinha I, deprived of most of what he had gained by his successful soldiering, died of blood poisoning in 1592. As Dharmapala had freely donated his territories to Philip II, it was with some show of legitimacy that Pedro Lopez de Souza arrived in Ceylon as General Conquistador, and the reduction of the Kandyan kingdom was attempted. .

Though the Portuguese captured Kandy and sacked it more than once, they were unable to consolidate their hold on it. Kandy with its threefold protection of forest, river, and mountain, could not be kept even by soldiers by now accustomed to marching barefooted in jungle infested by leeches, or 'bloodsuckers' as Ribeiro more picturesquely calls them. Lopez de Souza's expedition in 1594 began as a triumphal march to Kandy, to which he conducted the young princess Dona Caterina, the sole heiress of the Kandyan kingdom. But the General Conquistador was unable to maintain himself at Kandy against the hostility of the whole country. He retired and on the way back to Colombo was surrounded by the Sinhalese at Gannoruva and decisively defeated. This was the first of the military catastrophes of the Portuguese arms in Ceylon. It should have taught them the futility of trying to subdue the Kandyan kingdom with the arms and resources they had at their disposal.

In 1597 the wretched Don Juan Dharmapala died. He had been through his long reign of forty-six years only the shadow of a king. A devout Christian, he stands out of the cohort of corrupt and brutal Portuguese soldiers and officials surrounding him as a better man and Christian than any of them. That he should have been able to suffer the indignities, insults and humiliations put upon him so long was the greatest tribute to his Christian patience.

Philip II was proclaimed king of Ceylon by Don Jeronimo Azavedo, and the kingdom of Kotte ceased to exist even *de jure*. At Malvana a specially convened assembly of the Mudaliyars (or military officers commanding the lascarins) and nobles of the island was asked by which laws they preferred to be governed—'those of the kingdom of Portugal or by those of the kings of Cotta'. Queyroz states that the Sinhalese unanimously chose their own: 'by those of Raju (the king), according to their way of speaking, because they had been brought up in them'.

The Malvana Convention was as little representative of the people of Ceylon as Buckingham in Shakespeare's *Richard III* of the citizens of London. The reality, however, was plain. The

Portuguese would do as they pleased in those parts of Ceylon under their control. As for the laws and customs of the country, they were neither interested in them, nor were they going to be restrained by them, even if they did know what they were or how they operated. The testimony of Queyroz dispels the claim that the 'people of Ceylon' had anything to do with the fantastic proceedings at Malvana, or that the latter had any other significance than that of daubing force with the semblance of legality: 'Never, however, did they (the Portuguese) take pains to find out what these laws and customs were; nor were they ever reduced to writing like our ordinances: nor were they ever published so that all might come to know them; nor was any order given to the Dissavas (the Portuguese administrators of provinces) and other captains nor to the *foreyros* (renters or leasors of land) of the villages, so that everything was left to the good or evil conscience of each, and there was none to gainsay them in anything however evil it be, and however contrary to the laws and customs of the country, save the Ministers of the Royal Exchequer, who received orders according to the laws of Portugal; and some under pretext of war, others on pretext of being *foreyros* and others on the pretext of revenue or service of the King, who were at all times the biggest thieves in our conquests, moved by ambition and self-interest, for the most part had no other law than sin, nor any order save ambition.' There could be no more convincing proof than this of the extent of the dislocation of the social and economic system of old Ceylon by the Portuguese.

Before the end of the century the Dutch had appeared in Indian waters. In 1602 they were in touch with the king of Kandy. The Portuguese were losing control of the seas. Their ships were sacrificing seaworthiness and manœuvrability to size. Their unwieldy hulks, built in the shipyards of Goa and Daman and in addition poorly fitted, were designed to transport the loot of India overseas. Even the private loot of officers and members of the crew—the euphemism *caixas de liberdade* or 'liberty chests' was used of them—was allowed to encumber valuable deck space and interfere with access to guns. The smaller and speedier Dutch and English ships outmanœuvred the Portuguese carracks and mounted heavier guns. In 1612 Captain Best with two Indiamen, *Red Dragon* and *Hosiander*, beat off four Portuguese galleons and twenty-six frigates. Sea power was slipping out of their hands.

Their soldiers, however, fought with the desperation of men who realized that what they had taken by force could only be retained by greater force. The long state of war with the Kandyan kingdom, the inhumanities of generals like Azavedo, startling even in an age inured to brutality, are to be read as the confession of their failure to mobilize anything in Ceylon in their support. Their accusations of perfidiousness, so often levelled against the Sinhalese, sort ill with their own record of dishonourable dealing with the people of the country and their dependence on native mercenaries who often had no alternative but to share the fate of their masters. Their courage as soldiers, remarkable though it may seem, was only the instinct of the animal at bay, for in spite of the temporary successes of their arms under Azavedo and Constantine de Saa, an upright but bigoted Captain General, the odds were against them, and they fought with the savagery of beasts who knew they were cornered.

In 1628 Rajasinha, the youngest son of Senerat the king of Kandy, was assigned the Kandyan kingdom as his portion. The resoluteness of his hatred of the Portuguese led him to use the Dutch to get rid of his foes. In 1630 de Saa's force was cut to pieces near Vellavaya in Uva—the second of their major disasters in Ceylon. In 1637 the Dutch, who had been investing Malacca, had such a control of the Indian Ocean that they could blockade Goa at will.

In the following year the third and last of the great disasters of the Kandyan war befell the Portuguese. On March 28th, Palm Sunday, the army of the Portuguese General Diogo Melo de Castro was annihilated at Gannoruva. It was in this same year, 1638, that Rajasinha II signed a treaty with the Dutch, giving them certain trading rights in return for help in ridding Ceylon of the Portuguese. The end was not far off, but the fanatical fighting power of the Portuguese postponed it for another twenty years. Negombo, captured by the Dutch in 1640, was re-taken, and though there was peace in Europe between the Dutch and the newly restored kingdom of Portugal, the Dutch refused to be bound by its stipulations outside Europe. Galle fell to them in 1640, and after a desperate struggle Colombo capitulated in 1656. Ribeiro who came out to Ceylon in 1640 as a boy of fourteen, with neither noble birth nor connections to help him, describes the conclusion of the siege in which he took part: 'At three o'clock on the afternoon of the 12th May, 1656, we came out of the city, seventy-three very emaciated soldiers, all that remained there, including some with broken arms and minus a leg, and all looking like dead people. . . . We then entered the house where we met the (Dutch) General and Major who received us very warmly and gave us a toast in wishing us farewell, saying we must stay there and that before it was late they desired to go and receive the infantry and their lordships the Generals. We replied that their lordships could go to meet the Generals, but that all the soldiers were there before them. At this they changed colour, a great sadness following the cheerfulness with which they had received us.' The Dutch had been halted nine months at Colombo by a small garrison of which this was the miserable remnant.

After another long siege Jaffna, the last Portuguese stronghold in Ceylon, was taken in 1658 by the Dutch who kept possession of these forts, besides those they had, contrary to Rajasinha's instructions, built at Batticoloa and Trincomalie.

Ribeiro was convinced that the Portuguese had failed because 'we were unwilling to leave anything outside of our control; we were anxious to lay hands on everything in that huge stretch of over five thousand leagues from Sofalo to Japan'. He was thinking of the huge extent of land and ocean which the Portuguese had tried to dominate, but his words could well be used to point the moral of their connection with Ceylon. They laid forcible hands on everything. There was nothing they touched that they did not destroy. They were in the vanguard of European exploitation of the East and unconsciously they fulfilled their role of delivering the first concentrated blows at the foundations of the already shaken feudal economy of Ceylon.

With the advent of the Portuguese another stage in the running down of independent Ceylon was reached. When Marco Polo's ships touched at Ceylon at the end of the thirteenth century, its ruler was the Malayan Candrabhanu, and fifty years later when Ibn Batuta visited the island and made his pilgrimage to Adam's Peak, there was a kingdom of Jaffna, an

Indian chieftain ruling over Raiyagam, a king of Gampola, and Parakrama Bahu V at Dedigama.

Yet the chance of the arrival of the Portuguese in Ceylon, and the one hundred and sixty years during which the story of the island was connected with the rise and fall of their sea power in the Indian Ocean, cannot be thought of only as the speeding up of the inevitable death agonies of independent Ceylon. Their connection with Ceylon meant much more than the acceleration of a process which would have worked itself out with them or without. What would have happened if they had not arrived in Ceylon belongs to the futilities of the might-have-beens of history. The results of their rule over some parts of the island between 1505 and 1658 seem to be clear.

They brought Ceylon fairly and squarely into the world of the commercial rivalries of western European powers operating in the Indian Ocean. This in itself was a change of portentous significance. Very little which happened in Ceylon up to this time could be attributed solely to events in the island. South India, Peninsular India, the world of Eastern dynastic and trade rivalries had changed the course of events in Ceylon. Now the decisive influence was going to be exerted not by the comparatively familiar and known potentates of an Indian world, but by the sea power of European nations.

The immensely profitable trade in Eastern spices, drugs, silks, textiles and luxuries, so long controlled by Eastern Mediterranean powers like the Venetians, whose ships transported what had been brought overland and by Arab traders sailing the Indian Ocean, was sooner or later going to be disputed by new entrants into the field. In the fifteenth-century Italian science and Italian mariners still led the Western world, but the rise to power of the Ottoman Turks threatened the stability of the eastern corner of the Mediterranean. So Spain and Portugal at its western corner were to benefit from the genius of Italian seamen. When Vasco da Gama set out in 1497 as leader of a Portuguese expedition sailing south-west in search of India, he was heir to nearly seventy years of careful preparation in Portugal—exploration, the development of navigational skills, of ship-building and of map-making. And most importantly, German and Netherland banking houses were alive to the prospects of the route which they knew must be discovered. When da Gama arrived on the east coast of Africa, the rest was easy for the trade routes of the Indian Ocean had long been established by Hindu and Arab mariners.

Within ten years of da Gama's voyage western European banking houses had shown their practical interest in the direct route with the East. The commercial exploitation of the East by European nations, restricted up till now to the profits on handling and carrying what Oriental traders provided, enters on a new phase. Naval power enabled the Portuguese first to establish trading stations. They were then committed to military forts required for their protection, and for the maintenance of their forts or fortified positions, sea power was needed.

All this was not without its consequences for the way the story of Ceylon could develop. Ceylon was not simply the world's only supplier of cinnamon (indeed except for a coarse variety found in South India, there was no other source of supply available), it was an island lying strategically across important trading routes soon to be scoured by the ships of every western European power.

The Portuguese were not only mariners and soldiers intent on exploiting the wealth of the East. They were also rulers of a fair portion of the western maritime provinces of Ceylon for close upon seventy years. True they ruled over a small part of Ceylon; they were continually at war with the kings of Kandy, and with other aspirants to power in the low country. But the best part of Ceylon was undoubtedly theirs—all of the seaboard on the western coast from Matara to Mannar, and the whole of the Jaffna peninsula. That theirs was the richest slice of Ceylon was acknowledged by the old king of Kandy, Senerat, in the grim story told by Queyroz of his reaction when the head of Constantine de Sa was brought to him after the catastrophic defeat of the Portuguese at Vellavaya: 'They carried the head of the General in triumph to Candea where the King was, still ill, and when it was brought to his presence, addressing it he said: "How often did I ask thee not to make war on me, nor destroy my lands, but to let me live in peace, the Portuguese remaining absolute Lords of the best part of Ceylon." '

What the old king could not understand was that the Portuguese as exploiters of the wealth of the country could not rest content with only a part of it, even though it was its 'best part'.

Theirs was the first stage of colonial exploitation. It lacked some of the refinements of later capitalistic exploitation, for they put nothing into the countries where they had trading posts but money for soldiers and fortifications to ensure control of the wealth of the country, and for ships to carry it away. In pursuit of this main interest of theirs they actively interfered in the laws, customs and traditions of the country. They were, like all Europeans of that time and later, contemptuous of Sinhalese and Tamil culture and traditions. They had strong colour prejudices. All the evidence from their own sources points to the unsystematic way in which they stripped the country of its wealth. They first substituted themselves for the kings and over-lords in the feudal economy and then perverted it to suit their own ends. Their native nominees in the army learnt so quickly from them that they were more versatile oppressors than their masters. It was for this reason that the lascarins asked for Portuguese captains in the memorial Queyroz quotes them as presenting to the Captain General.

As for the *tombos*, or land registers, they compiled of areas under their jurisdiction, though they recorded traditionally held tenures, they could be set aside at will, and what was suitable to the rulers substituted. Queyroz notes that in 1631 the Vedor da Fazenda, or Comptroller General, made a new *tombo* in Jaffna because the old one exempting certain cultivators from service was 'harmful to the service of the king'. The lascarins, in their petition already referred to, stated that 'all we possess they enter in the *tombo* and take from us, even robbing the areca from our gardens'. This illuminates one of the uses to which the *tombo* could be put. It was often another mode of extortion.

As a consequence of their rule, and not by design, the maritime provinces and Jaffna, which received the brunt of their impact, developed differently from the Kandyan kingdom. These parts were softened up and became the more easily accessible to the process of change. The spread of Christianity by Portuguese missionaries, the gradual opening of schools, the natural anxiety of the inhabitants of these parts to secure for themselves the advantages of freedom from persecution and taxation which Christianity conferred, the desire of status seekers for the dignity of Dons and for Portuguese names marked a small part of the country.

The discontinuity of development in the two areas of Ceylon still weighs in the political balance of forces in the island. Rural Ceylon moved less far from its feudal world of ideas than the western coastal regions and Jaffna. It remained closer to the past which was slower in its departure there than in regions ruled by western European powers.

The Roman Catholicism of the Counter-Reformation touched Ceylon through the various Portuguese Orders who were invited officially to the island by Bhuvanaika Bahu VII. As professed by its evangelists it was a bigoted and arrogant faith as contemptuous of paganism as it was of Islam. But it had some success, catching the Buddhists of Ceylon at the nadir of Buddhism in their country. The Roman Catholic religious, much more anxious than the soldiers to complete the spiritual conquest of the island, were often the sympathetic supporters of the natives of the country against the worst excesses of the soldiers and the administration.

Much more successfully acclimatized by the Portuguese were the various plants and fruit-trees they brought to Ceylon from their other Eastern and American possessions. A number of fruits and plants, now imagined to be indigenous, like the guava and the chilli, owe their introduction to Ceylon to the fidalgos. For this part of their conquest of the island nothing but gratitude can be recorded.

CHAPTER 7

Agents of Change—Overkoopman

One hundred and thirty-eight years of Dutch rule over the coastal regions of Ceylon were like a wave slowly gathering force in the early years of the seventeenth century. It toppled and crashed over the shores of the island towards the middle of the century, and then withdrew, leaving new markings in the sand and a few land-locked pools. The tide of Dutch commercial energy which had washed the littoral of Ceylon was not without its effect even on inland areas which it did not touch. When the wave retreated at the end of the eighteenth century, the island was littered with the driftwood of the ruins of the old and the imperfections of the new.

The story of the Portuguese in Ceylon has some touches of saga to relieve its depressing record. The reader comfortably outside the realities of life on the seas and continents into which they burst in the sixteenth century can derive some quickening of spirit from such things as Camoens, even in English translation. There is nothing heroic, however, in the story of the Dutch in Ceylon. Theirs is the comparatively dull ledger of an *Overkoopman* (senior merchant) anxious to secure the best dividends for the shareholders of the company, dubiously squaring legitimate commercial honesty with the dictates of an elastic conscience, and occasionally perplexed that neither balanced as they ought to have done. The Memoirs and the Instructions of Governors General and Councils of India are only infrequently exciting. As men and women the Dutch hardly touched Ceylon as the Portuguese had done. In extenuation of the cruelties of the latter it might be said that their cruelty was that of human beings. Into it entered something of the passion of human contact. The Dutch had a penal code which was severe and frightening; theirs was the inhumanity of a code.

After all, there had been a Sinhalese poet to celebrate the
virtues and triumphs of a Portuguese General, miracles were
recorded of some of their religious, one of their commanders
was deified, while the sinister reputations of others are still
remembered. The unflattering colours of common day light up
the figures of Dutch Governors, their *Hoofd Administrateurs* or
Controllers of Revenue, and their Senior and Junior Merchants.
Out of the mass of papers and publications after their 138 years
in Ceylon there is nothing to set beside Queyroz's *Spiritual Conquest of Ceylon* in the meticulous passion with which it ruminates
on the past and what might have been. But during the years of
Dutch connection with Ceylon change proceeded apace, and
by the time they surrendered to the English in 1796, it was
clear that an old age was on the way out.

Events in Europe forced the Dutch into Eastern waters. In
1585 by the order of Philip II of Spain, who was also king of
Portugal, their ships in Spanish waters were seized since they
were in rebellion against Spanish domination. In 1594 a further
blow was directed at them, when their ships were denied access
to Lisbon. Philip II was crippling the economies both of Spain
and of Portugal, for what caravels and carracks were transport-
ing from India was on arrival in Europe distributed by Dutch
shipping. The Dutch had already built up a long tradition of
seamanship. They had proved themselves as herring fishers in
the dangerous waters of the North Sea, and since the discovery
of the Indies—both East and West—their ships had had the
largest share of the carrying trade of Europe. So important was
this commerce that it had continued even through the vicissitudes of their revolt against Spain.

Forced by the situation in Europe either to outflank the Portuguese and the Spanish by trying to find a way to India via a
north-east passage, or doing as the Portuguese had done and
sailing south, it was not long before they had fitted out an
expedition to India via the Cape of Good Hope. It was not
difficult to repeat the Portuguese achievement, for their enterprise was based on cartography, mariners' instruments, and
routes, winds and currents in the Indian Ocean already known
for several centuries to Hindu and Arab mariners. There was a
a further incentive to sailing south. Jan Huyghen van Linschoten, a Hollander, had been in the entourage of the Cardinal

Archbishop of Goa and had spent six years there. The second part of his *Itinerario* was published in 1595, and this was a compilation of Portuguese routes. This 'directory' was used by the first Dutch expedition to India in 1595, when four vessels set out for the Cape, and then, following Linschoten's advice, made for Java, reaching Bantam. The Dutch Government had ' "stipulated that the ships should as much as possible avoid conflicts with the Portuguese, and seek friendly intercourse with the inhabitants". Now, Linschoten had pointed out the great importance of the trade with Java, and had remarked that "there men might well traffick without any hindrance, for that the Portingales come not thither because great numbers of Java come themselves unto Malacca to sell their wares". So it came about that the Dutch ships chose the route to the Strait of Sunda, and Java was the first Indian country reached by them. It happened, however, that Linschoten had erred in assuming that the Portuguese did not come themselves to Java, for when the Dutch arrived at Bantam, the Portuguese merchants there were the principal cause that their first endeavours to open the trade were unsuccessful.'

Besides making practicable, through his *Nautical Directory*, the projects of sailing to India and grabbing some part of its extraordinarily profitable trade, Linschoten in his account of his six years in Goa had shown how remunerative this was. Even with the corruption of Portuguese officials, from Viceroys down to the sentries at forts, the Eastern trade used to bring in a million cruzadoes a year to the revenues of the king of Portugal. According to Linschoten's account, the first of the three years spent in India by the Viceroy was taken up with repairing and furnishing his house which had been stripped by his predecessor. The second 'to gather treasure, and to looke unto his profits, for the which cause he came into India. The third and last year to prepare himselfe and set al things in order, that he be not overtaken or surprised by the new Viceroy when he commeth, but that he may return into Portingall with the goods which he had scraped together'. The private fortunes of Portuguese Viceroys and Governors were notorious. Don Francisco de Lima, who was Governor of Mozambique and died in 1678, amassed such a fortune that he left a million cruzadoes to the Misericordia in Lisbon. Despite these 'scrapings' and despite the fall in the prices of pepper and spices on the European market, even at the worst times they were being sold at ten times their cost in India.

In 1602 the various Dutch companies interested in the Indian trade were amalgamated into the United East India Company which received a charter from the States General. This charter in effect secured a financial government interest in the company, and also gave it, in the name of the States General, the right to make treaties, to build forts, to mint currency, to appoint governors of territories and judicial officers and to levy troops. The United East India Company therefore had the powers of a sovereign state. Seventeen 'holders of command' represented the various local boards comprised in the company, and a committee of ten conducted the company's business with the States General. The effectiveness of the combination of commercial efficiency with government support and authority gave the Dutch company in its early years a great advantage over all other forms of exploiting the wealth of the East. The English East India Company was a chartered company too, but it lacked the active government support the Dutch company enjoyed. It is understandable that Queyroz, in the 1680s, considering the prospects of recapturing Ceylon and setting the Portuguese in the East on their feet again, planned for the future a company resembling the Dutch. He felt that it was 'settled by commonsense and disinterested reasons, that it is only by a Company that one can maintain and recover India or at least Ceylon; and that by means of it we can get the better of Holland, just as she got the better of us by means of her company'. With commendable foresight he was in favour of inviting Asian potentates to invest capital in this company.

In the same year the United East India Company was formed, Admiral Sebald de Weert on its instructions entered into negotiations with Vimala Dharma Surya, the king of Kandy. Nothing came of these talks, for de Weert succumbing to what was then regarded as the national vice of the Hollander, drunkenness, behaved offensively in the king's presence and was later killed with a number of others in his suite. In 1609 a twelve-year truce in Europe between the Portuguese and the Dutch, which, however, allowed the latter to 'negotiate with other princes and peoples outside Europe', helped the Dutch with their commercial expansion in the East at a time when their ships were able to defeat the Portuguese in European waters and hold up their trade with the East and America.

In this year came the first official attempt at colonizing the Dutch possessions in the East Indies, for a fleet of nine ships set out under the command of Pieter Both, nominated by the States General as the first Governor General of Netherlands India. He was succeeded in 1617 by J. P. Coen, a very able merchant and administrator. In 1621 the new city of Batavia, to take the place of Jacarta, was founded. It became the capital of the Netherlands Indian Empire, well placed strategically to control the Indian Ocean and Far Eastern routes, with a good deep-water harbour. It would only be a matter of time now before the Dutch could strangle Portuguese trade in the East, and attempt, in the face of competition from the English, to establish a monopoly in it for themselves.

In the meantime—between 1612 and 1615—Marcellus de Boschouwer spent three years in the Kandyan country trying to persuade the king, Senerat, to sign an agreement with the Dutch Company in return for aid from it against the Portuguese, who had advanced to Kandy and burnt the city. Senerat, like Rajasinha twenty-five years later, was ready to agree to most of the Dutch demands, if only he did get the help he wanted against the Portuguese. But nothing practical came of these negotiations either. The Company was too much involved in Java and the islands. Boschouwer's later defection from the United East India Company led to his bringing out an expedition from a Danish East India Company. But before it could reach Ceylon he died and Senerat had made peace with the Portuguese. All the Danes could do was to secure a treaty with the king allowing them to build a fort at Trincomalie, which they had to abandon.

By 1636, however, when Rajasinha II called on the Dutch in Pulicat in South India for help against the Portuguese, they were ready, now that Malacca was invested by them and their eastern flank was secure, to intervene in Ceylon in order to secure for themselves the monopoly of the cinnamon trade—its most valuable product. Linschoten had described it as the 'best and finest', and '(at the least) three times dearer in the price' than that obtained elsewhere. Paludanus, in his notes to his friends *Itinerario*, proclaimed that it 'healeth, it openeth and strengtheneth all the inward parts, it is somewhat attractive, stretcheth the mawe and digesteth the meate, it is also used against all kinde of poyson that may hurt the hart . . . the water and Oyle of Cinnamon doe greatlie strengthen all the inward parts, as head, hart, mawe and lyver.'

The Dutch Company was, at first, interested only in the cinnamon of Ceylon. Its dealings with Rajasinha between 1636 and 1656 can be understood in that light. Anxious to obtain a foothold in the island, from access to which their ships could at least hinder the Portuguese, but unable to take on their garrisons without help from the Sinhalese king, their emissary, Admiral Westerwold, signed a treaty with Rajasinha in 1638. By this the Company was assured of the monopoly of the trade of Ceylon in return for Dutch help against the Portuguese. The king bound himself and his subjects not to trade with any other nations, European or Oriental. An article of the treaty stipulated that forts captured by the Dutch from the Portuguese should be garrisoned by the latter only 'if the king so desired'. This vital clause, 'if the king so desired', was deliberately omitted in the Dutch copy of the treaty and was the first cause of trouble between the two contracting parties.

By the treaty the Dutch recognized Rajasinha's claim to be ruler of the whole island of Ceylon. But the king surrendered the economic control of both the Kandyan kingdom and the rest of the island by assigning to the Dutch the sole right to exploit its trade. True the South Indian traders of Tanjore were allowed to continue their trade with Ceylon, but in effect the king encompassed himself in the net the Dutch constructed.

As long as the control of cinnamon-producing areas was not involved, no trouble was likely between the signatories. Batticoloa which was the first of the Dutch 'possessions' in Ceylon was not an area where it grew. But after the capture of Trincomalie the Dutch refused to hand the fort to the king's army. Though the hinterland produced no cinnamon, the harbour was too valuable to the Company to be given up. In those parts where cinnamon was trumps—on the southern and western coasts—'the real intentions of the Dutch came to light and differences arose between the allies. With the conquest of Galle and Negombo (in 1640), in both of which districts there grew the invaluable cinnamon, serious disputes arose as to who was to be the controlling power. The King demanded that the places be returned to him to be administered by his officers as they had been conquered by the Dutch on his behalf. Realizing the immense value of the two ports, if they were to control the cinnamon, the Dutch had decided on sticking willy-nilly to these places.'

Rajasinha looked upon the Dutch as allies who, if they were assured of certain trading rights, would help him to achieve his purpose of driving the Portuguese out of the island. This he was helping them to do. The Dutch saw in the treaty the opportunity for which they had long been waiting and which they now could seize. To them, both king and treaty were a convenient mode of securing the best cinnamon in the world at the source of supply. It had long been a principle of European nations that treaties entered into with Oriental and African potentates could not bind them as treaties between Christians might. From the operations of law and morality which were supposed to regulate the conduct of Christians, Moors and Gentiles were expressly excluded, 'because if the principal part of (man, namely) the soul is condemned, the part which it animates cannot be privileged (to have) the benefit of our laws as they are not members of the Church'. The Dutch in suppressing the vital clause in their treaty with Rajasinha were only acting according to the logic of this belief. Their conduct can neither be defended nor justified, it could only be described as being no blacker than procedures already known in Portuguese times and assured of a long continuance.

In the years which followed this treaty two principles regulated the Dutch in their conduct of affairs in Ceylon: the good old plan that 'they should take who have the power, and they should keep who can'; and the sacred duty of providing profits for the Company. In 1640 Portugal, now free from Spanish Hapsburg domination, concluded a truce with Holland for ten years suspending hostilities between the two nations and allowing each to keep what it had acquired. The Dutch refused to agree that the treaty was binding on them in the East. They used the opportunity to consolidate their position in Negombo and along the coast before they were ready to treat with the Portuguese.

In 1644 an eight-year truce was signed between the Portuguese and the Dutch in Ceylon, despite the previous treaty between the latter and Rajasinha. A few months later the two European powers concluded an agreement of mutual protection against the kingdom of Kandy. But as the Dutch could not retain what they had taken from the Portuguese in face of the hostility of the king, they had to treat with him. In 1649 a new treaty was signed between Maatzuyker, the Dutch Governor of Galle, and Rajasinha which repeated the conditions of that signed between Westerwold and the latter eleven years previously. This time the clause missing in the Dutch copy of the treaty was incorporated in it.

When Colombo, after its heroic defence by the Portuguese, fell into Dutch hands in 1656, their attitude to Rajasinha was soon sufficiently clear to him. Far from making Colombo over to him as Hulft, their Director General who led the assault on Colombo till his death, had repeatedly promised, within seven months of its capture the Dutch drove the king and his forces from their positions outside the fort. From that time till his death in 1687 there could be no semblance of peace between them and Rajasinha. They profited from his own troubles with his subjects cautiously to extend their territorial gains; he did everything possible, in spite of their control of the coastline and their forts established at strategic points, to cause disaffection in their territories and to attack them whenever he could. To the majority of people in Ceylon he was its ruler, and the Dutch were in the districts they occupied only as protectors of the country accredited by him—a position in which they acquiesced as they had no legal right to be in Ceylon. One of their Governors, Van Goens the Younger (1675–9), described himself in letters to Rajasinha as 'the King's Governor of Colombo'.

At various times in negotiations with the king they claimed that they held their forts only until such time as he discharged his debts to them—the expenses of their campaign which they prepared with the skill and the honesty of a shady accountant. Quite early too they asserted that they had conquered the lands from the Portuguese who were the legal owners by the donation of Don Juan Dharmapala.

The position was cleared up long after Rajasinha's death. In 1766 Falck negotiated a treaty with King Kirti Sri, after a campaign in which Kandy had been taken and sacked but the Dutch had barely got away from the hill-country with the remnant of their forces. The Company was recognized as entitled to the sovereign possession of the territories it held, the king ceding to it of the coastal area of the Kandyan kingdom an extent to his 'breadth of a Sinhalese mile'. Its revenues, however, had to be paid to him by the Company. He was acknowledged as sovereign ruler of the rest of the island. Salt, from which the Company's blockade had often cut off the king's subjects, was to be freely available to them, and the Company was allowed to gather cinnamon from various districts belonging to the king. The contracting parties also solemnly pledged themselves to assist each other if they were attacked, and the king and his nobles were not to enter into any correspondence with any European nation.

But by this time neither peace with the Kandyan king, nor the assurance of the fixed supply of cinnamon, could help the Dutch power in Ceylon. Their sea power in the Atlantic had declined. It was ebbing away in the Indian Ocean, and in thirty years nothing was left to them of all they had gained in Asia but the East Indian islands where the United East India Company had made their first settlements.

Keeping what the Dutch held in Ceylon was indeed the preliminary to the sacred duty of providing profits for the Company. Cinnamon and areca which were the bases of the profits had to be gathered and the Company's monopoly secured against any interlopers. Elephants, trapped in the jungle and tamed, were another valuable article of export, for which, as for the cinnamon, the Dutch were dependent on the king's goodwill. As the Batavian authorities did not include the cinnamon trade in the Company's balance sheet in Ceylon, if there were to be any profits at all its economy had to be diversified and the costs of its establishment reduced. These two considerations decided the course of the story of the Dutch in Ceylon.

Cinnamon grew wild, and a great deal of it was obtained from the king's territories. It could not be gathered without the labour of the Chalias, the caste to whom this duty had been assigned. The cutting and peeling of cinnamon was difficult and dangerous work entailing several months in the year in damp and elephant-infested tropical jungle. The Chalias with a sharp

knife cut the shoots, and peeled the bark from them. When
dried these became hard, tubular, sheaths or quills. Conditions
of employment and the harshness of the penalties enforced if
the quota was inadequate turned most of those employed in the
work into hardened and desperate characters, who were a constant source of difficulty to the Dutch. There was constant strife
between the two, and more than once the rebellions of the
Chalias threatened Dutch control of the territory lying outside
their fortified positions.

The severest penalties were enacted by the Dutch to protect
the cinnamon plant and to maintain their monopoly both of its
growth within their territories and trade in its products. It was
a capital offence to damage or to destroy the plant and also to
sell or export the quills or its oil. A Hollander was in charge of
the Department, called the *Mahabadda* or the great revenue, the
peelers being controlled by their Mudaliyars. It was the most
important item in the revenue of the Dutch Company, and the
quota needed could not be obtained without work in the king's
territories. In order to put pressure on him to allow their
Chalias to peel cinnamon in his jungles, the Company often
blockaded the Kandyan kingdom, interfering with its trade and
cutting off the king's subjects from their supplies of natural salt
made by evaporating sea water in *levayas* or salt-pans on the
southern, eastern and north-western coasts, all of them controlled by Dutch shipping. But blockade to be effective must be
expensive, and the Dutch preferred, when necessary, to put up
with the most humiliating and obsequious shifts to get cinnamon by placating the king with yearly embassies, presents, and
acknowledgements of his power. Even after the Dutch succeeded in cultivating cinnamon in the Company's gardens in
the middle of the eighteenth century, they still were dependent
on the wild supply.

In the attempt to ensure the loyalty of its employees and the
small Dutch element in the towns, certain rights of private
trade had for a time been conceded to them. But this did not
stop the corruption which both the Portuguese and the Dutch
seemed unable to control. To read the Instructions of the
Governor General and Council of India to the first Governor of
Ceylon is to realize how deep-seated and ineradicable commercial dishonesty was. 'The principal qualifications', the Governor

General and Council decided in 1651, 'required in the Superintendent of the Cinnamon Peelers are honesty, unselfishness, wisdom and justice'. Had holiness been added the only adequate candidates for the post would seem to have been the knights of *The Faerie Queene*.

Cinnamon for Europe and for India, elephants, areca nuts and the whorled chank shells for the Asiatic trade were for long the pillars of the Dutch export trade from Ceylon. But maintaining their monopoly against other European nations, notably the English, and the ubiquitous Asian traders was a difficult and expensive undertaking. In addition to the export trade, and indeed necessary to it, was the lively import trade of the whole island—the rice, the Indian textiles, which had been for generations in the hands of South Indian traders. To monopolize the latter it was necessary to control not only all the trade in the island, but also in the Bay of Bengal. Even if this could have been done, the local trade was beyond the skill and experience of the Dutch. It had so long been the family business of the Malabari and the Moor that Dutch attempts at prohibiting them from trade, and even transferring groups of Moors from the western to the eastern coast, failed to achieve anything but the breakdown of the trade. Arasaratnam's study of *Dutch Power in Ceylon (1658–1687)* shows how Dutch attempts to monopolize the Asian trade of the Bay of Bengal led to similar dislocation. 'Monopoly created more problems than it solved. Its effects on the people of Ceylon were no less important and in turn created new problems for the Dutch. . . . There was a good deal of coastal trading within Ceylon itself, undertaken by the islanders, as for example, from Jaffna to Batticoloa, Galle to Batticoloa, Jaffna to Manaar, etc. The function of this petty trade was to provide one place with goods that it lacked from another which had them in abundance. All these were affected by the Dutch trade policy. Thus a number of avenues of bye-employment, which had partially sustained the people, were now closed. These were important for the common man because he had supplemented his income from the land by these means. And income from the land was, in this period, a most uncertain and inadequate one because of the breakdown of the tank system and the dependence on rains.'

More important, attempts had to be made to produce new

sources of revenue in the island, and also to increase the food supply as rice had to be imported from South India, Bengal and even from Batavia. In the Jaffna district which was quieter and better controlled than almost any other part of their territories, the Dutch very soon tried to introduce weaving and the dyeing and painting of cloth. For this purpose weavers and printers were settled in Jaffna from the Coromandel coast. The root which produced the red dye—*chaya* or Indian madder—was produced in Jaffna, and until the beginning of this century the distinctive Jaffna printed cloths were an article of trade. The Reverend Philip Baldaeus was apprehensive of the bad influence of these heathenish calico printers from India on his flock: 'It is further to be feared, that in time there may be a promiscuous copulation betwixt the Christians and Pagans, which must needs produce direful effects in the church.'

A start was made with the cultivation of pepper, as there was a good market for it both in Batavia and in Europe. Coffee was tried out with success by Rumpf (1716–23), and land was made available by the Company for the cultivation of both. Coffee was not drunk in Ceylon at the time, and, whether on account of the absence of a local market or on account of falling prices in Europe, its cultivation was not attractive, and was not persisted in.

More and more land was being planted with coconut during the long armed truce, as it might be called, which prevailed between king and Company. Sugar-cane was tried in the Maritime Provinces in the West, and tobacco near Negombo.

To save money and shipping space the Company tried to increase the local supply of rice. In the first years of Company rule slave labour from Tanjore was used to re-settle and cultivate the rice-fields ruined by the long wars of the Portuguese with the king. In connection with these attempts and also to transport cinnamon, the Dutch in the eighteenth century built a number of canals using the rivers and lagoons on the western coast.

For all these attempts at diversifying the economy the Company made available their lands and lands which they had resumed on the death or disappearance of their feudal holders. As a result there came into existence well-to-do officials and semi-officials loyal to the Dutch because their status and wealth depended on them. The wealth and influence of the Sinhalese Mudaliyars was increasing. Goonewardena notes that 'the Dutch hoped to counteract "attachment to the king" by giving the chiefs such material advantages under their rule that none of the chiefs would wish for a change of government. "The richer they are, the trustier they must become, as their wealth is like a security of their loyalty", said the Batavian authorities. Therefore, in addition to maintaining the chiefs in their old positions and privileges, they were given liberal grants of land, particularly out of the confiscated Portuguese properties.' It is of this group of people at the end of the eighteenth century that Pieris remarks in *Ceylon and the Hollanders* that 'the King's money revenue was probably less than that of some of the Mudaliyars in the Company's service'. The British in their first years in the Maritime Provinces came up against their wealth and influence and distrusted and disliked it.

Like the Portuguese, the Dutch in the territories they administered substituted the Company in the place of the king as the sole holder of land. Existing service tenures were not interfered with except in the interests of the Company's trade. The *tombos* were continued and revised. But it was clear from the instructions issued to the *tombo*-registrars that 'the work should be done without detriment to the Company'.

As the Dutch began to insist on documentary title to land before 'ownership' could be established, the *Landraad*, a court empowered primarily to hear land disputes, performed the useful service to the Company of determining through its assessors the true picture of what land could be claimed by it, and what services it was entitled to from holders of land whose claims had been established. Of course the 'native chiefs' who were members of the *Landraads* did often succeed in getting more land than was their due, but as the Dutch were dependent on them for their dealings with the people in their territories this could scarcely have been avoided. Though in the main the institution of customary service tenures was accepted, whenever these could get in the way of the Company's plans for the commercial development of land, change was made.

The Dutch were therefore uncompromising on the subject of tenures which seemed needlessly complicated and vexatious. It was decided very early by the Governor General and Council of

India that in the Colombo *Dissavani*, or Administrative District, 'because nearly all the lands in this jurisdiction are depopulated, abandoned, and laid waste, we have no need to follow any old laws, customs, or practices of the Sinhalese in cultivating them'. With every attempt at introducing new crops land was made over to the Company's servants with which in the main they proceeded to do as they liked, the hierarchy of native officials being the biggest beneficiaries.

In their process of clearing up the administration of their territories for the development of the Company's trade, the Dutch created other tribunals. The highest of these was the *Raad van Justitie* at Colombo, to hear criminal and civil suits, from which an appeal could be made to its counterpart in Batavia. Roman Dutch law was introduced in these tribunals in addition to the traditional laws of the country. One of the legacies of the Dutch to the British was the codification of the customary law of the Tamil country, called the *Thesavalamai*. The most influential part of the Dutch connection with Ceylon was the legal institutions they had set up in the country.

The Portuguese had been exploiters of the country's resources whose rights had been backed up by soldiers. This mode of operation was much too costly and wasteful for cautious merchants. War could be considered as the logical extension of diplomacy only when conciliatory means had failed. Even so its expense filled the Company's Governors and Commanders with horror. The elder Van Goens in his Memoir (1675) to his son who succeeded him as Governor commented: 'It can easily be seen what a mischievous and horrible thing war is, and what prejudice this Government has suffered thereby; and although through God's goodness we have overcome all this evil and now are in a better position than before, all our efforts should be directed in future to reduce our expenses by a well-regulated establishment and to increase our profits by faithful economy.'

By the end of the eighteenth century the sharpest contrast existed between life in the small Dutch territories and in the Kandyan country, which after one hundred and fifty years of war against the Portuguese and the long-continued economic blockade by the Dutch had been reduced to a state of ruinous penury. Since the death of Rajasinha's grandson Narendra Sinha in 1739 the Kandyan kings belonged to a South Indian dynasty from Madura, and the court grew more and more Malabar. After the death of Kirti Sri who was an ardent Buddhist, a noticeable split was developing between the Kandyan chieftains and the court, and soon the most influential among the former were intriguing with the Dutch, and then with the English.

Though the Dutch may have brought off some successes against the internal enemy in their economic war against the Kandyan king and the Moors, they were unable to maintain control of the seas in competition with the external foe—the English and the French. The three Anglo-Dutch wars, fought in the second half of the seventeenth century, had left Dutch sea power weakened. Their navy had been defeated in European waters by the English. Merchantmen had formed an important sector in both navies, but Blake realized that the armed Indiaman was not to be reckoned a decisive factor in European naval warfare, though it was still enormously effective in African and Asian waters. At the opening of the Third Anglo-Dutch war (1672–1674) the warships of a foreign power for the first time appeared in Indian waters—those of the French under de la Haye. The ease with which they proceeded to set themselves up in the Bay of Kottiyar near Trincomalie showed that before long European naval strategy would be applied in the Indian Ocean. De la Haye's excursion made no difference to the history of the island as an episode in itself, but it was important as a straw which showed the way the wind was blowing. Control of the Bay of Bengal and the Indian Ocean was necessary to the power dominant on the Indian mainland. Trincomalie which could provide control of both was therefore going to be a valuable prize.

During the War of Austrian Succession (1743–8) the French, with Madagascar, Mauritius and Pondicherry as bases, were ready to challenge English sea power in the Indian Ocean. The French fleet laid siege to Madras and captured it. Had Dupleix on the mainland been ready to act, the termination of the European war would have left the French the major power in India.

By the middle of the eighteenth century the English, having wrested the initiative from the French on the mainland and having obtained control of the Atlantic, were gradually reaching the stage when they could take whatever they chose to have in Asia. It was not the armed Indiaman alone, adaptable, well built, and trim, which finally turned the scales and gave England the mastery of the Indian Ocean. Naval squadrons from home had to be used to deal with the last threat to English shipping from Indian naval concentrations like those of the Angrias, and finally the French.

The English Company at Madras was showing an interest in the trade of Ceylon and the possibilities of the harbour of Trincomalie. During the Seven Years' War one of their civilians, John Pybus, at the Kandyan king's request, had sailed to Kottiyar, and from there had gone on a diplomatic mission to Kandy. As he had little to offer and wanted for the English Company exactly what irked the king to have to concede to the Dutch, nothing came of his long and tiresome vigil at the Kandyan court. But the Dutch had been warned and were the more anxious to seal off the Kandyan kingdom from sea-borne intruders.

In 1782, during the War of American Independence when the Dutch were drawn into fighting on the high seas through English interpretation of contraband laws, they were considerably chagrined at having Trincomalie pass out of their hands first to the English and then to the French. No sooner had the English taken it than they sent Boyd on a mission similar to Pybus's to the king of Kandy. But as the king had just died the chieftains were unwilling to negotiate with anybody except an envoy accredited by the king of England. Boyd, a civilian from the Company at Madras, was not deemed important enough.

The capture of Trincomalie by the French under Suffren was one of a series of exploits which could not alter the turn of events in Eastern waters during the war. The British were too strongly entrenched in India to be dislodged, even though temporarily the advantage lay with Suffren in the Indian Ocean. At the Treaty of Paris in 1784 Trincomalie was returned to the Dutch.

In 1793 war between republican France and England drew the Dutch in Ceylon once again against their will into the struggle. The French overran the Low Countries in 1794 and the Stadtholder fled to England. He was urged by the English to instruct the Governors of Dutch possessions in Asia to accept the protection of English forces against probable French attack. The Company at Madras was not slow to push their advantage home. This time Trincomalie and Ceylon were within their reach. In 1795 the Madras government invited the Dutch in Ceylon to seek British protection for the duration of the war, at the termination of which their settlements in India and Ceylon would be returned to them. But before any reply to this request could possibly have been received, an English expedition from Madras had reached Trincomalie. Andrews, a civilian in the Madras government, was appointed ambassador to Kandy. He informed the king that a large force had been sent against the Dutch and proposed a treaty between the king and the English.

The efforts of the Dutch Governor at temporizing were not successful, and the English proceeded to take Trincomalie after a brief encounter. In the meantime Hugh Cleghorn, a Scots professor who combined empire building with a passion for the role of a secret agent and a keen eye for the main chance, secretly persuaded Comte Charles de Meuron, the proprietor of a European regiment in the pay of the Dutch and forming the core of the Dutch garrison of Ceylon, to transfer it to the British on terms arranged between them. The loss of these soldiers must have contributed to the capitulation of the Dutch in Colombo, though the whole story has not as yet been satisfactorily pieced together. From the very outset the Madras government was determined to present Angelbeek and his Council in Colombo with a situation in which they would have no alternative but to surrender. This would explain the instructions to Stuart who commanded the British forces in Trincomalie to make sure that Batticoloa, Jaffna and Manaar were in his hands before Agnew, the Madras government's emissary, reached Colombo with its second letter to Angelbeek.

While the Dutch power in Ceylon was collapsing a treaty was signed in Madras in February 1796 between the British Company and Rajadhirajasinha's envoys, by which the former would move into the position of the Dutch as 'protectors' of the Kandyan kingdom, with all the privileges in trade enjoyed by them. The king was confirmed in the sovereignty of his kingdom (which excluded the Dutch settlements), he was to be given a 'situation' on the coast and the right to use a certain number of ships for trade. But this treaty, signed before Colombo was in British hands, was ratified neither by the king who wanted much more, nor by the British, who discovered that they got all they wanted without the inconvenience of giving Rajadhirajasinha anything at all. There was certainly nothing to be gained by the East India Company's granting the Kandyan king the very valuable concession of a 'situation' on the coast which the Dutch had not allowed him to possess.

In spite of a show of defiant refusal to consider the second British request for the temporary cession of Dutch Ceylon to them, Colombo surrendered with hardly any resistance. On 16th February 1796 the British took over the Dutch Company's possessions in Ceylon. They had displaced the Hollanders by playing the old English country game of fast and loose with both their European rivals and the Kandyan king. The former were deprived of all they had acquired in their one hundred and thirty-eight years in Ceylon, and though they might have hoped to regain some part, or all, of it in any future European settlement, the Madras government was determined to thwart these expectations. The Kandyan king was left with no brighter prospect than that which the Dutch had opened up before Rajasinha II in 1656. The Kandyan kingdom before long would have to save itself from its new friends and protectors.

Dutch rule left an impression on the island which remains to the present day, because it was based on principles of colonial development which endured long after the Dutch left Ceylon. To them it was fundamental that a colony should pay its way. To this end all their theory and practice were directed. Everything they did in Ceylon—the customs of the country they were disposed to observe, their fiscal policy, their management of the cinnamon monopoly, their use of a subordinate native hierarchy the better to secure their power, their agricultural planning, their attempts to raise commercial crops, their school system— all were taken over by the British who showed how well they could be made to work.

The contribution of the Dutch to the story of Ceylon will then be found not so much in conventional assessments of the results of their rule—neither in the system of Roman Dutch Law they instituted, nor in the mixed population they left behind, nor in their cuisine which still survives. It will be seen

133

rather in the function their administration performed. The Dutch bridged the awkward gap between medievalism and nineteenth-century colonial rule in Ceylon with a pioneer structure which the British modernized.

CHAPTER 8

Agents of Change—Lieutenant Governor

With the British in possession of the coastal areas of Ceylon in 1796 history seemingly repeated itself, for once again after a lapse of centuries the paramount South Indian power had intervened successfully in the politics of the island to establish itself there. To look back on the events of the last decade of the eighteenth century in Ceylon is to have familiar patterns catching the eye in both the larger and smaller time-scales of history.

In the larger time-scale the British, as the power emerging victorious out of the struggles of the South Indian kingdoms, naturally won a foothold in Ceylon. In the smaller time-scale they replaced the Dutch in Ceylon, as the Dutch by reason of their superior sea power displaced the Portuguese. To one European trading company succeeded another. In the same scale the Sinhalese king found, as Rajasinha II had discovered to his cost, that he had gained nothing by supporting the invader. And nobles and pretenders were going to intrigue more conscientiously than ever before to secure some advantage for themselves.

But history never really repeats itself. The design appears to be the same, but the fresh social and political situations which make up history trace new patterns. First and most important, the British were much more than the emergent paramount power in South India. They were not an Indian power, and their might in India was only part of a growing world empire. In the course of the next twenty years they were going to be engaged in wars with their French rivals to decide who was to rule Europe and the seas and so control the world.

135

The paramount South Indian power in 1796 was different from the Pandyans and the Colans of old time. Ceylon was no longer the cache which South Indian armies would rifle and then retire homewards because of more important concerns there. Strategically Ceylon was of greater value to the English than it had been to either Dutch or Portuguese. It was a link in the chain which was going to bind India and the East to British domination of the seas. Even if there had been nothing of commercial value in Ceylon, Trincomalie was a key with which the Bay of Bengal and the Indian Ocean could be locked. In 1802 the younger Pitt described it in Parliament as 'the most valuable colonial possession on the globe . . . giving to our Indian empire a security it had not enjoyed from its first establishment'. As long as the warship was to decide the control of the seas Ceylon would continue to fit that description, even though in actual fact Trincomalie was not developed as a naval base for several decades.

Furthermore, the East India Company was different from the United East India Company of the Dutch, not so much in its objects or policies, but in the stage of evolution it had reached in 1796. It was rapidly becoming the arbiter of the destinies of millions of human beings and the possessor of great stretches of territory. A trading company had been transformed into an empire, and the government of England had accepted, if Pitt's India Act of 1784 is remembered, responsibility for its possessions. Besides, the home country which was rapidly industrializing itself could logically make of its new acquisitions something different from what they had been in the old pattern of the seventeenth and eighteenth centuries.

As for the kings of the last remnant of independent Ceylon, the world which had changed all around them and had left the scars of change on court and nobleman was not for long to be kept out by pathless forest and high mountain. It is a rueful truth that neither king nor peasant can go on making bad bargains indefinitely, unless his purse is deep. Accounts have sooner or later to be settled. The Dutch with their blockade of the coast had begun the economic ruin of the Kandyan kingdom, it would soon be written off as an independent political entity.

Soon after the Dutch surrendered Colombo, Galle and Matara

fell into British hands, for their garrisons had been withdrawn, and the Kandyan forces which might have intervened to claim them retired, rather than provoke a conflict with the British, whose advance along the coast to Colombo they had been supporting. Rajadhirajasinha had both an army in the field and supplies for the British who could have made use of both had the need arisen. But they called upon neither, and the king, disappointed with the terms of the treaty signed by the Madras government, refused to accept it. He had good reason to feel that he had got little out of his support of the invaders.

The first twenty-five years of British rule in Ceylon seem in retrospect an era in which no great changes were initiated by the new rulers. In the first few years the uncertain political future of Ceylon may have accounted for British policy, for in any peace settlement in Europe the Maritime Provinces, taken from the Dutch, might despite the best efforts of the Madras government, have been handed back to them. In addition, the British with the French war on their hands had other things to occupy them than the task of working out a considered programme for their new possessions. In 1796 therefore the Madras government of the East India Company administered the Maritime Provinces.

But once they were made a colony of the Crown in 1802, even though they were still subject to the control of the Company and its Court of Directors, a significant principle of change had been introduced. The Governor of Ceylon, appointed by the Crown would naturally have his responsibility to the country he was administering and his own ideas as to how his mandate was going to be carried out. Whether Ceylon of the Maritime Provinces was fortunate in its first four Governors or not, they considered themselves placed in the island to rule, and they were all of them men with definite notions and ambitions of how they wished to rule. They were not free agents, there were multifarious authorities to be consulted, to be referred to, to be placated, authorities on the spot in Ceylon, in India and at home in England: the military, the Madras government, the Governor General in India, the Ceylon Agent in London, the War Office and Parliament. But they were not the officials of a trading company and in the last resort the Governor of Ceylon could be, even for the brief interval between despatch and the

137

reply to it, an autocrat. It was he who ultimately decided and acted. Round him were a cloud of witnesses who recorded and wrote with such fervour that sometimes it is difficult to tell what really happened. Practically all those who served in Ceylon in any position of responsibility in the early nineteenth century wrote about what had been done, what ought to have been done and what ought not to have been done. Most of them were the 'men' of some important personage or other in India or England. The past was history they had helped to make, and their interest in it was that of parental ambivalence.

The outstanding event of these first twenty-five years—the unification of the island through the annexation of the Kandyan kingdom—paradoxically took place against the wishes and the express injunction of the authorities in England, who were not anxious to encumber themselves with fresh responsibilities and new demands on the revenue of Ceylon. But with the Kandyan kingdom part of the British possession of Ceylon, a new scheme of things had to be moulded. The government of Ceylon tried, as will be seen, to carry its new fief as a separate entity, but substituting the Governor in Colombo and his Agent in Kandy for the king of Kandy was unsatisfactory, and radical changes had to be made.

For a long time the Kandyan wars and the conduct of the principals in these historic events were the main interest of the numerous tribe of Europeans who wrote about Ceylon in the early nineteenth century. But in the story of the Maritime Provinces the Kandyan wars fall into the sphere of foreign affairs. In home affairs the overall picture is of a see-saw between the reforming zeal of governor or official to tidy up administration, or at least to reduce it to known and manageable quantities, and a social organization which seemed to obey very different laws. In the end a fair balance seemed to have been struck, though it was clear where the weight of the government's interest lay.

The East India Company's principle of keeping out English settlers was extended to Ceylon which was a Crown Colony in which there were to be no colonists from the home country, nor could, by the same rule, land be held by a Britisher for more than seven years. This remained unaltered during the first twenty-five years of British rule. When this was altered, it was only one of the many great changes which accompanied the passage from the old to the new.

The British took over from the Dutch an extent of territory stretching from the north of Ceylon all along the coast to the banks of the Valave Ganga on the south, with Trincomalie and Batticoloa on the eastern coast. By the terms of the capitulation of Colombo, the Dutch had been guaranteed their paper money and their pensions, but they were sullenly awaiting a turn favourable to them in negotiations going on in Europe and were of no help to the British.

Dutch Ceylon had been administered by Dutch Disavas and a hierarchy of Sinhalese Mudaliyars and minor native officials. Apart from the Company's own gardens and lands, land was held, it will be remembered, in a complex mixture of traditional Sinhalese service tenures and all but private ownership where the old tenures had fallen into desuetude. Several decades of peace, the Dutch Company's stimulation of rice-growing and commercial crops and the agglomeration of small urban populations gave the south-western coast and Jaffna an air of prosperity, though the population was living very close to subsistence level. Population was increasing, and there was a scarcity of specie.

Among Mudaliyars and traders, both Moor and Tamil, there was definite prosperity. The fortunes of this small group of functionaries particularly in the early years of British rule should provide a revealing study, for though they did not make policy, they provided the British official with the only glimpse of the reactions of the ordinary man to British policy he was likely to have. It was clear that the mass of people lived in a world in which they could maintain themselves without depending on money for what they wanted. They were desperately poor, but as this had been their lot for centuries, no one troubled to remark on it until, exasperated, they resorted to violence.

The Maritime Provinces were taken over by the Madras government and administered by its military commanders. Pierre Frederic de Meuron, now raised to the rank of Brigadier General for his services to the British Crown, knew how the Dutch had governed Ceylon, and he was in touch with local feeling as it was represented by the Mudaliyars and others in the service of the Dutch.

The civilians of the Madras government in Ceylon, a small caste extremely touchy about their rights and privileges and resentful of the powers assumed by the military, looked after revenue and internal administration. They were given executive and judicial powers in all matters connected with revenue, and these they proceeded to use. The combination of executive and judicial powers was well known in Ceylon. This in itself would not have been objectionable, if the powers had been used by officials who knew the country and its people and could at least understand their language, and if traditional checks had operated.

But Andrews, the Resident and Superintendent of Revenue, was not interested in the latter, and was suspicious of the powers of the Mudaliyars which he was determined to diminish. As a first step service tenures were abolished. These were felt to be the foundation of their influence.

Madras administration in the first two years of British rule can be understood if the context of the military and political situation is remembered. The country was controlled by the military, apprehensive of the Kandyans and of the possibility of some French diversion in Indian waters. The few civilians knew neither the country nor its language; they could get no help from the Dutch who did. So a variety of expedients was resorted to in order to make sure that the cost of the military occupation would be met by revenue. The modes of taxation and revenue collection were a heterogeneous mixture of Madras procedure, bits and pieces of Dutch practice where this seemed advantageous to the official concerned, and the use of minor native officials from Madras who were given special powers. In the prevailing confusion so wide a latitude was allowed the collector of taxes that, at a time when most officials were venal, corruption became the rule. Taxes were farmed as most taxes were in Dutch times. The Madras officials were not accustomed to farmed taxes and the renters were given a free hand. A new tax, assessed on the possession of coconut trees and payable in silver, brought discontent to a head. Silver was more than could have been extracted from the ordinary inhabitant of the Maritime Provinces. A few months of Madras rule led to serious disturbances in the Sinhalese districts administered by the government. No taxes at all could be collected, the army had to be called out to put an end to the rioting, and the military were alarmed that their difficulties would be increased by Kandyan intervention. A Committee of Investigation was appointed in June 1797 to report 'on the state of the Revenue, and other important matters on the Island of Ceylon'. Meuron, its President, was able by being conciliatory and firm to end the disturbances. Lord Hobart, the governor of Madras, saw for himself when he visited the island that the new taxes would not do, and that the old system of assessing and collecting dues would have to be restored.

In 1798 the proposals of the Committee of Investigation were accepted. As a result there was a return to service tenures, the Mudaliyars were reinstated, and the Dutch land courts were revived. In October of the same year the first Civil Governor appointed by the Crown, the Honourable Frederic North, a son of the Earl of Guildford, arrived in Ceylon. He had only slender experience of any kind of administration as Secretary of State to the Viceroy of Corsica during its military occupation by the British in 1795–6, but he possessed all the qualifications necessary for a colonial governor. He belonged to the right family, was wealthy, had been educated at the right places, and had represented a pocket borough in Parliament. With him arrived in Ceylon nine officials—three of them just thirteen years old—of his own choosing, who were with one exception, Cleghorn, going to be his men.

He was to be Governor and Commander-in-Chief of the Maritime Provinces of Ceylon and its dependencies. The Governor General of India and the Directors of the East India Company were to have control, and all the revenues of the provinces were placed under the direction of the Company. Though North was Commander in Chief, there was a military Commander of the British forces in Ceylon whose authority over them and over British forts in the provinces was supreme. There was also the Commandant at Trincomalie responsible for it.

These restrictions on powers he was anxious to employ in the new theatre, where he was ambitious as a philhellene to play the roles of Solon and Theseus, irked North, and he soon set about getting rid of the 'Madras Click', as he called it. He wished to introduce some order into administration, to replace the medley of systems of ownership of land by registering them

141

in the name of a single owner, to organize the revenue system and to reduce the Kandyan kingdom into the position of a feudatory of the British Crown. He was much too small a figure for the part he assigned himself; much more was required than his good conceit of his powers and his undoubtedly good intentions. These liberal notions of his, which differentiated him from the Dutch governors of the past, were his greatest handicap, because they urged him to impulsiveness.

The Madras officials looked upon him as an intruder in spheres properly theirs. He disliked them and very soon battle was joined. Most of the Madras officials were in trouble on account of their dishonesty. Before long North was rid of them, though he was singularly lenient to his own men when they were found to be similarly unreliable in their management of public funds.

Within three weeks of his arrival in Colombo North addressed himself to the problem of the Kandyan kingdom. Rajadhirajasinha had died in the previous year, and the new king, Sri Vikrama Rajasinha, was a nominee of the Chief Adigar Pilima Talauva. North sent the king the usual flattering and obsequious letter. Whatever his intentions were when he wrote it, three months later he was intriguing with Pilima Talauva, to whom, in his own words to Mornington in 1799, he disclosed 'a distant glimmering of my own desires'. What illumination the king's Chief Adigar received in this fitful light will never be known. Pilima Talauva's disappointment in the king who was proving to be no puppet may have led him to intrigue with North, who saw in the Adigar the agent through whom his designs on Kandy were to be achieved.

The tortuous story of the intrigues has been well set out by the late Sir Paul Pieris in *Tri Sinhala*. Most of the evidence consists of North's secret diaries, his letters and despatches and the replies to them. The few scraps available on the Sinhalese side are mostly in translation, ever likely to be unreliable, in English documents. It is difficult to evade the conclusion that North's impulsiveness decided his policy. Pilima Talauva was hardly the fiend he was represented as being by English writers of the time. He was nothing more than a clever and ambitious schemer. Sri Vikrama Rajasinha may have been no angel: he was certainly not the Cretan tyrant to be outwitted by a new

Theseus destined to found another Athens in the Kandyan country. North knew what he was about when he was intriguing with the chief minister of a friendly power. Pilima Talauva realized that the British would never place him on the Kandyan throne. Opportunistically therefore he decided to play a double game with the king and with the British, relying on his own abilities to secure much more than he could get from either party in the resulting confusion.

The intrigues on both sides continued. North installed a suitable pretender to the Kandyan throne, Muttu Swamy, who was in Jaffna, while he kept trying, without explicitly promising Pilima Talauva anything but continuation in his office as Adigar, to secure a treaty which would make the kingdom a protectorate of the British with a garrison stationed in Kandyan territory and a military road from Trincomalie to Kandy. It is difficult to believe that he could have expected terms like these to be considered by a king who was invited to barter the only thing he had—the independence of his country—for the gift of protection which he did not want.

North felt an important step had been reached when the king agreed to accept General MacDowall with these proposals as British ambassador to Kandy. When these very naturally were turned down by the king's ministers, North was left with no other possibility of having his way than by removing the king and his 'perfidious' ministers. To him the Kandyan king was 'beneath all contempt'. As for his army, both MacDowall and Davie were of the same opinion; the latter, even after his capture and imprisonment in Kandy, was certain that 'with one hundred men (not Malays) I would bid defiance to the whole Kandyan force, as long as we had meat to eat'.

Carried away by being told what he was anxious to hear about disaffection among the king's subjects by both Pilima Talauva and the host of spies employed by the British, North expected a quick end to any Kandyan war. There was no great difficulty in finding cause for hostilities and the First Kandyan War was on. In January 1803 MacDowall advanced with an expeditionary force to Kandy, which was evacuated by the Kandyans. North's puppet, Muttu Swamy, was formally set up as king, but there was no popular support whatsoever for him, nor had the king's forces which had withdrawn been defeated by the British, who were completely isolated and in difficulties about food. Pilima Talauva, corresponding as busily as ever with the British, must have been as surprised as themselves at the turn events had taken.

MacDowall had to retire to Colombo on account of ill health, leaving Davie in command of the garrison at Kandy. Disease and the elements worked the final ruin of the British. The Malay troops were suspect and the lascorins were deserting. With the onset of the monsoon in May the position of the British was no longer tenable. MacDowall had recommended the evacuation of Kandy, and no other course seemed open to Davie. He left Kandy before North's formal order to retire was received.

On the 24th of June 1803 the remnants of the British army and Muttu Swamy were intercepted by Kandyan forces on the banks of the Mahaveliganga. The pretender had to be given up in spite of Davie's attempts to save him. He was taken to Sri Vikrama Rajasinha and executed. As for the English officers and men, they were either executed or shot; some may have shot themselves rather than fall into the hands of the Kandyans. The sick left behind in the hospital at Kandy were put to death. Davie and three others escaped with their lives, Davie ending his days in the Kandyan kingdom, the king having graciously allowed him two wives.

The First Kandyan War had proved once again that the hill country with its malarious climate and its lack of roads could not be held by inadequately supplied European troops against Sinhalese guerrilla tactics. Davie's 'as long as we had meat to eat' desolately echoes the predicament of European forces unsupported by an efficient commissariat. The experience of his men resembled in miniature that of the Grand Army in Russia. The hedgehog defeated the fox as decisively as climate, the refusal of the people to co-operate with the invader, and the guerrilla tactics of the Russians had destroyed Napoleon. Had there been a Kutusov on the Sinhalese side the British would have been left with only Colombo and Trincomalie, which their sea power would have saved from the general rout. But there was not, the Kandyan counter-attack was held, and the war dragged on desultorily for two years longer. British troops kept destroying villages, confiscating cattle and terrorizing the unfortunate inhabitants on the border.

As for North, he developed neurasthenia, and in a spate of recriminations against the tyranny of the king and the perfidy of the Adigar asked to be relieved of his post. But no replacement was forthcoming till 1805, when he left Ceylon for the more congenial occupation of travelling as a milord on the continent of Europe.

Clear enough though the political and military lessons of the 'First Kandyan War' were, the British were spared the necessity of learning them, for the kingdom divided against itself was going to be delivered to them by disaffected chieftains. North's escapade contributed little to its ultimate fall.

By contrast with his military and political exploits North's administrative policy was significant for the future. The impulse was provided by his enthusiasm for change which he could not bring about, hindered as he was by inadequate staff and the difficulty of understanding the complexities of land tenure and social organization. He took up with particular interest the recommendations of the Committee of Investigation relating to the Judicial establishment, and in Alexander Johnston there was a man equally liberal in his views, and as anxious as himself to press on with civilizing legal procedure and organizing the administration of the law. The changes made still remain in broad outline the features of the legal system of the island. The Supreme Court, with its judges recruited from England (only recently discontinued), Town Courts (later District Courts), Appeal Courts, and the right of appeal to the Privy Council in England, together with Roman Dutch Law, still continue.

The organization of the Revenue departments and education made a special appeal to North. His general attitude on these subjects is well expressed in his opinions of landholding by service tenure: 'to men of liberal sentiment and enlightened minds . . . an onerous and disgraceful servitude'. His own policy on all matters was described by his friends on the spot as 'having been executed for the intellectual and moral improvement of the Sinhalese'.

North's policy with regard to schooling reflects the general trend of the work of the administration in all spheres. There was change, but no great departure from methods tried out and found practicable by the Dutch. What was most significant was not what was actually achieved, but the indication provided of the direction of British policy.

North built up the Dutch system of education and in extending it laid the foundations of an organization which was to last with its major characteristics unchanged for nearly one hundred and fifty years. The Dutch schools had been in the main an agency for proselytism. The incentive to school-going was provided both by the fines imposed for non-attendance and by the rule that employment in the Company's service was restricted to baptized Christians. It was hoped that the schools would act as centres of some sort of cultural diffusion. One institution—the Seminary at Colombo—imparted higher education, the medium of instruction being Dutch. It was merely a training-ground for native missionaries. The subjects taught were alarmingly impressive: 'Latin, Greek, Hebrew, Natural Theology, the Passions and their government.' Higher education was not really the interest of the Dutch. Intent as ever to subordinate everything to the profit of the Company, the Dutch looked at their educational programme in the words of an early Governor, Maatsuyker (1646–50), as 'work whereby God's glory was promoted and the Company's position is at the same time assured'.

North's achievement may not seem to have been much more than this. Cordiner, the first Colonial Chaplain and one of North's men, was as delighted with the speed with which the children of the old Dutch Orphanage acquired the manners and appearance of British children as van Imhoff in 1740 had been astonished at the ease 'with which the little black fellows chatter in Latin and construe Greek'. And North himself suggested to the Court of Directors a scheme of 'sending . . . natives to England to receive a learned education and episcopal ordination, a regulation which (as I have had the honour to state in a previous letter) I consider as highly advisable not only in a religious but in a political point of view'.

The difference in programmes so much alike is to be sought in the character of the British administrator and the background of British political institutions. North himself, in spite of his remarks quoted above, was not moved by the same theological and religious ambitions as Maatsuyker. Before he came to Ceylon he had been received into the Russian Orthodox

Church, but in the island he was officially an Anglican. He was interested in religion only as one factor among others in schemes of moral improvement. And British political institutions would prevent them from discriminating officially between the Christian and the pagan. North saw practical administrative advantages in education. To him the schools, particularly the three Superior schools established in Colombo for Sinhalese, Tamils, and Europeans, were 'likely to produce in a much shorter time than I expected a set of well-qualified candidates of all the offices which are attainable by Burghers or by natives . . . and those of an inferior description are beginning to diffuse in their neighbourhood the spirit of industry, religion and morality and attachment to order and the present government'.

Quite early the principle was laid down that a knowledge of English and the fact of attendance at a school could be made immediately remunerative. This notion received stronger support when the Governor decreed in November 1801 that the only petitions he would receive would be those translated into English at the Academy on the payment of a fee. Later, when the home authorities insisted on economy and the finances of the Academy were considered, it was proposed to pay pupils a part of the translating fee.

As in England schools were part of the Ecclesiastical Establishment, so they were run for the most part by the various missionary bodies which set themselves up in Ceylon in the first and second decades of the nineteenth century. The missions had their partisans in Parliament, and awkward questions could be asked there in order to keep officials in Ceylon aware of their duty. Of course the missionaries were fervent, and naïve, proselytizers, but if they could not baptize those whom they taught, there was at least 'moral reformation' to be hoped for.

The trend is seen very early, in Cordiner's wish to find for the Colombo Academy a man who would speak English to its pupils. He was found—in 1802—in the person of Andrew Armour, the first of a long line of English teachers who worked in Ceylon with the intention of improving the Ceylonese by infusing them with English modes of thought and conduct and English examples. He was, unlike most of his successors, a man of few intellectual attainments, but he possessed the saving

147

grace of belief in his work. His régime gave rise to the highest hopes of the success of the policy of 'the intellectual and moral improvement of man'.

In 1802 the Peace of Amiens confirmed the Maritime Provinces in British possession, and they were made a Crown Colony, and an Agency for Ceylon was set up in London. In Colombo a Consultative Council and a separate Civil Service, distinct from that of Madras, were established. Ceylon's was the first overseas Civil Service responsible to the Crown.

In 1805 Sir Thomas Maitland, the son of the Earl of Lauderdale, took North's place as Governor. He was given a special mandate to restore 'the seemingly hopeless state of Ceylon's finances'. 'Honest Tom', as he was known to his military colleagues, was an able and practical person, temperamentally very different from the impulsive North. As a soldier who insisted on discipline, he was caustic in his condemnation of North's enthusiastic schemes and intensely suspicious of anything which increased expenditure and of departments likely to drift out of the personal ken of the Governor. He chased no will-o'-the-wisps with regard to Kandy, but he saw, as Pieris points out, how important it was to control the supply to the Kandyan kingdom, of 'foreign luxuries' so often requested by Kandyan noblemen and the king. This could be used as an instrument of political pressure. War with the Kandyan king, for whom and for whose forces Maitland had the greatest contempt, was out of the question because it was both pointless and expensive. Nor would he consent to involving the British government in the elaboration of an embassy to the king, without which a formal treaty of peace, and consequently the release of Davie, could not have been secured.

Without actually undoing North's schemes he curbed expenditure on them, because he was scornful of their pretentiousness. One of his despatches (quoted by Colvin de Silva) ran as follows: 'In truth, in everything that has been done in the island the same principle (as in North's plan for a Land Registry) prevailed; it has been one constant scene of writing fine plans home and doing nothing here except inventing places of no utility as far as related to the country and to provide out of the King's Orders for a set of favourites unworthy of the situations they held.' (Maitland to Edward Cooke, 19th October

1805.) He reorganized North's departments, suppressing a few which seemed to provide no advantage but to the holders of office in them. He was a thorough administrator, and was determined to stamp his own efficiency on Civil Servants and others in the government hierarchy. It was his insistence on efficiency which made him wary of the Mudaliyars. He had an orderly mind, and his tidying up of the administration gave the Maritime Provinces six years of peace during which roads between coastal stations were being built, trade was prospering and, to judge from the increasing volume of imports, there was some rise in the general standard of living of the urban population.

When Maitland left Ceylon in 1811, he was accompanied by the two sons of Mudaliyar de Saram. Their destination was Trinity Hall, Cambridge. They were the first students from Ceylon who have owed their training to English universities. Their number and their influence on their native land were at first negligible, but from the end of the nineteenth century they were among the strongest agents of social and political change.

Robert Brownrigg, the son of an Anglo-Irish country gentleman and the protégé of the Duke of York, succeeded Maitland as Governor and Commander-in-Chief. He was a soldier who had seen service in America and Europe. Although he had assured the Secretary of State that he intended to continue Maitland's policy of leaving well alone so far as Kandy was concerned, increasing trouble between the king and his Adigars, and the Civil Servant D'Oyly's correspondence with numerous Kandyan chiefs, gradually led Brownrigg too to fish in the troubled waters of Kandyan politics. Before long he was as feverishly excited as North had been at the prospect of landing the biggest catch of all—the conquest of the Kandyan kingdom.

In 1811 Pilima Talauva, in trouble once too often, paid for his misdemeanours with his head. He was succeeded as Chief Adigar by Ehelapola, who had been in correspondence with D'Oyly since 1808. The share of this inscrutable Englishman, who had learned Sinhalese and could speak and write it, in encompassing the ruin of the Kandyan kingdom has yet to be determined. On the surface he appears to have been—right throughout his career from North's time till his death in 1823—nothing more than the conscientious official engrossed in his duties and interested in Kandyan institutions. He had gained

149

the goodwill of some of the Kandyan chieftains and one of them entrusted his family to his care. He was assiduous in his letter-writing—to the chiefs, and to the Governor—but hardly anywhere does he betray anything more than the feelings of the good Civil Servant.

Most of Sri Vikrama Rajasinha's nobles were in touch with the British, whose description of him as a tyrant seems at variance with the reasons for his unpopularity with his courtiers, for the king was anxious to restrain his chieftains from exercising their powers arbitrarily and to the detriment of their tenants. British observers soon after the fall of the kingdom noted that this was one of the reasons for the disaffection of his nobles. The Chief Adigar, Ehelapola, kept sounding D'Oyly as to what the British would be prepared to do to put an end to what he termed 'the injustices' of the king. But he found D'Oyly sphinx-like and as ambiguous as the Delphic oracle. The British had learnt a lesson and were not going to be inveigled into any adventure in the Kandyan hills on the promises of any chief.

They waited while the disaffection, to which they had given momentum through their intrigues with the chiefs, gathered force. Ehelapola was deprived of his Dissavani and his honours in 1814. He tried to raise his people in Sabragamuva against the king and failed. He then crossed the frontier into British territory and placed himself under their protection on the 23rd May 1814. He had left his wife and family in Kandyan country and Sri Vikrama Rajasinha proceeded against them with the utmost rigour of the Kandyan law. The execution of the children and the reported forcing of the mother to pound their heads in a mortar with a pestle before she herself was drowned, were the subject of ballads and the main episode in the enormities listed by Brownrigg against the king.

The evidence for this particular detail in the execution of Ehelapola's wife and family—the forcing of the mother to pound the heads of her children—has been reviewed by Pieris in an appendix to *Tri Sinhala* and found unconvincing. The inhumanity is familiar illustration of the cruelty of various Portuguese, Dutch and Sinhalese commanders. Not quite the same story, but something close to it, was picked up by Robert Knox in the seventeenth century when it was repeated of Rajasinha II. The sexual fantasy lurking in it could have given pleasure to a psychopath. But Sri Vikrama Rajasinha was no psychopath. Quite apart from various practical difficulties in the story—such as the unusual size of the mortar which would have been required—its gory trimmings are more likely to have been corroborative detail familiar in folk belief about the activities of *yakkhas* than the sadism of any human being.

The Second Kandyan War followed upon the usual convenient pretext. Brownrigg would have liked to use as *casus belli* the punishment meted out by the king's court to some British traders taken in Kandyan territory and punished with mutilation as spies. But the Prince Regent would have no punitive action taken against the king on this score. Brownrigg was not to act unless British territory was invaded. He had already decided to invade Kandyan territory himself; his plan of campaign, prepared with Ehelapola's help, was ready. As the man on the spot he could decide when British territory was invaded.

This happened, according to his view, when the king's forces chased a band of insurgents across the border. Brownrigg proclaimed that the war then undertaken was on behalf of the oppressed Kandyan people who were to be protected, and the Second Kandyan War had begun. It was over in forty days. The veterans of the Peninsular War in Brownrigg's forces were not put to the test because the king's army under the Adigar Molligoda, who was in communication with the British, kept retreating all the while until the Adigar could safely give up his pretence of opposing the British advance and come over to them. This he did when his wife and family were safe. On the 18th of February the king was captured.

On the 2nd March 1815 at the Audience Hall in Kandy where the king used to receive his ministers, Brownrigg received the submission of the Kandyan chiefs. The terms of the agreement between the chieftains, on behalf of the Kandyan people, and Brownrigg, on behalf of the British crown, were proclaimed though nobody in Kandy appeared to be greatly interested. This agreement—the famous Kandyan Convention—was signed a week later. Six years later Brownrigg, now a baronet, was given leave as 'Conqueror of Kandy' to bear the crown, sceptre and banner of the kingdom of Kandy in his arms. By that time there could have been no manner of doubt, even in the minds of chieftains who had scarcely grasped the significance of the proceedings in the Audience Hall in 1815, that the independent kingdom of Kandy had ceased to exist.

CHAPTER 9

The Break-up of the Old

When on that March afternoon in 1815 Brownrigg, as representative of the British crown, met the Kandyan chiefs in the Audience Hall and the Kandyan provinces were formally ceded to the British, the royal umbrella (in the old picturesque phrase) had been raised over the whole island after the lapse of three hundred and fifty years. The last ruler who could claim suzerainty over all Lanka was Parakrama Bahu VI, the king of Kotte. The new ruler was the British king, George III, in Shelley's phrase of 1819 'old, mad, blind, despised, and dying'. Even if Kandyans, chieftains or people, had known or cared about the British ruler, it would have made little difference to them. Brownrigg, as his representative, was king. To many Kandyans the *Devenni Rajjuruvo*, (deputy or assistant king) was Ehelapola, the former Chief Adigar whom Brownrigg placed on his right hand at the Audience Hall.

Whatever the chiefs might have thought of the terms of the Convention which they signed, it was self-evident to Brownrigg and to the British that the Kandyan kingdom was rightfully theirs. They had been asked, according to Brownrigg, to overthrow the power of the legally constituted king by his nobles. Now that this had been effected, the nobles through the Convention yielded the British king the sovereignty over the kingdom. Brownrigg's Proclamation which launched the Second Kandyan War had insisted on the unanimous demand of the people of more than half the Kandyan kingdom to be taken under British protection. This war, like most others, was a just war: 'for the deliverance of the Kandyan people from their oppressions; in fine, for the subversion of that Malabar dominion which, during three generations, has tyrannized over

153

the country'. Its object was to ensure to the chiefs and the people their rights and liberties: 'to the chiefs the continuance of their respective ranks and dignities, to the people, relief from all arbitrary severities and oppressions, with the fullest protection of their persons and their property; and to all classes, the inviolable maintenance of their religion, and the preservation of their ancient laws and institutions, with the extension of the blessings resulting from the establishment of justice, security and peace, which are enjoyed by the most favoured nations living under the safeguard of the British Crown'.

This was an ambitious guarantee of the *status quo* with a promise, or a threat, of unimagined blessings in the future. It was hardly a statement of Brownrigg's intentions with regard to any future constitution for the Kandyan kingdom. As a political document it came under fire from the *Edinburgh Review* of June 1816, which was rightly sceptical of the high-minded principles on which the British proceeded against the legitimate sovereign of a country. He was '*dethroned* for mismanagement, *cashiered* for offences committed against his subjects, *called to account* for his actions, and *punished* for his abuse of power'. It went on to say that 'it would puzzle anyone, however, to find a defence for this interference, which should not justify us in other acts of interposition nearer home'.

Now that 'the most sweeping forfeiture' had been entered against the king of Kandy and he had been removed, the twelve Articles of the Kandyan Convention outlined the future pattern of the administration of the Kandyan provinces. 'The Great Chiefs no doubt understood the implications of the Treaty; but the Sinhalese version was embodied in complicated sentences whose elucidation taxes the skill of the student'—so Pieris in *Sinhale and the Patriots*. It is much more likely that the implications of the Treaty were just what the chiefs failed to understand, not because of its abstruse language, but because they were unaware of what has grandiloquently been called the 'dynamic of history' or who gets the power to push about whom. Some of them had certainly invited the British to help them in their rebellion against the king. To get rid of him was more important than discriminating between all the possible consequences of having the British in Kandy. One of them, Ehelapola, hoped that he would be invested with royal power.

There is no evidence that any of them foresaw that, since the king had gone, their own rights and privileges were going to be undermined by the process of a new system of rule founded on the theoretical assumption of the equality of all men before the law and the inalienable rights of property in a money economy. The people in the Kandyan kingdom were the people of the chieftains, their tenants and men. As such they were properly excluded from any share in the proceedings between Brownrigg and their betters. One section of the community, the *bhikkhus*, the most important of them related to the chieftains, had to be considered. One of them had actually drawn down the Union Jack run up on a flag-pole outside the palace. It was for their benefit, and also a politic extension of the statement in the Proclamation, that the fifth Article of the Convention declared that 'Buddhism and the Agama (the religion) of the Devas were inviolable', and that the *sangha*, its places of worship, shrines and ceremonies were to be protected.

This clause, with its reference both to Buddhism and to popular cults, was an acknowledgement on the part of the British of responsibilities soon to place them in difficulties with the powerful missionary organizations in England. The clause was expedient, for it would lull the chiefs into acquiescence. The Evangelical lobby in the House of Commons was uneasy, however, and immediately inquired about the sense of the word 'inviolable' in Article 5. Did it exclude missionary activity on their part in the Kandyan kingdom? About this Brownrigg was clear. It did not.

The sacred Tooth Relic of the Buddha, an object of immense popular devotion and the guarantee of the political stability of the kingdom, was brought back to Kandy and installed in the Dalada Maligava on the 24th April 1815 with appropriate ceremonial in which D'Oyly, as the representative of the British monarch, took part, making an offering to the shrine in the name of the British Governor. Pieris quotes him as writing with 'deep relief' to Brownrigg: 'We have this day obtained the surest proof of the confidence of the Kandyan nation and their acquiescence in the dominion of the British Government.'

But was this so? The implications of the Convention should have been clear to D'Oyly who had sufficient knowledge by now of Kandyan social structure and of British intentions to realize that two or three articles were contradictory. Article 4 reserved to the chiefs and minor officials 'the rights, privileges and powers of their respective offices'; Article 12 referred to arrangements for trade between the Kandyan provinces and the rest of the country. By Article 8 civil and criminal cases involving Kandyans were to be tried as they customarily were; Article 6 abolished various forms of torture and mutilation (which were customary). Freedom of trade would affect the income of the chiefs, and British law would not allow some of the procedures of the Kandyan code.

No specific economic or political issue precipitated the crisis in which the old Kandyan order expired—the rebellion of 1817–18. Outwardly everything seemed quiet. The Kandyan Provinces were separately administered. D'Oyly, by this time almost 'native' in his habits, seemed to be performing all the duties of the post of British Resident, to which he was appointed in 1815, with acceptance—giving audiences, easing the transition between old and new, trying his best to restrain the military in the discharge of their duties, and compiling copious notes on ancient usage. Ehelapola had turned down offers of both rank and money and had been refused some of the king's revenues in reward for his help to the British, but was apparently satisfied with the distinction of the title of 'Friend of the British' and the promise of a jewelled miniature of the Prince Regent. He was regarded with some suspicion by both Brownrigg and D'Oyly as a man who hankered after the show of royal dignity. Indeed the ex-king Sri Vikrama Rajasinha on his voyage to Madras warned the civilian Granville against him, with a remarkable insight into his psychology. The king remarked of Ehelapola's treachery to him: 'He owed me a debt of gratitude which he never could repay, and therefore took up arms against me. I ought to have known that this was the natural consequence of a sovereign placing a powerful subject on a level with himself. I twice gave him his life when he ought to have forfeited it to the laws of his country. It was impossible for him to love me afterwards, and I ought not to have confided in his professions of loyalty and attachment.' Simon Sawers who was Agent at Badulla when the rebellion began left the following manuscript notes which were used by his friend Henry Marshall in his *Ceylon*, published in 1846: 'The chiefs and higher classes of the Kandyans were greatly offended at what we called the impartial administration of justice, whereby the privileges and civil distinctions of caste were practically extinguished: but however general this inimical feeling to the English was throughout the whole country, it was not sufficiently strong to subdue the jealousy of the chiefs towards each other. In short, the outbreak of the rebellion in the province of Velassy was purely accidental, and the chiefs and people of the other provinces were as much taken by surprise as were the English authorities.'

The chiefs and the important *bhikkhus* were restive and ill at ease. Whatever they understood of the Convention, and of their Sovereign Lord, the king who ruled through Brownrigg and D'Oyly, rancour had been put into the vessels of their peace, and they came out against the British at a moment's notice. The trouble first started in the remote and wild regions of Uva and Vellassa, and then flamed through the Kandyan provinces like a chena fire. A pretender to the throne—one of a series manufactured by disaffected chieftains during the next eighteen years—supported even when later discovered to be an ex-*bhikkhu* from the Maritime Provinces, was set up by the rebels, for anything of their own, even a fraud, was preferable to the *ersatz* product offered by the British.

The Kandyan country was held through a series of forts in a wilderness as yet unprovided with roads. Militarily the forts could be defended, if they were supplied with food. Some had to be evacuated because their garrisons could not be provisioned. It was disease and not the guerrilla tactics of the enemy which took the heaviest toll of the various British detachments. In most engagements between small regular army groups and the rebels, the superior fire and discipline of the former enabled them to hold off the latter though they were outnumbered. The position grew serious because of the difficulties of supply. But reinforcements from India and the organization of supply lines decided an issue which was never in doubt militarily. The rebellion failed because it was impossible for the rebels with their pitiful resources to achieve more than disrupting communications, forcing the British to give up some of their forts and harassing their movements. Even if the rebels had been united, as they were not, little more could have been expected from them than delaying temporarily the British development of the Kandyan country.

The chiefs who were entirely responsible for the rebellion were suspicious of each other. Molligoda, the Chief Adigar, kept out of it entirely, though, on his own statement, he knew very well what was in the air. Before the trouble became wide-spread Ehelapola was arrested and moved to Colombo. He may have known of conspiracy, but he was not a party to the insurrection. In 1825 long after everything was over he was exiled to the island of Mauritius. The three leaders of the rebellion were Keppitipola who knew of the real identity of the pretender, Madugalle, and Pilima Talauva. The British policy of systematic reprisals against villages known, or likely, to be helping the rebels took the heart out of the rising. Some of the lessons taught the hapless villagers are recounted by Marshall who was in Ceylon in those years. He described Major Macdonald's decision to impress on the villagers in Uva the folly of continuing their struggle: 'With this view the work of devastation commenced; the houses of the inhabitants were forthwith set on fire and burnt to the ground, and all the cattle, grain, etc., belonging to the people, were either carried off by the troops or destroyed. The inhabitants appeared to be horror-struck at the devastation thus produced: they ceased to shout at the troops or to fire upon them; while they were seen on the neighbouring heights, and close to the skirts of the plain, gazing in silence on the flames which consumed their habitations, and the driving away of their cattle, they having had no time to remove any part of their property.'

When the Tooth Relic, which had been spirited away from Kandy in 1818, accidentally fell into British hands, the heart went out of the guerrillas and the ineffectual struggle seemed no longer justified. The leaders were captured, and two of them, Keppitipola and Madugalle, were beheaded. Their skulls were sent to Scotland, presented to the Phrenological Society of Edinburgh by Marshall. Keppitipola's was returned to Ceylon only recently. It was ceremonially buried and now, amid the dingy statues of British governors, has found a place in the national monuments at Kandy.

The rebellion should be viewed as the last involuntary twitchings of the already dismembered body of Kandyan political independence. The political and economic structure of the kingdom allowed the ruler and his feudal chieftains the luxury of minor forays among themselves. But the long-continued war against better-armed European powers, who could rely on their sea power to jeopardize Kandy's supplies of necessaries, was too great a strain. Trade between Kandy and the outside world was never completely cut off. It could not be. But the hardship of economic distress added to the devastation of war was beyond the resilience of the economic structure. The world into which the Kandyans—kings and chieftains—had been introduced in the seventeenth century was not of their making. Both king and noble reacted to it with a desperation which showed a failure of understanding. The nobles began intriguing with the Dutch and the British, until in the end they found themselves committed not only to selling their country but also to delivering the goods. It is impossible, however, to think of them as either patriots or traitors. What impelled them to the courses they took was neither love of their country nor a deliberate disregard of its integrity. The times were too much for them. They were not thinking of country, perhaps they felt themselves *vis-à-vis* Sri Vikrama Rajasinha to be Sinhalese who could not put up with a South Indian's curtailment of their powers. D'Oyly and Brownrigg certainly saw the possibility of this when in the first three Articles of the Convention the word 'Demala' was used three times to describe Sri Vikrama Rajasinha and his line. The chieftains were conscious of their rights and their privileges; they were the people. Their rebellion in 1817 was not a war of national liberation, but the struggle of the drowning man to clutch at a straw. As the dominant political force in the old order they went under shortly after the king had been removed.

How far the Kandyan kingdom had fallen from its high estate as a hierarchic feudal society is revealed in the circumstances of the capture of the king. He was taken by the Sabaragamuva men of Eknelligoda who was in the van of the British advance. It is ironical that Eknelligoda should have been reproved for his lack of consideration shown to the king by a 'Sinhalese from the British Settlements who acted as interpreter to the English officers'. The following is taken from the Englishing of his account of what happened: 'I stepped forward and said: "Nilame, you Sinhalese were up to this very day and hour subjects to and honouring this king, styling him with such epithets as 'God', 'Lord', 'Parent', and so forth; whereas we cannot be expected to show him the same regard for the reason of our having been subject to foreign administration from the days of our ancestors. He is your king, your god, your master and your parent. Now what is only necessary is to .take him; and it is not right for you to bind, insult, or injure him." ' The Kandyan kingdom rose against itself. It destroyed itself.

The rebellion against the king in 1814, as well as that against the British in 1817–18, were motivated by personal reasons. The political independence of the kingdom went in 1815; shortly after the political significance of the chiefs as direct rulers in the kingdom lost its meaning. In the reorganization of the Kandyan provinces the chiefs, down-graded and now the agents of the British in their dealings with the villager, still kept some social importance and patronage—a reflection in the comparatively minor sphere to which they were relegated of the great prestige and power of the British official in the most important affairs of government. The old titular ranks of Adigar and Dissava, shorn of their major administrative functions, were never abolished. Their existence gratified the status seekers, but the actual power the chiefs wielded was a shadow of what it had been. Never could it compete with that of the white ruler who was now the *Rajjuruvo*. Nevertheless over great areas of the Kandyan provinces, tracts unvisited by the British official on circuit, Adigars, Dissavas, Ratemahatmayas and Koralas still held sway. Away from these areas they trotted behind G.A. and A.G.A. (Government Agent and Assistant Government Agent), apparently content with their minor role in the new hierarchy.

In his Minute of 25th September 1818, Brownrigg in effect acknowledged the extent of his error in believing that one part of the old system—the privileges of the chiefs—could survive the destruction of its head and the substitution for it of the British power. The Minute is instructive for it reveals some of his predilections: 'The system of administering the Government of these new possessions through the medium of native chiefs holding high privileges, which they conceived to be very little controlled by the Articles of the Convention, was inefficient to establish the due authority of the Supreme Executive power of the British Crown, for any of the purposes of securing its stability, collecting its revenues, or ensuring the well-being of its subjects by protection from oppression or a full administration of justice. . . . His Excellency contemplates with a sanguine expectation of deriving pleasure from their being brought into action that these several principles, combining a great deal of civil liberty, and the fullest security of property, will soon be well understood and voluntarily acceded to by both chiefs and people of the Kandyan provinces.' He should have known that the stability of the kingdom did not really depend on the chiefs who accepted the sovereignty of the British ruler. If it had, even in the two years between 1815 and 1817, Kandy would not have been a garrison town, and no forts would have been needed all over the country. He was convinced now that 'civil liberty and the fullest security of property' were boons which the ordinary man in the Kandyan provinces would appreciate. There is such a strong tincture of eighteenth-century political thought in the phrases used that it is not surprising that they should have been meaningless to the Kandyan peasant. He was not free in the old social structure, neither was he a serf. He was bound to a traditional system which, despite its vicissitudes, afforded him the only security he could understand. How could he understand what a precious heritage was bestowed on him in theory, when in practice little difference was going to be made to him or to the way he lived for decades yet? Some of the awkwardnesses of service tenures could no longer be insisted on, but the benefits of British rule hardly touched him. For more than a century the world of the peasant was going to be dominated by the same figures of yore. Of course this had been his destiny and he could cheer himself up for all the shortcomings of the present with an idealized picture of the better days of the past. Living on a subsistence level, the great mass of people in the Kandyan country was going to benefit much more slowly than the rest of the island from the opening up of the hill country which followed the establishment of British rule. The feast to which they were bidden in 1818 with its tidbits of 'civil liberty and the fullest security of property', was one to which their appetites were unaccustomed. Right throughout the nineteenth century, and almost up to the present day, they remained unsatisfied spectators while others gorged themselves with the scraps which fell from the tables of their masters. When they became a political force and could understand, even vaguely, the power given them by the vote, their stomachs rumbling with hunger, they were going to overturn the tables, ignorant of what they wanted and unable to set up anything in place of what they spurned, but convinced that things were better in the only past they could remember.

The rebellion over, the administration of the Kandyan provinces was reorganized. Brownrigg construed the rebellion as public repudiation of the Convention by the chiefs. The government could therefore proceed by the Proclamation of 21st November 1818 amending the Convention to set up direct British control of the country, using the chiefs for the subsidiary function of ensuring that its orders were being carried out on the unimportant periphery. The army had been there and was still there to ensure civilian control of the new areas soon to be connected by road with Colombo and other provincial and military centres. The most significant departure from the normal in these years was really a topographical change—the work of the Royal Engineers and the members of a military Corps of Pioneers organized in 1821. The first Director of Island Works, a military man—Lieutenant-General John Fraser —was appointed in 1820, and under his supervision, in the governorship of Sir Edward Barnes, military roads linked Kandy with Colombo, with Trincomalie and Matale, and with Kurunegala.

The roads were built with the help of compulsory labour— the traditional system of *Rajakariya* or work in the king's service. As they were toll roads they soon paid for their cost of construction. They reduced distances between strategic points enormously, and though their surfaces were rough and in the monsoon they often degenerated into quagmires, they allowed wheeled traffic and put an end to the slowness and wastefulness of palanquin travel. Metalling of road surfaces was not begun till 1841. Lord Valentia who visited Ceylon during North's administration paints what is on the whole an agreeable picture of palanquin travel between Galle and Colombo. But it was unbearably slow, and in spite of the cheapness of labour (the cooly was paid six cents a day, thirteen being needed for each palanquin) extravagant. North on his circuit from Colombo to

Tangalle needed 160 bearers for himself and his suite. Already in 1814 there was a road to Galle which the *Gazette* of May 11th described as a 'fine road . . . the greater part of which rivals the turnpikes in England, perfectly practicable and easy for travellers'.

The new roads placed military control of the Kandyan provinces firmly in British hands. No longer would it be possible for guerrilla tactics to isolate garrisons or hold up the movement of troops. Some of the bridges on that first military road to Kandy stood until quite recently, when the demands of a much heavier volume of traffic superseded the efficient structures of Captain Brown. His best-known piece of work, designed by Fraser, was the satinwood bridge over the Mahaveli Ganga at Peradeniya. Though it did not live up to the claims made for it by the engineers and had to be dismantled quite early, the beautiful sweep of its arch was in better harmony with its surroundings than the bridge which replaced it.

It took some time before Kandy, still a village by any standards, developed into a town. The garrison, the civilians, and the administrative centre it became brought trade and expansion to the old capital. The Moors who had been redoubtable supporters of the British during the rebellion were first on the spot. They had been trading there before, now under British patronage they became a thriving colony. Gradually the numbers of other traders increased too. The wealth of a number of low-country families was made in Kandy, out of contracts for supplying the government with timber and with the farming of arrack rents. An indication of the comparatively strong grasp of the Kandyan provinces soon after the rebellion is provided by the announcement of the first Race Meet held in Kandy in 1821. There were minor disturbances in 1821, 1822, 1823 and 1824. But these were nothing more than outbreaks of mob violence soon localized and easily suppressed. That of 1824 was the ingenious frame-up of some 'conspirators' by an Interpreter Mudaliyar who was after their land. Risings such as these in the nineteenth and twentieth centuries were sudden bursts of violence which took government officials and their advisers by surprise, followed by army, police (and sometimes volunteer police) retaliation as sharp and unnecessary as official understanding of the situation had been inept.

Malaria and dysentery had seriously troubled Kandy's first settlers from the Maritime provinces. Malaria, however, was no longer what it had been when the fever started what Sinhalese guerrillas completed. The credit for this should be given to Sri Vikrama Rajasinha who began the process of stripping his capital of one of its ancient defences when he drained the marshes and constructed the artificial lake beside the old palace and the Temple of the Tooth. Malaria and cholera would continue to afflict the growing town, but the lake fed by streams put an end to one marshy area where mosquitoes used to thrive. This pleasant sheet of water with its earthwork and stone railing in the Kandyan style round it, the islet which used to be a miniature pleasure garden of the king's and the octagonal *Pattirippuva* (now housing a library) were a striking tribute to the artistic talents of the last king of Kandy. The new town has nothing like it.

The Kandyan provinces, still separately administered, were divided into eleven provincial districts in 1818, each under an Agent who was British and under whom British officials served. At the head of the administration was a Board of Commissioners to whom Brownrigg delegated his executive and judicial powers. Government Agents presided over the new courts. In the background, in an advisory capacity only, were some chiefs to whom the British official could apply for advice on local custom. The Supreme Court, with its civil jurisdiction restricted to Colombo and to Europeans all over the island, and the Provincial Courts were a feature of the Maritime provinces only. The Burghers, now loyal subjects and the first large group to acquire a knowledge of English, were providing these courts with lawyers. To the law courts were streaming litigants, witnesses, petition drawers, bailers, and lawyers in such a tide that it seemed to British observers that the native of Ceylon was incurably litigious.

In the royal gardens at Hanguranketa coffee had been found growing. Brownrigg had sent some of the coffee to England and favourable reports of its quality were an incentive to the attempt to grow it on a large scale in the Kandy district. Some plumbago or graphite was shipped to England in 1825 and the prospects of trade in it too seemed bright. It was doubtful whether the cinnamon monopoly, now in the hands of the

Ceylon government since the East India Company's monopoly had been terminated in 1821, was going to be buoyant enough to float the economy of Ceylon. Exports from Ceylon were beginning to suffer from the competition of inferior grades from elsewhere and the greater cheapness of cassia on the European market.

The usual revenue-producing stand-bys could no longer be depended upon. The pearl banks had been so unscientifically and unsystematically fished that no settled revenue but only windfalls, like the first three fisheries which enabled the Madras government to recoup itself for the expenses of the Ceylon campaign in 1795-6, could be expected. Elephants had ceased to be a profitable export in a country where the clearing of the jungle for roads was soon to set limits to the wild life that once ranged it. Army men, civilians and planters later were to begin the *battues* which decimated Ceylon's wild life. A major in the Ceylon Regiment was reported to have killed 800 elephants in the twenty years he spent in the island—an average of nearly an elephant a week. What was left the village poacher despoiled.

Ceylon's financial problems in the 1820s have a familiar present-day ring: the chief article of export, the commercial crop of cinnamon, was faced both with competition from other sources of supply and with world fluctuations in price. The balance of trade was against Ceylon and imports were increasing. If the establishment was to be maintained—the heaviest item of expenditure was the army—economies would have to be effected and new sources of revenue discovered.

In 1822 Robert Wilmot, the Under Secretary for the Colonies, moved in Parliament the appointment of a Commission to investigate the affairs of the Cape and Mauritius: 'Such a Commission might indeed be less necessary in the island of Ceylon, but government had no hesitation to extend it to that island likewise, in order to satisfy the public regarding the manner in which its resources were managed.' (Quoted by G. C. Mendis: *The Colebrooke-Cameron Papers.*)

It was not until 1829 that one of the Commissioners, William Colebrooke, arrived in Ceylon and set to work immediately with his questionnaire. He had served in the army in Ceylon, and had had experience of colonial administration in India. He was joined a year later by a Scots barrister, Charles Cam-

165

eron. Their report 'on the whole state of each colony', as Wilmot had phrased it in 1822, 'into its whole civil government, into the extent to which its different offices might be diminished, both in number and salaries; into the state of its laws; and also into the practical administration of its justice', published in 1831–2, was a momentous set of papers.

The report was significant on many counts. In the first place it reiterated what had been stated often enough before in the short connection of Ceylon with the British crown, that Parliament had the right to assure itself how the colony was managed. This may not have meant much in practical terms to the sum of the individual happiness of each Ceylonese, but it set up a tradition of the responsibility of Governor and British officials to a body which could be invoked by the native inhabitants of the colony—a court of appeal in their way of thinking as distant, incalculable and disappointing as the Privy Council in lawsuits, but still a useful safeguard.

In the second place, the pace and direction of development in Ceylon, as it could in the last resort be decided by Parliament, did sometimes reflect the climate of opinion at Westminster and not only that of British officialdom on the spot in Ceylon. It could also take very different views from those of Whitehall. The man on the spot in the East because he knew, or thought he knew, his Colony, could react coldly to Parliament, to itinerating members of Parliament, to Commissions, and to officials from Whitehall. Barnes, who was Governor when Colebrooke was expected in Ceylon, could not contain his dislike of the Commission of Enquiry, and his tart replies to the questions put by the Commissioner reveal the wounded *amour propre* of the official who knows what is good for the people he governs and is sceptical of well-intentioned cranks from Whitehall: 'Whatever Utopian ideas Theorists may cherish of universal fraternity without regard to Colour, Religion or Civilization, or whatever notions Levellers may wish to see adopted I am definitely of opinion that this people cannot nor ought to have in any existing circumstances any greater share in the Government than they have at present.' Robert Wilmot, who had initiated the work of the Commission of Enquiry when he was Under Secretary, now in 1832 Sir Robert Wilmot-Horton, Governor of Ceylon, was equally mortified. In his letter to the Secretary of State for the Colonies, in which he enclosed letters and communications from public servants, a merchant and a missionary, he pledged his word that he could not 'hear (and I have made ample enquiries) of one single public servant, or one influential individual expressing the slightest approval of the views and recommendations of the Commissioner, commented upon in these letters, but on the contrary I hear but one voice of reprobation'.

The official on the spot may have had an interest in showing that the intruder from Whitehall was wrong, but if the fate of some of Colebrooke's proposals is remembered—notably his Civil Service reforms which left the service in disarray—Wilmot-Horton was justifiably pettish about his report.

But whether the man on the spot was ready to co-operate or not, the wind of change from England was going to blow exactly where it listed. The small industrialist from the Midlands was going to be the dominant figure in the new age when England had had a flying start in industrialization. In the nineteenth-century race for markets her manufacturers, if they needed a philosophy, could fabricate one out of the natural laws of the new Science of Political Economy, the egalitarianism of Benthamism and Evangelical glorification of self-help. Bentham's 'felicific calculus' justified the freedom of all human activities uncontrolled by forces imposed from outside, for inevitably what was best for the greatest happiness of the greatest number would decide. The older view of the individual restrained by and functioning within an ordered society was exploded. In the new dispensation governments would hold the ring, and allow natural laws to decide what was most useful and therefore what was best.

Cameron certainly was a Benthamite. As a Scot and a barrister he probably drank deeply of the radical notions of his time. But Colebrooke—a soldier for most of his life before he came from Ceylon—was scarcely any kind of theorist. Where did he get his ideas from? He had been in Java between 1811 and 1816 when Raffles was Lieutenant Governor there. He was not on Raffles's staff, but had served as Military Secretary to his rival Gillespie. But he knew what Raffles had done in Java. Raffles had abolished the traditional system of forced cultivation and of forced labour; 'he had regulated modes of raising revenue; and had remodelled the administration of justice while retaining Dutch colonial law'. What Colebrooke proposed for Ceylon was on the lines worked out in the Dutch Indies nearly twenty years previously; and as Colebrooke saw things such changes would be humane and economical.

Dr. Mendis draws attention to two points in the report—its relation to trends by no means novel in Ceylon and its clearing of the ground for the subsequent building-up of a new economy. Some of its proposals 'had been anticipated much earlier by others like North, Johnston and Brownrigg'. The schemes North tried to hatch out were those of eighteenth-century moral improvement slightly addled, but they were of a liberal strain. Sir Alexander Johnston, who was Chief Justice in Ceylon, had struck a blow for the emancipation of slaves, had introduced the jury system, investigated local law and custom, and was an enlightened reformer. As a boy in Madura in India he had learnt Tamil, and he was an indefatigable compiler of information on legal systems. Brownrigg, through his wife, was a firm believer in the peaceful revolution to be made through education.

Colebrooke and Cameron were given an opportunity which none of the three referred to above had, because they were, in a sense, placed above the highest authority of all—that of the Colonial Governor. They did not forget 'the primary aim for which the Commission was appointed'—economy and the balancing of the budget. Their radical changes were not so radical after all, but combined a practical concern for the reduction of expenditure with elevated morality. In effect their proposals: the incorporation of the Kandyan provinces in the rest of the administration; the abolition of *Rajakariya*; the end of the cinnamon monopoly and reduction in customs duties; a common system of law for the whole island; the spread of English education; the institution of a Legislative Council and an Executive Council—were not in themselves revolutionary.

Not all their recommendations were accepted, but their principle was approved. Cameron's interjection in his report on Judicial Establishment and Procedure sets the tone of the earnestness of the whole report: 'I trust I shall be pardoned for making in this place a remark which has often pressed itself upon me. That the peculiar circumstances of Ceylon, both physical and moral, seem to point it out to the British Government as the fittest spot in our eastern dominions in which to plant the germ of European civilization, whence we may not unreasonably hope that it will hereafter spread over the whole of those vast territories.'

Its practical reality rises to the surface in frequent remarks like these: 'the discouragement to private capital of a Colonial Government's concern with the commerce of the island'; 'the relief of the island from a system which has checked the industry of the people and the prosperity of the settlement'; 'it does not appear that the natives are indisposed to hire their labour on moderate terms, where regular employment is held out to them'; 'in the present state of the country there is no private capital applicable to the restoration of ancient works, or the clearing of lands; nor can the government afford assistance to any extent in the execution of these useful works. The policy, therefore, of giving the utmost encouragement to Settlers from abroad is unquestionable'.

The report was not the instrument by which commercial development of the island was initiated. Coffee, the first large-scale commercial crop which succeeded cinnamon, had already been planted in Ceylon on plantations in the Kandyan country. And long before the Commissioners' Report was published Kandyans were growing coffee in their home gardens, and the export from Ceylon was increasing.

But it has been estimated that 'the reforms recommended by Colebrooke and Cameron turned the course of the history of Ceylon in the modern direction'. It was time in the 1830s to announce the beginning of a new age, for its evidences were everywhere. Before we go on to consider how the new enters the story of Ceylon, it will be well to look back once more at the old, now presumably on its way out.

CHAPTER 10

Between Old and New

The old and the new find an appropriate representative in the figure of Robert Knox, a Londoner born within the sound of Bow Bells, who spent eighteen years in the Kandyan kingdom between 1660 and 1679 and wrote the best account of it there is in *An Historical Relation of the Island of Ceylon* (1681). The country he wrote of had not changed very much when the British captured Kandy one hundred and fifty years later. Even now in the remote byways of the old kingdom something of the life Knox described survives. E. R. Leach in *Pul Eliya, A Village in Ceylon* (1961) writes that the technique of fishing with a plunge-basket as Knox described it is still practised in this Nuvarakalaviya village. And Ralph Pieris in *Sinhalese Social Organization* (1958) states that 'even two centuries after Knox's account, the ecology of this province (Nuvarakalaviya) has remained unchanged'.

The outstanding events in Knox's story should be set down as he remembered them: 'This Booke was wrote by mee Robert Knox (the sonn of Robert Knox who died one the Iland of Zelone) when I was aboute 39 years of Age. I was taken prisoner one Zelone, 4th Aprill, 1660. I was borne one Tower Hill in London, 8 Feb: 1641. My Age when taken prisoner thare 19 years: 1 Month & 27 dayes. Continewed prisoner thare 19 years 6 month 14 dayes So that I was a prisoner thare 4 Month & 17 dayes longer then I had lived in the world before, & one the 18 October 1679 God set mee free from that Captivity, being then with the Hollanders at Arepa fort to whome be all Glory & prayse. Robert Knox, 1696 in London.'

(Knox was never in a prison in the Kandyan kingdom; his father, himself and some of the members of an English ship were captured by the king's men when they had gone ashore in the Bay of Kottiyar. They were taken to the Kandyan hills, and were moved from village to village, where as the king's 'captives' they were looked after by the villagers.)

His is a record of the old made by a man whose countrymen were going to be nearly a hundred and fifty years later the agents of the new. This turn of the future he did not see, his was not a speculative mind, he was too much immersed in the reality around him to be able to project himself into the future. There is observable in his record the clear difference between the attitudes of a seventeenth-century Englishman and those of the world in Ceylon to which he was confined, a difference which held good a century and a half later. Knox's prejudices, limitations, deficiencies belong to the seventeenth-century Englishman he was, but in his 'relation' of Ceylon he can occasionally transcend these by his great natural gifts—his power of observation and his ability to see the essentials, even in the differences from what he was accustomed to and what he found in the strange land where he wandered at liberty though a captive.

His account of the Kandyan kingdom could even be given the particular value of anticipating some of the attitudes taken to Kandyan society by his countrymen in the early nineteenth century. That his attitudes were sometimes prejudiced and ill-informed is clear, but he was closer in time to the Kandyan and in the ability to understand him than his nineteenth-century compatriots. His errors are not very serious.

He was probably wrong in believing that the white man or the Christian was reckoned of honourable estate by the Kandyan. He wrote: 'All Christians either White or Black are accounted equal with the Hondrews (*Hamuduruvo*—those of honourable caste). The Whites are generally Honourable, only it is an abatement of their Honour that they eat Beef, and wash not after they have been at Stool; which things are reckoned with this People an Abomination.' Knox certainly mistook for a general rule what was probably true in exceptional cases only. Some Christians may have arrogated to themselves, because they were useful to the king and so placed in special positions in the army, a dignity to which Kandyan society would have given them no right whatsoever. Besides, those outside the hierarchy could satisfy their self-esteem by reckoning themselves superior to the members of an institution from which they were excluded.

Whites or Christians in the king's service, or in the collection of 'captives' Rajasinha II delighted in keeping, could regard themselves as favoured. But Knox states accurately that differences in personal habits must have placed them beneath the contempt of their neighbours. In the interleaved copy of his book to which he added numerous notes in 1698, he writes: 'At our first Coming, we thought they highly respected us, to pour water on our hands, to wash them after we had eaten, & wondred they did not to thare Commanders, but by the time we understood the reason, the sent of beefe was quite wornn away from our hands & mouths, so that they did not deny to honour us with thair pots to wash our hands but not to put them to our mouths to drink.'

Knox did see very clearly how life was bound up by caste, but he took some time to learn how it worked. For instance, he was not long enough there to know that he could not expect the neighbours to help him with the burial of his father who died within a year of their capture. But he was able to hire help. Later he realized, as he stated it, that 'handling the Dead makes people unclean'. He saw too, but only later, that his father's 'black boy' who was taken captive with them could not refuse to serve them because they too were captives. As long as Knox did not know this the boy was refractory. Knox did not understand how caste came into being, for, as we shall see, he looked upon the system of landholding with which it was bound up as a 'politic' invention of the king's to provide himself with what he needed. This rationalization of the aetiology of caste is understandable.

In political sentiment Knox appears to have been anti-Royalist and even Whig. He was born in 1641, the year in which Strafford was executed and strife between Parliament and English Royalists could not long be delayed. He was besides a Londoner and his family interests were in the trade of the capital. The Knoxes were of good middle-class origin; the father was a captain in the service of the East India Company. Knox's mother was a devout Christian, much given to the reading of the Bible. Knox himself seems to have been a sturdy believer in the doctrine of good works as the surest promise of the aid of divine providence. He was certainly uninterested in politics, but must have grown up as a boy in a household more sympathetic to the Puritan cause than to the Royalist. His comments, in the *Autobiography* discovered later, on the deaths of the Dauphin and the Emperor of Germany from smallpox: '14th April 1711 Dyed the Dauphen of france of the Small pox aged 50, & one the 17 ditto died the Emperor of Garmany of the Small pox also, in the 33 yeare of his Age, by which I observe that the greatest of Mortalls, who by some as estemed as Gods vice Gerents, & have the sole power over Nations, are afflicted & cut of by the most odious desease that falles one the meanest of theire subjects; wheare is now theire pretended power to Cure deseases with a touch of theire fingers' are the caustic reflections not of a political Leveller, but of the moralist on the levelling tendencies of Death. The acid of Knox's re-marks bites into a superstition disappearing at about that time in England that the sovereign by divine grace had the power of 'touching' and healing the victims of tubercular scrofula. Anne was the last English sovereign to keep up the rite.

To Knox all 'great ones' were subject to the disease of pride which deluded them. In this connection he delivered himself of the not very original pronouncement that 'Death does not make any difference or exception betweene the degrees of quality and dignity that men make, from the King on the throne to the Beggar that layeth at his doore, but as they were made of the same Dust of the earth to the same they shall return.'

Though Knox was no Republican he looked on the feudal society he described as being a tyranny by comparison with what he was accustomed to in England. English lawyers at the time had arguments strong enough to arraign a king for mis-government and to sentence him to death. Though the English penal code of the time was rigorous and grievous punishments were executed, English common law and the rights of members of Parliament, or of the city with its legal charter, would make an Englishman feel he was better protected by a code of law than any Kandyan by the force of custom. When Knox wrote: 'Here are no Laws, but the Will of the King, and whatsoever proceeds out of his mouth is an immutable Law. Nevertheless they have certain antient usages and Customes that do prevail

173

and are observed as Laws; and Pleading them in their Courts and before their Governors will go a great way,' he was as fair as he could be. His sympathies would naturally be with a system in which codified law defined rights and liberties.

As for his account of the king who was the incarnation of the country, whom he never met face to face, he gives us the image of the man as it was stamped on the imaginations of his countrymen. Knox had the offer through a Mohotalla of being given employment as a 'secretary' in the court, but his desire to get away if he could from the Kandyan country led him to prefer the obscurity of life in a village to the insecurity of the court. He therefore turned down these 'fair proffers'. He was summoned to the court, but fortunately for him neither king nor Adigar remembered that he was in attendance at Kandy praying that he would not be admitted to the king's presence. And so was safe.

The portrait he gives of the king, even the fantastic drawing made on his instructions, is a conventionalized picture of a capricious ruler of men, modified by Knox's own appreciation of a strong man. Of the greatness of this 'Politian' (in the seventeenth-century sense of 'schemer'), as Knox called him, there could be no doubt. Knox's prejudices incline him to give a darker shade to the ruthlessness with which he dealt with his enemies, but the main lines of the portrait present us with the strong man who needed all his powers to rule a country beset with foes and full of 'Great Ones' who were not to be relied on.

The ceremonial costume of the king can appropriately be described only by such a word as the American 'personalized'. It was extracted out of many modes and was the creation of Rajasinha himself. 'His Apparel', wrote Knox, 'is very strange and wonderful not after his own Countrey-fashion, or any other, being made after his own invention. On his head he wears a Cap with four corners like a Jesuits three teer high, and a Feather standing upright before, like that in the head of a fore-horse in a Team, a long band hanging down his back after the Portuguez fashion, his Doublet after so strange a shape, that I cannot well describe it, the body of one, and the sleeves of another colour; He wears long breeches to his Anckles, Shoes and Stockings. He doth not always keep to one fashion, but changes as his fancy leads him: but always when he comes

174

Rajah Singah the King of Ceylon.

abroad, his Sword hangs by his side in a belt over his shoulder: which no Chingulays dare wear, only white men may: a Gold Hilt, and Scabberd most of beaten Gold. Commonly he holdeth in his hand a small Cane, painted of divers colours, and towards the lower end set round about with such stones, as he hath, and pleaseth, with a head of Gold.' (The last king of Kandy, when he set out for Madras, affected a fashion which must have owed a great deal to the memory of Rajasinha's attire according to Granville who described it.)

There are numerous incidental remarks in Knox of the strange humours of the king. These strike a balance between the tyrant and the human being. He could be revengeful and cruel, yet he could be indulgent of any remissness on the part of his nobles. 'At uncertain times he will send out a Spy by Night, to see what Watch is kept. Who once finding one of the Great Men asleep, took his Cap, his Sword and other Arms, and brought them to the King; who afterwards restored them to the Owner again, reproving him, and bidding him take more heed for the future.' Like Haroun al Raschid 'he used in the night to disguise himself and walk abroad in the Streets, to see al passages, but now he will not adventure so to do'. The uncertainty which attended his ceremonial appearances must have been a sore trial to his 'Great Ones'. Knox's description of the court chasing the king points to the pleasure Rajasinha must have derived from his contrariness: 'But when he is minded to go abroad, though it be never so little a way, and he seldom or never goes far, Order is given some time before, for all Soldiers of his Guards which are a great many, it may be Thousands, together with a Dutch and Portugal Captain with their Flags and Soldiers, Drummers, Trumpeters, Pipers, Singers, and all belonging, such as Elephants, Horses, Falkeners with their Faulkons, and many others, to stand at the Gate in a readiness to attend his pleasure. And tho he means not to come forth, yet they must wait in this manner, until he give order, that they may depart to their houses. Commonly all this assembly are gathered together at the Palace three or four times before he comes out once. And oftentimes he comes out when none there are aware of it, with only those that attend on his person within his Palace. And then when it is heard, that his Majesty is come forth, they all run ready to break their necks, and place themselves at a distance to Guard his Person and wait his pleasure.'

Knox considered the king a man of 'Spirit'. There was a strong strain of nobility and greatness in Rajasinha. If he took delight in the 'windy Titles' given him, it is not difficult to imagine the satisfaction of a man of spirit in the exhibition of the pusillanimity of those who used them in addressing him. The Dutch could never understand Rajasinha. At times they felt they could get their way with him by humouring him as they might a petulant schoolboy with trifles like coloured marbles. But they could never be sure what he would do. Knox noted how often they were deceived: 'Yet at other times, upon better Consideration, he will not be Flattered, but falls upon them at unawares, and does them great damage.'

Knox was wrong as were most people in the kingdom and the Dutch about the fate of Rajasinha's son. It was assumed that he had either died or been put to death, but shortly before Rajasinha died, in 1687, he presented his son, the future Vimala Dharma Surya II, to his court. Knox's comment on the impression he may have given his reader, that he had 'incerted a lye' into his *Historical Relation*, is interesting, for in the reference to the old king is perhaps a trace of some personal feeling towards him: 'I thinke I neede not doubte of any Readers pardon that I have incerted a lye, for if they themselves had bin upon the place they might as safely have bin deceaved as myselfe, but I must Confesse it is some Injury to my old Master Raja Singah whose Tyranny without this Act was not inferiour to any. . . .'

Knox came closer in sympathy to this king than to any other 'great one' he knew. He was received in audience by Charles II in 1683 and had an hour's conversation with him. But no mention is made by Knox of the honour done him or of this meeting. To him Charles II was apparently not as impressive as the Kandyan king.

His account of the country and the people could be considered as a description of the land which the English took over in 1815. It was undeveloped, most of it in high forest, with insufficient well-watered arable land in the valleys for the crops of its population. The king's wars, the internal troubles between nobles and king, disastrous though they may seem now to the functioning of the kingdom, were no doubt a strain, but part of the pattern of life to which the peasant was accustomed. As he looked at the Kandyan country Knox had in his mind's eye the England of his time. By comparison with it the tenurial system he observed was stagnant, it was devoid of the incentive he reckoned necessary to all thriving societies. In such a state what could it profit a man to toil, if there was no expectation of enjoying the fruit of his labours? Yet his incidental remarks and his account of his own activities show that the system was not as rigid as he described it as being. He had the good sense to see that the indolence of the Kandyans, of which the nineteenth-century European accused them, was not entirely due to instinctive sloth: 'Yet in this I must a little vindicate them; For what indeed should they do with more than Food and Ray-ment, seeing as their Estates encrease, so do their Taxes also? And altho the People be generally covetous, spending but little, scraping together what they can, yet such is the Government they are under, that they are afraid to be known to have any thing, lest it be taken away from them. Neither have they any encouragement for their industry, having no Vend by Traffic and Commerce for what they have got.'

Old Ceylon was an agricultural community holding land in lieu of services performed. 'The payment of rent' which Knox speaks of was most often a percentage of the crops raised on the land and not money. Knox thought that the system of feudal land tenure he described was the special device of the king's by which he maintained himself in power in a country in which all sources of wealth were agricultural: 'But because Policy is a necessary endowment of a Prince, I will first shew in an instance of two, that he is not devoid of it. The Countrey being wholly His, the King Farms out his Land, not for Money, but Service. And the People enjoy Portions of Land from the King, and instead of Rent, they have their several appointments, some are to serve the King in his Wars, some in their Trade, some serve him for Labourers, and others are as Farmers to furnish his House with the Fruits of the Ground; and so all things are done without Cost and every man paid for his pains; that is, they have Lands for it; yet all have not watered Land enough for their needs, that is, such Land as good Rice requires to grow in; so that such are fain to sow on dry Land, and Till

other mens Fields for a subsistence. These Persons are free from
payment of Taxes; only sometimes upon extraordinary occasions, they must give a Hen or Mat or such like, to the King's
use: for as much as they use the Wood and Water that is in his
Countrey. But if any find the Duty to be heavy, or too much for
them, they may leaving their House and Land, be free from the
King's Service, as there is a Multitude do. And in my judgment
they live far more at ease, after they have relinquished the
King's Land, than when they had it.'

Caste with its strict hierarchy decided a man's status for life.
At the head were the farmers, those who tilled the fields. Knox
called them 'Hondrews' or 'honourable'. He saw that there
were various grades among them. Next to them came the
artificers—skilled workers in gold, metals, artists, who had their
pride in their profession and of whose temperaments the caste
above had to be wary, for the work of the skilled artisan was
necessary to them. Knox quite plainly sets out the immobility
of caste: 'No Artificers ever change their Trade from Generation to Generation; but the Son is the same as was his Father,
and the Daughter marries only to those of the same Craft; and
her Portion is such Tools are of use, and do belong unto the
Trade: tho the Father may give over and above what he
pleaseth.' Elephant-catchers and Keepers, as artificers of
another sort, were reckoned equal with Smiths, but they did
not intermarry.

Below them were Barbers, and as the scale went lower Pot-
ters, then Washers of Clothes, then makers of Jaggery (the
natural sugar of the palm), then the 'Poddah' (Paduvo)—
'Husbandmen and Soldiers, yet ar Inferior to all that have been
named hitherto. For what reason neither I, nor, I think, themselves can tell: only thus it falls to them by Succession from
Predecessors, and so will ever remain', Knox comments. Still
lower were weavers, who included astrology in their activities,
besides drumming and dancing. Below them Basket-makers,
and then mat-weavers. Last of all came outcasts or Rodiyas,
who lived by begging.

All the above except the Rodiyas tilled the fields, but the land
they cultivated had certain duties attached to it—services to be
performed by the various castes. These were obligatory on the
holder of the land. In the Kandyan country where the system

of land tenure was not interfered with, as it was in the territories ruled by the Portuguese and the Dutch, the social distinctions of caste persisted longer. Heydt observed that one of the attractions of Christianity in the Dutch provinces was the opportunity it provided the person of inferior caste to evade these social distinctions: 'Yet often their unpleasing pride moves them to change their religion to Christianity to obtain one or another loosening of the rules of dress (if it be not from hunger). Also if they get the opportunity to marry Europeans of a certain standing, or render them good service in their households, then they may be allowed to have a Tampat or Tallipot leaf carried behind them.'

Knox noted how strictly apparel and social usage differentiated castes one from another: 'All below the Couratto or Elephant-Men, may not sit on Stools nor wear Doublets, except the Barbar. . . . Neither may any of these ranks of People, either Man or Woman, except the Potter and the Washer wear the end of their Cloth to cover their Bodies, unless they be sick or cold.' The social system in England permitted movement upward. Those who made their money in trade could be ennobled, but in Kandy no one in the castes below the Hondrews could ever hope to improve his status. 'Riches', he wrote, 'could not prevail with them in the least to marry with those by whom they must eclipse and stain the Honour of their Family'.

This was more or less a closed society, adequate to a static agricultural economy in which money was scarce and of little importance. 'Their Manufactures are few: some Callicoes, not so fine as good strong Cloth for their own use: all manner of Iron Tools for Smiths, and Carpenters, and Husbandmen: all sorts of earthen ware to boil, stew, fry and fetch water in, Goldsmith's work, Painters work, carved work, making Steel, and good Guns, and the like.' There was some specie in the Kandyan kingdom, but very little indeed. 'All sorts of Money is here very scarce: And they frequently buy and sell by exchanging Commodities.' The static nature of the economy can be inferred from Knox's comment: 'They have a small Traffic among themselves, occasioned from the Nature of the Island. For that which one part of the Countrey affords, will not grow in the other. But in one part or other of this Land they have enough to sustain themselves, I think, without the help of Commodities

brought from any other Countrey: exchanging one Commodity
for another; and carrying what they have to other parts to
supply themselves with what they want.' Trade with the world
outside was in the hands of the Moors.

The nature of this old world, gradually changed during the
nineteenth century as a result of contact with the new, should
be held in mind, if the strain to which the mass of people in the
Kandyan kingdom were subjected is to be understood. The
Kandyan provinces covered the greater part of the island. They
were sparsely populated and supported fewer people than the
western and southern seaboard and the northern peninsula.
The land was mostly in forest, and sometimes the names of
coffee and tea plantations recall a hazy picture of what must
have been effaced. Black Forest Pussellava brings to mind the
dark foliage of the tall *doon* trees (*Doonia Zeylanica*) which grew
to a height of a hundred feet; High Forest, Kandapola, the
dense but not tall growth of virgin forest at elevations of 5,000
feet and above.

These forests—royal domains—provided the villager who
tilled the rice-fields on the slopes of the mountains and the
valleys with common land. On their fringes cattle were grazed,
and by custom there were rights of cultivation in the forest and
in the land bordering it. Strips were cleared and burnt, and
crops raised to supplement the peasant's food supply. In the
nineteenth century the highlands were opened up. This could
only be done by men with money to spend on changing the
use to which the land was put. They could only be Europeans
or people of the island already moving away from the strict
social stratifications of Sinhalese society. By the 1820s there
were in the Maritime provinces people sufficiently weaned
from custom to secure some profit for themselves out of the new
order and ready to fare farther afield. The highlands of the
Kandyan country provided the scene for the enterprise of
European planters and the traders of the low country, Sinhalese and Moors, who followed in their wake.

The old way of life gradually was effaced, but something of
its spirit lurked underground, revealing itself in the feudal
nobleman who could most accurately measure the extent of his
loss in the form of a hankering after the past; and in the peasant
in an apathetic dissatisfaction with the present. Life in the

Kandyan country has been written about in a variety of ways. To the European in the nineteenth century it was either 'nasty, brutish, and short' in the Hobbesian phrase, or the natural condition of those who lacked the great moral virtue of self-help. To others who flood it with the mellow light of the pastoral myth, its other worldliness and the certainties its rigid social structure afforded would seem today much more desirable than the rootlessness and complexity of the urbanized life which has replaced it. Ananda Coomaraswamy, who looked back on it with the mystical temper of the artist identifying the beautiful with the good, took up the many exquisite examples of the work of its craftsmen and glorified it almost elegiacally: 'Such an organization of society seems strange already, even in the East, so rapid has been the "progress" of the nineteenth century. There was no trade in land, nor did agricultural labourers work for hire. Craftsmen made no goods for sale and kept no shops. "Riches were little valued nor made any the more honourable." Yet there flourished a prosperous agricultural community, a pure and intellectual religion, and a highly skilled and intelligent race of craftsmen. It is probable that in respect of most real advantages the Kandyan villager was better off in the eighteenth century than he is now.' (*Medieval Sinhalese Art*, Kelmscott Press, 1908.)

The Englishman in the early nineteenth century did not see any of these things in it. He was convinced, whether he was administrator, soldier or missionary, that the best future for Ceylon was one which he was planning, from which he himself hoped to benefit, by that rule which offered rewards to enterprise. Those who did gainsay him—the feudal noblemen and their men who resisted change—were moved by just as sincerely held convictions as to where their profit lay.

Of secondary interest in Knox's fascinating book is the account of his own activities in the Kandyan country: those of an Englishman who had chosen a profession quite unusual in its inland regions—the mercantile marine. Knox was an 'adventurer' in the old meaning of the term, the man who takes the risk of staking his money on ventures which could turn out profitably, and his cast of mind differed from that of most of the people he met in Ceylon. Being an outsider in Kandyan society, he had to make his way in the world, as he chose to do, in ways different from those usually pursued. He had no advantages, except the precarious rights of being a privileged detenu maintained at royal expense. He was not therefore entirely unprovided for, and like any true-born Englishman (he had both Scots and Scandinavian blood) he was tenacious of his few rights and privileges.

He worked hard to improve his condition, engaging in activities which must have impressed Defoe who knew his story, since they could now be described as Crusoe-like occupations—fishing, breeding goats, and even, following Biblical precedent, gathering the ears of 'corn' as he walked through the fields, not for food but for his private business. He displayed strong commercial instincts which must have distinguished him from his lazy compatriots and from the less business-like Kandyans. He engaged in barter, developed skill in bargaining, and was able to 'buy' an English Bible not with the only piece of money he had but with a cap. (Though it must be admitted that this was the result of the advice of his 'black boy'.)

His later career in the Kandyan kingdom could be exaggerated into illustrating in very simple terms economic processes as we know them. He used his skill and labour—the knitting he had learnt from his servant—to produce caps. He sold his caps for money—'Nine pence a piece in value English money, the Thread standing us in about three pence.' Over-production brought prices down and he felt the pinch of necessity: 'But at length, we (himself and his English friends) plying hard our new Learned Trade, Caps began to abound, and Trading grew dead, so that we could not sell them at the former price: which brought several of our Nation to great want.'

Later, however, trade boomed and he built a house and bought an estate. He was advised by his neighbours to marry. But war—a sudden Dutch incursion into the king's territories —ruined him, and he lost both his house and his estate. He started all over again, collecting the moneys owed him by former debtors. He again bought a piece of land, and settled down with three other Englishmen who decided not to marry, but to keep themselves free from any ties so that they could escape from the Kandy country if ever the opportunity presented itself.

Trade cycles in caps—his sole commercial product—once

again hit his prosperity, but this time he had profited from experience and took up 'banking' (usury). This he saw as the easiest and most profitable way of making a living. His capital was not money but grain, the rate of interest on which he lent 'corn' being 50 per cent—the usual rate in the country. He discovered the justification of all those who have been at some pains to justify their high rates of profit: 'As the profit is great, so is the trouble of getting it.'

When he left the Kandyan kingdom, taking off towards the north with another Englishman and ultimately reaching Dutch territory near Aripu, he abandoned his home and estate, an old man who was his watcher, and a girl by the name of 'Lucea', the daughter of one of his fellow captives, who looked after his household. In 1698 he was in Cochin as commander of an English ship and met there one of his fellow prisoners who had been set free after Rajasinha's death. He wrote to those of his friends still in the Kandyan kingdom, entrusting his letter to the Dutch commander at Cochin. He gave them news of relatives and friends of theirs, with the only consolation he knew of—trust in God—and reflected that at their age it would be difficult for them to support themselves at home: 'I have often mentioned your Case to the English East India Company but without effect, therefore I advise you to rely onely upon God who worketh all things after the Councell of his owene will, & Consider the difficulty of aged persons to gitt a living as the 2 now in England doe find it.' For himself, he found 'a man in his Native Country amounge his Relations is not free from trouble, many of which I was free from whilst one Zelone, in so much that I still Continew a single Man. I have heere with sent my picture to the Girl I brought up, Lucea, and you know that I loved the Child & since have no cause to hate her. We have had Strainge Change of governments in England since you left it, as King Charles the 2ᵈ, James the 2ᵈ who is now living in france & flead from his throne, & now happie under King William the 3ᵈ; Prince of Orange, and at present all Christendom is at peace.'

There are two sources of interest in the story of this Englishman who knew the Kandyan kingdom—his energy, and the points at which his career anticipated the careers of those Englishmen who followed him there in the nineteenth century.

His energy was the *élan vital* of the man who believed in himself and was as sure of himself as any 'Hondrew'. This enabled him to turn the extreme situation in which he found himself as a young man of nineteen into limited success. If one believes in the life force it must have elected Robert Knox as one of its vessels.

His career, though it was not a paradigm of the various roles the Englishman has played in Ceylon, touches them at many points and recalls them in the determination with which he pursued his interests. He was, if the exaggeration is permissible, many things Englishmen later were to be—the owner of an estate (thought precious small by later standards), capitalist, banker. By tests still valid he must have done exceedingly well, for he was twice bankrupt in Ceylon, yet he rose superior to circumstances. Like his successors he was a bird of passage; he organized his own club in Ceylon; and what he did, using his privilege as the king's captive, later Englishmen were to do on an immensely greater scale, having an advantage over Knox in that they were the new 'Hondrews' of the English king's kingdom.

Modern Ceylon

CHAPTER 11

Plantation Economy

O f the transformation of the economy of Ceylon by the British in the nineteenth century, it might be said that everything the Dutch tried to do the British did better. This remark, taken from another context, throws into sharp relief the essential difference between the British and the Dutch as colonial powers. It could be seen in the contrast between the development of Netherland Indies and peninsular India. The British way was better because it was grounded on such liberal ideas as the emancipation of slavery, and the absence of religious persecution; it was less autocratic, and it did contrive, in spite of tensions, to maintain good relations between rulers and subjects. However rigid and unsympathetic British colonial officials may have been, they had some sense of responsibility towards the people they ruled, and at some time or other— later perhaps than sooner—they were subject to pressures exerted constitutionally from England.

Besides all this the British in Ceylon possessed an advantage denied to the Dutch: the control of the whole island. Already in the 1830s Ceylon was provided with strategic roads and a garrison sufficient to remove the slightest possibility of successful uprising on the part of the native population. For decades after the fall of the Kandyan kingdom a military force was maintained and paid for out of the island's revenues, greatly in excess of the colony's requirements, and without reference to any systematically worked out plan of imperial defence. (There was in fact no co-ordinated scheme of imperial defence until the 1880s. The Colonial Defence Committee met for the first time in England in 1885.) Ceylon was not thought of as a link in a chain requiring military and naval force related to other demands besides those of internal security. Governors in

189

Ceylon wished to keep the military establishment, for which the colony paid, at full strength. Even so, in 1848 when the Governor was alarmed, troops were sent for from India. One result of this top-heavy military establishment was that a far too numerous force with time on its hands was, at the least opportunity, only too ready to demonstrate with inordinate zeal how badly needed it was. Superior British efficiency, when contrasted with that of the Dutch, depended both on the character of the British official and the complete political and military control of the whole island.

The economy of Ceylon was transformed by coffee as a large-scale plantation crop. Between 1834 and 1835 its economic pattern changed from that of subsistence agriculture and the exploitation of its forest resources (cinnamon which was also cultivated in the Maritime provinces) into the plantation economy of today. The Dutch had grown coffee in Ceylon in the eighteenth century. They were not unsuccessful at it, and as much as 100,000 lb. was produced. But it was not developed, the lowlands were unsuitable for its cultivation, and there were larger and easier profits in cinnamon. There was some cultivation of the coffee berry in the Kandyan kingdom; but it was casual. The enterprise and personal energy of Englishmen like Bird and Barnes in the early twenties were responsible for the beginnings of the plantations later to become the mainstay of the island's economy.

Coffee was the key-signature marking the transition from old to new Ceylon, and not constitutional and legislative enactments. The new tune to which planters, government, and the populace adjusted their steps was coffee and 'the unexampled prosperity' (to use the stock phrase of those times) it brought to all those associated with it. Not only the European planter who owned most of the plantations benefited; coffee sent money downwards from the hills into the Western and Southern provinces. It brought into being practically everything associated with modern Ceylon—its characteristic economy, its changed social structure, its altered landscape and even its political development. Coffee means little or nothing to present-day Ceylon dependent for the bulk of its revenue on tea, rubber and coconuts, but there was nothing these products have brought about in Ceylon's economy which coffee had not set up before.

The plantation 'industry' came into being and developed, like most British institutions in Ceylon, not as part of a systematic plan, but as uncoordinated private enterprise which, as it was European, could claim government support. Neither Whitehall nor Westminster showed, until later in the story of coffee, extravagant interest in the development of the island's plantation economy. Nor was the city of London committed to large-scale investment in this venture overseas. I. H. Van Den Driesen in his exhaustive study of Ceylon's coffee industry commented on the fact that 'almost throughout the whole of the coffee-planting era in Ceylon, Britain was capital-shy, so far as investment in the Colonies was concerned.' The coffee industry owed its origins to a number of Europeans, who with their small capital and their influence with the government in Ceylon were able to begin clearing the forested highlands and planting coffee. Conditions outside Ceylon—the difficulties of the West Indian coffee planters and the increasing popularity of the drink in England and Europe—enabled a small undertaking to become a fair-sized industry.

The first coffee plantation in Ceylon was that of George Bird in Gampola in 1824. He was an Army officer who was given a part of the royal lands of Sinnapitiya and Veyanvatta. The land was Crown land and Bird was in default for some part of the purchase price. Sir Edward Barnes, the Governor, using his own private means, planted land in Gannoruva. These plantations were opened up by Sinhalese village labour and by the use of *Rajakariya*. Other plantations by civilians and military officers followed, but it was not until the 1830s, when the duties which favoured the West Indian planter were removed by Parliament, that the rapid development of coffee growing began. In the early 1840s there was a coffee boom which lasted until the world financial depression of the late forties. Lieutenant de Butts, whose *Rambles in Ceylon* was published in 1841, gives a balance sheet of the 'Estimated Expenses of Establishing a Coffee Plantation of Three Hundred Acres in the Island of Ceylon for Fourteen years'. With an initial capital of £2,201 and a further £2,216 for the second year, the coffee planter would begin to show a profit in the third year. At the end of his fourteen years, with his plantation sold, he would be the richer by £28,516. Butts was a fribble who knew nothing about Ceylon, but his schedule incorporated some of the extravagant hopes of the coffee planters in those years.

When trade recovered coffee was on its feet again. From the fifties until the late seventies, when the blight of *Hemileia vastatrix* destroyed the coffee industry of Ceylon, it was king. It was being produced on large plantations in the highlands by the European planter who bought the land he planted on; by the peasant who supplemented his income by the shrubs in his garden; and by the native small-holder on a smaller scale than the European planter. Between 1836 and 1840 50,000 cwt. were exported annually. In the boom exports reached 120,000 cwt.; in 1850 278,473 cwt., and in 1860 506,540 cwt. By 1875, in spite of new areas opened up, exports did not rise higher than 856,570 cwt. Then the decline began, and in 1886 they had sunk to 179,254 cwt. The acreage under coffee had dropped too, and first cinchona and then tea took the place it once held in the economy.

In the fifty years between 1830 and 1880 coffee so decided the direction of Ceylon's economic development that it is well to reflect on the differences it made to the island. In the highlands of the Kandyan country the pattern of landholding was metamorphosed. What used to be royal domain or *nindagama* became, wherever coffee could be cultivated, the private property of the planter. The village survived in the valleys and on the slopes where rice was grown, but the villagers lost their rights to raise subsidiary crops and to pasture cattle in what used to be regarded as common land. The opening up of the highlands by the coffee planter did not radically alter the peasant economy, but it introduced another type of economy developing beside it and so affecting it.

Land was needed in the highlands for the growing of coffee. The government proceeded to make it available by selling it at the upset price of five shillings an acre. It worked on the seemingly logical assumption that all uncultivated land, except where it could be proved to be private property, was deemed to be the property of the Crown. The difficulty of providing proof of ownership according to the demands of a new legal code, and the rights of customary usage, were overlooked. The chief beneficiaries of land sales in the thirties came from the class of European government official, army man and civilian

3*a*. Trincomalie—early nineteenth century A.D.

3*b*. Colpetty from the Cinnamon Gardens—mid-nineteenth century A.D.

4a. Ancient and Modern—tea pluckers in the shadow of Adam's Peak

4b. Adam's Peak: waiting for sunrise on the summit

from India. No one else, except for an infinitesimally small number of Ceylonese, had either the money or the influence required. Among the new landowners were the Governor, Stuart Mackenzie (1837–41), with 1,120 acres; Anstruther, Colonial Secretary, 3,793 acres; Wodehouse, his assistant, 900; Turnour, the Treasurer, 2,217 acres; Buller, the Government Agent of the Central Province, 1,929. The Chief Justice and the Archdeacon were also coffee planters. So the hierarchy of officials responsible for planning land policy and legislation was an interested party.

New owners outside this circle not only obtained land cheaply, but through their personal influence with officialdom could arrange to get exactly what they wanted at generous terms. Many of them camped on the hillsides until their properties had been cleared. Some employed superintendents, retired army men generally, who made up for their ignorance of coffee culture by the terror of their rule over their workers. The soil was rich and the plantations throve. Sir Thomas Villiers wrote that the first crop from Black Forest, 167 cwt. or 21 cwt. per acre off 8 acres, 'sold in London for about 108s. per cwt., realizing £670 which was just about double the expenditure on the purchase of 105 acres of land, opening and clearing and planting, including the erection of a shed for storing, and a bungalow for his (the owner's) wife and family which cost £26'. Jenkins, who started in Madulsima, described his first purchases: 'Became a proprietor of 60 acres . . . what good could ever come of only 60 acres, with no adjoining forest to fall back upon? But never mind: an hour after I had bought it for a few bids over £60, I was offered £100 for it by some enterprising Moormen: this I refused, for if it was worth that to them it was worth that to me. . . .An adjoining piece of mixed *patana* (grass-land) and chena of sixty acres (which had been previously offered over and over again by Government for sale without finding a purchaser) I bought at upset price, thus making the place 120 acres. The first planted land bore over 12 cwt. an acre *when only three years old*. After the first crop I sold out for £3,000 and was glad to do so.'

Speculation in land followed, and the government attempted to introduce some principle by which sales of land and security of tenure could be regulated through the Crown Lands (Encroachments) Ordinance of 1840 and Ordinance 9 of 1841. Were the peasants as a result deliberately tricked out of their land by the officials who framed these pieces of legislation? It seems unlikely that the Colonial Office were parties to a scheme concocted in Ceylon to expropriate the peasant for the benefit of the coffee planter. But the general impression, still current in Ceylon, is that the coffee plantations made the peasant landless. He certainly was deprived of his supplementary sources of food, because his access to forest chena no longer existed. But was he in the 1840s actually dispossessed of his land? It would seem that the landlessness of the Kandyan peasantry was a later phenomenon. Then the peasant, without either money or influence, got the worst of the bargain, whether it was at the hands of the European planter or his own countrymen speculating in land or opening it out in commercial crops. There was nothing he could do in his corner of the Kandyan provinces but suffer the lot of all the unregarded poor displaced by the industrial changes of the nineteenth century. Van Den Driesen quotes the case of a coffee planter who is reported to have said that 'when he took possession of a property sold to him by the Government Agent of the Central Province, he found in the centre of it, a prosperous village. Being sorry for the poor villagers and not wishing to eject them, as they seemed to have been long resident in the place, he had on his own initiative, set aside a part of the land for their use. Adjoining planters had then voiced their objection to this, and some told him that they too had to deal with similar problems, but had successfully driven out the people who were in occupation.' If this was so, the disturbances of 1848, miscalled the Kandyan or the Matale rebellion, were the understandable results of the peasant's confusion and exasperation.

The planter was rationally pursuing his private profit. He had invested his money in the land and hypothecated his future crop. All he was concerned with was buying in the cheapest market and selling in the dearest. The peasant might have benefited directly from changed circumstances by selling his labour power to the planter, but his early experiences when he hired himself and was not paid for his labour (according to Tennent) dissuaded him. He was not yet landless and he had his own crop of rice to produce. In addition to the social pre-

judice which discouraged him from being a hired labourer at
work all day on the hillsides when the coffee berry had to be
picked, why should he have given up the usual round of the
life he was accustomed to for the doubtful benefit of uncertain
wages in money? The planter anxious for a labour pool looked
with unfriendly eye on what he interpreted as the pride, the
laziness and the independence of the peasant. 'Independence'
was at the time a word of sinister import; it betrayed a spirit
inappropriate to the poor.

The planter's labour problems were ultimately to be solved
in much the same way as the kings of ancient Ceylon had
solved theirs, when in the fourteenth and fifteenth centuries
there was cinnamon to be peeled in the royal domains. They
had settled their difficulties by the importation of a labour
corps from India. What would now be termed large-scale government action had been necessary to deal with the situation.

It was different in nineteenth century British Ceylon. The
government took no hand in the proceedings until much later.
The first immigrant labourers from India to work on coffee
plantations were imported by Bird and Barnes in 1828. Had
South India not been in a state bordering precariously on
famine throughout the nineteenth century, Ceylon would never
have been the Elysium of the immigrant cooly. Coffee did not
require a permanent labour force, so the first immigrants were
not settlers. They arrived for the harvesting of the berries, and
most of those who survived their expedition to Ceylon left with
what they had saved through denying themselves practically
everything in order to take something back home.

It was the work of the South Indian cooly which enabled the
planter to cultivate his land and keep it in production. The
plantations needed seasonal labour, and the planter, the producer of the greater part of the revenue of the colony, was
determined that this labour should be provided with as little
expense to himself as possible. He agitated the government to
undertake the whole project of providing immigrant labour
for work on the plantations. But the Colonial Office was not
ready to allow the Ceylon government, if it had been so inclined, to take over the responsibility. To have intervened in
this sphere would have infringed *laissez-faire* principles. The
view of the Colonial Office was that this was the proper concern

of those at whose special instance and for whose special advantage the labourers resorted to the island. But once immigration on a large scale had begun—between 1843 and 1859 903,557 men, women and children had come over to work on the plantations—both the Ceylon government and the Colonial Office had to insist 'that every attempt must be made to secure protection for the immigrant, not only as a matter of humanity, but also as one of public interest'. From this time onwards the Colonial Office and the Civil Servant in Ceylon did try to secure the immigrant from exploitation by employer and contractor. Even though little came of these attempts, it must be stated that Secretaries of State in England and Civil Servants in Ceylon did take a hand in trying to alleviate the lot of the cooly.

The story of the immigrant cooly in Ceylon during these years is melancholy reading. They swarmed across the strait from South India in catamarans and rafts to ports in North Ceylon. The rigours of the progress from there through jungle to the highlands; the conditions in which they lived and worked on the plantations and their own ignorance, which made them victims of their desperate compulsion to save what they could in the year or two they spent in Ceylon, worked havoc among them. Ferguson put the death-rate during the forties among the immigrants as 250 per thousand. Except for the Friend-in-Need Society's hospital in Kandy, there were no hospitals provided by planters or government for them. As for the Friend-in-Need Society's hospital, it depended largely on voluntary contributions and few planters were interested in its funds. In one year the death-rate there was 63 per cent of those admitted. The government was unwilling to provide what in its view the planter should have undertaken. As for the planter, a devotion to his own interest blinded him to his responsibilities. When the government did intervene to regulate relations between planter and cooly in Ordinance 5 of 1841, the effect of this 'first piece of labour legislation' was to enable the planter to hold the cooly to his contract. As Van Den Driesen puts it: 'The law strengthened the planter. He could ill-treat his coolies and suffer no ill effects, but if in desperation they deserted, he could get the courts to hold them to their contracts.' Those who fell sick on the plantation and were unable to work were driven out on a charge of idleness and left to die by the roadside and be buried by the Police—according to Tennant in his despatch to Grey of 21st April 1847.

The unconcern of most planters then, and later, could best be summed up in the dictum of H. W. Cave, writing of the living conditions of workers on tea plantations in 1900, because it expresses a point of view about the stranger in our midst common enough all over the world today: 'A coolie line is usually a long building of one storey only, divided into a large number of compartments. Each compartment accommodates about four coolies, and it is obvious that they do not enjoy the luxury of much space; but their ideas of comfort are not ours, and they are better pleased to lie huddled together upon the mud floors of these tiny hovels than to occupy superior apartments. Their condition calls for no pity or sympathy, as we shall see later; in many respects they are a favoured class.' Later Cave explained that 'compared with this condition at home the coolie is much better off here, where he is free, well housed, his food guaranteed him and medical comforts provided. . . .' Sabonadière, one of the best-known of the coffee planters, recommended the provision of rooms 12 ft. x 12 ft. to house ten coolies who would cook, feed and sleep in them.

It is an indictment of the Christian missionaries that they did little to protest against this treatment of human beings. Feverishly counting heads in their proselytizing activities they were too keen on converting the cooly and saving him from future damnation to have time for his wretched state in the present. The Friend-in-Need Society helped to the extent of its inadequate means, but as a semi-official body dependent on official patronage, it took no strong action but discussed such theoretic questions as 'Should the sufferings of the bad man be diminished?' What explains the difference between the courageous stand taken by the missionary in India against the social evils of Indian society and the silence of his counterparts in Ceylon with regard to the fate of the cooly and the peasant? It could only be understood on the assumption that suffering caused by the disruption leading to a social state the missionary approved of was accepted as natural and therefore inevitable, whereas all other forms of social evil, as being due to the depravity of human beings, had to be attacked.

On the question of the high mortality rates in the immigrant population the Colonial Office found itself unable to fix the responsibility on the planters or on the doctors in the few hospitals later provided. Van Den Driesen quotes one of Kimberley's subordinates writing: 'When we complain of mortality in these hospitals, the Doctors say it is the fault of the planters; when we complain of the condition of the coolies, the planters say it is the fault of the doctors; and between them we get little satisfaction.' The cooly got the worst of a system which treated him as a supplier of labour to be extracted from him at terms most satisfactory either to the planter who employed or to the *kangany*, or foreman, who recruited him from his village in India on a system of advances paid by the plantations. By the later *tundu* (chit of paper on which accounts were drawn up) system, 'money spent while recruiting, i.e. any cash inducement paid to the immigrant to come over, the commission paid to the *kangany*, the cost of transport from India and other expenses incurred in that connection were all treated as advances to the labourer. This debt would be subsequently increased by further loans for festivals, marriages, etc. or by credit purchases at a shop, in which in most cases the *kangany* had a vested interest'. No labourer was free to leave the plantation to which he had been recruited until the debts on his *tundu* had been discharged. He was in effect tied as a serf to the plantation. This system was abolished in 1921.

The unkindest cut of all was the accusation that, having exhausted themselves working on the estates, coolies did not spend the money they earned in Ceylon, but remitted or took their savings away with them to India. One of the early planters on Hunasgiriya wrote, in 1848, on what he termed the high rate of wages earned by the cooly: that wages were high 'is proved by the circumstance that a labourer in Ceylon can live on one third of his pay, and save two thirds, that he actually does so, and carries his savings, after remaining here a few months, away from the place where they are earned to another country: a state of things scarcely parralleled [*sic*] in any country'. Indignation has distorted the spelling of a comment still heard at the present time, when there is a stable labour force of Indian extraction in the island and as great differentials exist between its earnings and those of superintendents.

Plantation Economy

The presence of Indian immigrant labourers in Ceylon has been an interesting phenomenon of the last hundred and twenty-five years. Employed either on plantations, or on government roads and railways as unskilled manual workers, they were the first body of landless labourers who were not integrated into the community as earlier immigrants had been. Their work made possible the new economy of the island, but they were an alien minority in it, separated from the mass of people by differences of language, of social custom and of development. In the course of time those who settled in Ceylon and remained to work on its plantations, isolated from the life of the country by their conditions of work and habitat, continued as an alien group in a country which was their 'home'. The social problems involved by the existence of such a large group concentrated in particular areas were tackled very slowly by the government of Ceylon, as a result of the general improvement of the island's finances and pressure both by the Colonial Office and by the government of India. It is not the social problem, however, which defeats and has defeated various governments of Ceylon, but its political significance. Time, and constitutional change, transformed the cooly into both economic asset and political liability. The force of this will be noted when the story of Ceylon in this century is taken up.

Land and labour for the plantation economy were in the course of time provided. With them came roads to connect plantations with the port from which the coffee had to be shipped overseas. The roads built between Kandy and Colombo and those areas where coffee was planted were called into existence by the new industry. Neither in number nor in quality did they satisfy the planters' demands, so agitation through newspapers in Colombo and lobbying in Westminster set in motion the beginnings of political action for constitutional reform. The planting interest wished to secure an unofficial majority in the Legislative Council to impress the demands of the biggest revenue-producing section of the community on the government. Both the network of roads and the voluble political activity of those times were the result of planters' demands.

It is noteworthy that the first political agitation for change in the system of government should have been led by Europeans in Ceylon—George Wall, the representative of the planters in

the Legislative Council; Elliott, the Editor of the *Observer*; and
John Capper, the Editor of *The Times of Ceylon*. Their political
ideas could be translated into the old slogan of 'No Taxation
without Representation'. The taxes on coffee made up the
greatest part of the island's revenue, the planters who produced
it would therefore have the strongest representation in the
island's councils. The planting interest found allies in the
English educated minority, composed mainly of Burghers just
beginning to find their progress to the highest offices in the
land barred by official policy. As the drive in the agitation was
largely European, once the planters' grievances had been met
or coffee prices improved, political agitation languished. The
planter could afford not to trouble himself further about political advance when by the end of the century his position was
consolidated. The political movement which he then put into
cold storage was thawed and given animation by the new
generation of English-educated Ceylonese, lawyers most of them
like the Burgher agitators of the sixties, whose fathers had en-
riched themselves during the old coffee days.

In the evolution of Ceylon the roads and the political agitation were one stage in the story. Both established the importance
of the planting industry. From the sixties the politician in
Westminster was made to feel the pressure of the coffee interest.
In the eighties Ceylon was both a strategic and economic asset
in the overseas empire. British capital had been sunk in the
island. When coffee failed over a quarter of a million acres had
been planted with it; the hillsides had been cleared of forest; a
labour force had been assembled; the planter had been provided with a system of roads to the seaport of Colombo which
had been improved; there were excellent bungalows on the
plantations, and the old pioneering days were over. R. W.
Jenkins, who had been a coffee planter in the fifties, wrote in
1886: 'The new generation of planters, therefore find all these
good things ready to their hands, and have only to step into the
poor collapsed coffee planter's shoes and comfortable and
accessible quarters.'

So much was left that it was possible to salvage the economy
by using the wreckage. For by the seventies more important
than roads and a powerful interest ready to bring pressure on
the government in Ceylon and to lobby Parliament was the

capital provided by banks operating on a much wider scale than the earlier institutions and channelling money from India and England to the colonies. These banks and limited liability companies incorporated in England, part of a financial interest adequately represented in Westminster, enabled the European planter in the colonies to build a new industry on the ruins of the old.

An unwilling government had no longer to be prodded into interesting itself in the cultivation of commercial crops. The Planters' Association had been founded in 1854. Its membership was overwhelmingly European. By the end of the century it expressed the views of the most influential group in the island —its tea planters. The plantation economy was firmly established, and attempts had been made to grow other crops. The Botanical Gardens, an impressive memorial of British rule in Ceylon, had been moved to Peradeniya in 1821, and the work of its botanists and tropical agriculturists had always been two moves ahead of the foresight of the best coffee planters. To the government the only viable economy for Ceylon was one based on commercial crops for the world market. If one failed, it would be replaced by another.

Cinchona was first tried. The Indian government had acclimatized it there and it had done well. But its world price fell, and tea, already developed successfully in the hill country of Assam in India, was tried out in Ceylon on a larger scale than before and was successful. The Botanical Gardens' records show that tea seed had been imported into Ceylon from China in 1824, and from Assam in 1839. In the sixties a government Commissioner had visited Assam with a view to investigating its tea plantations. The shrub had been discovered growing wild there, and a hardy plant had been developed out of Chinese and Indian seed. Indian tea had done well on the London market.

Ceylon's first 'tea gardens' (as they were called for a time) were in the Ramboda district. This was in 1867. But only a few planters were interested, and in 1873 or 1874 a few packages of Ceylon tea were exported to England. Coffee prices were still so good that the effects of the blight on the yield were concealed by profits. Tea had several advantages over coffee. It could be grown on the highest elevations as well as in the lowlands, and it was an evergreen which could be plucked all through the year. Finally, tea was a more popular beverage in the United Kingdom than coffee, even in the best days of Ceylon's coffee, most of the tea coming from China.

Indian teas began to displace the Chinese on the English market. The trade, alive to the value of a new asset entirely in empire control, succeeded in blending a strong, deep-coloured beverage which was preferred to the China varieties. The vogue of China tea is remembered in the names given to the Ceylon blends—Souchongs and Pekoes—by which earlier tea-drinkers in England used to swear. The determination of the planter and the fertility of the soil were seconded by the skill of the blender. So tea became the major crop and the most profitable investment of the British shareholder in Ceylon's plantation economy. 'Approximately two hundred Companies were registered in the British Isles between 1880 and 1950 for the purpose of growing tea and rubber in Ceylon, and very few of them failed to pay yearly dividends of as much as 10 per cent for a decade or so.' The same American investigator quoted above estimated that a majority of the most profitable British tea plantations in Ceylon 'paid yearly averages running from 19 per cent up to 34 per cent during the half decade 1946–51'.

The first of the plantation crops, coffee, had made money for the successful planter, both European and Ceylonese. One of the earliest of the latter was Joronis de Soysa from Moratuwa. He invested the money made in selling arrack in the purchase of Hanguranketa, a plantation of over a thousand acres. This and others he possessed 'were all managed by young men selected by Mr Soysa from his native village, many of them his relatives, and he never had a European in his employ'. The plantation still belongs to the family. The Soysas from Moratuwa were engaged in a number of enterprises. Sir Thomas Villiers attributes the first (and short-lived) bank in Ceylon to the business acumen of this family. These were generous stewards of their wealth, and it is impossible to delve into the social history of the old Maritime provinces in the nineteenth century without returning again and again to Joronis, Susew and Charles Henry de Soysa.

The money made in coffee travelled all along the line from the hills to the low country and set up the fortunes of many others besides planters. In the courts land disputes were lining the pockets of Burgher lawyers; in the lowlands an army of carters, transport agents and clerks were doing well out of bringing the coffee from the plantations to Colombo and delivering supplies of rice needed by the coolies in the hills. The port of Colombo was being developed, and European commercial houses, most of them still in existence, had opened their doors. The growth of Colombo and small towns on the Western seaboard spelt the prosperity of landowner, timber merchant, builder and carpenter. For the first time since the connection of European powers with Ceylon it is possible to speak of a moneyed class among the inhabitants of the island. The mining of graphite (plumbago) was becoming a profitable small industry. The small number of those educated in English was increasing, and besides the 'upper-class' Mudaliyars and the lawyers (most of them Burghers) there were others making their way in the world. The machinery of government had to be enlarged and secondary schools were turning out the clerks and minor administrators required in the new departments of what was to become in the next century the greatest 'industry' of Ceylon—its government service.

The new moneyed group was able in the eighties and the nineties, with its capital and its land, to peg a claim in a new industry then beginning—the planting of rubber. In 1881 the *Observer* had a note that 'a sample of rubber taken from a "Ficus" in the Matale district and sent to a London broker has been reported on most favourably as very suitable for commercial purposes, and worth 2s. 3d. per lb. All reports seem to agree that the demand is practically inexhaustible, provided rubber could be supplied a little more cheaply than at present'. The Dutch had tried the *Ficus Elastica* as a producer of rubber in Java, and the Indian government since it had successfully acclimatized the cinchona, or quinine tree, from South America, was interested in procuring rubber seeds from Brazil.

It was Sir Clements Markham, an Assistant Secretary at the India Office, the man who had already purloined or kidnapped the cinchona tree for India, who was responsible for getting it rubber as well. The exploit was carried out by Mr. (later Sir) Henry Wickham who had gone out to South America at the age of twenty. The story of his successful adventure has often been told; in recent years Vicki Baum streamlined it into best-selling fiction with a solid background of fact. Before Wickham succeeded in 1876 there had been seeds exported stealthily from Brazil to Kew. Of the first lot of 2,000, 1,000 were taken by Sir William King to the Royal Botanic Gardens at Calcutta of which he was Director. But apparently the seeds did not do well in the climate of Calcutta. Wickham himself had sent seeds to Kew twice, but these had failed to germinate.

In 1876 a combination of circumstances gave him an un-looked-for opportunity which he seized. Self-confident, re-sourceful and vain, he had a flair for an adventure such as this and he triumphed. He was invited to dinner, together with some other Englishmen, by the captain of the *Amazonas*, an ocean liner which was suddenly deserted by its supercargoes and found itself without freight for the return voyage. Using his contacts with Kew and Markham, Wickham chartered the ship on behalf of the Indian government, gave its captain a rendez-vous at the confluence of the Amazon and the Tapajos rivers, and set an army of Indians collecting as many rubber seeds of the *Hevea Brasiliensis* as it could.

The ship was loaded fore and aft with the seeds carefully packed in baskets. The next stage was getting clearance from the Brazilian authorities. With the help of Green, the British consul at Para, Wickham interviewed the head of the *Alfandigo* and obtained permission from him to clear a ship 'anchored out in the stream, (with) exceedingly delicate botanical speci-mens specially designated for delivery to Her Britannic Maj-esty's own Royal Gardens at Kew'. The interview with the Brazilian official called for all Wickham's talents as a play-actor in real life. It was 'most polite, full of mutual compliment in the best Portuguese manner'.

The weather was remarkably good and the ship arrived at Havre, from where Wickham dashed to Kew and arranged for a night goods train to convey his precious freight to England. In June 1876 the orchid houses at Kew were cleared to receive the seeds, and 'a fortnight afterwards the glass houses at Kew afforded (to me) a pretty sight—tier upon tier—rows of young Hevea plants—seven thousand and odd of them'.

This time it was decided by Sir Joseph Hooker that the plants should go to the Gardens in Peradeniya, Ceylon. 'A consignment consisting of 1919 plants was sent to Ceylon in thirty-eight Wardian cases, in charge of a gardener, and 90% of them reached Ceylon in excellent condition. Some were subsequently forwarded to Malaya, and from the seed bearers raised in Ceylon and Malaya the present plantations are descended.'

Wickham lived to a great old age, a tireless speaker and writer, convinced that his knowledge of the tree and of processing rubber was far far superior to that of any scientist or technologist. He later described himself as 'Sometime Commissioner for the introduction of the Para (Hevea) India Rubber Tree for the Government of India'. In 1911 the Planters' Association of Ceylon and the Rubber Growers' Association presented him with $5,000 and an annuity. In 1920 he was knighted by George V, and in 1926 on his eightieth birthday he received gifts of $25,000 from an American millionaire and $40,000 from the Straits government. He visited Ceylon in the twenties and had the pleasure of being photographed beside the trees grown of the seeds he had smuggled from Brazil.

If Wickham had not succeeded in 1876 it would not have been long before someone else brought rubber seeds to the tropical dependencies of the British Empire. As a matter of fact in the year after Wickham's success Cross, a gardener from Kew, brought seedlings of *Hevea Ceara* and the *Castilloa* from South America, and these in time went to Ceylon and Malaya. But beside Wickham's his was hardly a story that gets headlines.

It took some time for rubber to be developed in Ceylon. For some years, the *Ceara* tree was persevered with, and results were disappointing. Little was known about the cultivation of the tree or how the precious milk should be extracted. Between 1881 and 1891, though seeds were freely distributed, the yield was poor. When it was proved that rubber did not require a marshy ground for cultivation, and that *Hevea brasiliensis* was more successful than the others, it gradually established itself. When Parkin, the scientific adviser to the Gardens at Peradeniya, discovered how to tap the trees and get a good yield in rubber-milk, its cultivation spread. It was grown in the low country—in the hinterland of the western coast, and in the valley of the Kelani river. In the cultivation of rubber, which did not require elaborate and expensive machinery and for which land in the lowlands had to be opened up, the new capitalist class of the country could take a hand. It was not slow to seize its opportunities. By 1912 225,000 acres were planted in it.

By 1914 tea, rubber and coconuts were the mainstay of the economy of Ceylon. Its social and economic picture had been as radically altered as its landscape, and it is difficult to take up the story of Ceylon at any point after 1833 without remembering the change the plantation economy was making to the island.

CHAPTER 12

Pax Britannica

In the sixty-seven years between 1848 and 1915 a new Ceylon came into being. Between the Ceylon of 1848 and that of 1915 there were no great basic differences. What was coming up to the surface in 1848 had covered and mantled the whole pool in 1915. The island was a British colony; its plantation economy was firmly established; the opening of the Suez Canal increased its commercial and strategic importance; small towns were springing up all over it; secondary school education in English was producing a new moneyed and landowning class, and these were years of tranquillity. What life was stirring in the depths of the pool seemed to be of no consequence.

After nearly three and a half centuries the island was completely at peace; there was no threat from overseas and no strife at home. There had been longer periods of peace before but they belong to the days of ancient Ceylon, and of them little is known, the absence of positive information as to how people lived being perhaps the surest indication of the quietness of the country. This period of calm in the nineteenth century can be described in terms of the idealized concept of the virtue of British rule in the East—the security and peace its alien rulers afforded to subject peoples within the framework of the empire.

The two terminal dates compass a period of law and order, but both were years in which there were civil disturbances in the island. In both years local discontent suddenly flared up. The villager, in justifiable resentment at the threat of economic distress and prevailed upon by dissatisfaction with his plight, went beserk. Both occasions were misjudged by the British rulers, and, with the co-operation of the army and planters in 1848 and again in 1915, the government proceeded to go beserk

207

on its own. The disturbances in 1848 were magnified into 'the Kandyan Rebellion', those of 1915 into a deliberate conspiracy to stab the empire in the back when it was involved in a world war. Neither was rebellion or a conspiracy. They were the periodic explosions of ignorant masses exasperated by real (and imagined) grievances. For the excesses on the part of the administration which followed disturbances only too easily put down, there is little excuse. The rulers were out of touch with the ruled. This, in spite of all the material benefits of ordered and orderly British rule, was its greatest condemnation. In spite of all it achieved, it failed to identify the people of the country with it.

But most of the items on the credit side of British rule in the island are entries to be chalked up to these years. If there are any at the present time who look back with longing to a haven of calm which they knew in their lifetime, they are recalling their own and their fathers' memories of these times. This feeling is not restricted to a particular class or to a region. Even the villager in the undeveloped North Central Province shared it. Leach in his book on Pul Eliya noted that the oldest inhabitant of the village in 1954 'claimed that the Pul Eliya villagers of those days (i.e. the nineteenth century) led a life of leisured ease'. He put down their forgetfulness of the reality of pestilence and famine in the nineteenth century to the 'very high valuation set on the traditional way of life, especially by the older members of the present-day population'. The greatest boon afforded by the traditional way of life seems to have been its ordered and hierarchic society, such as the British provided too. As will be seen, they imposed on a carefully graded society a small ruling class paternally interested in the welfare of the ruled, and assured of the certainty that they alone knew how this was to be achieved.

But the beginning and the end of this period were full of alarms and excursions. In 1848 suspicion of new taxes turned the peasantry in the Kandy district, sore at the expropriation of land in the great extension of the planting economy, into brushwood which agitation set aflame. Captain John Macdonald Henderson, of the 78th Highlanders, who was with the troops sent to Matale, gave his own account of how the 're-bellion' came about. 'New taxes were determined upon some

5. The Esala Perahera at Kandy, 1939

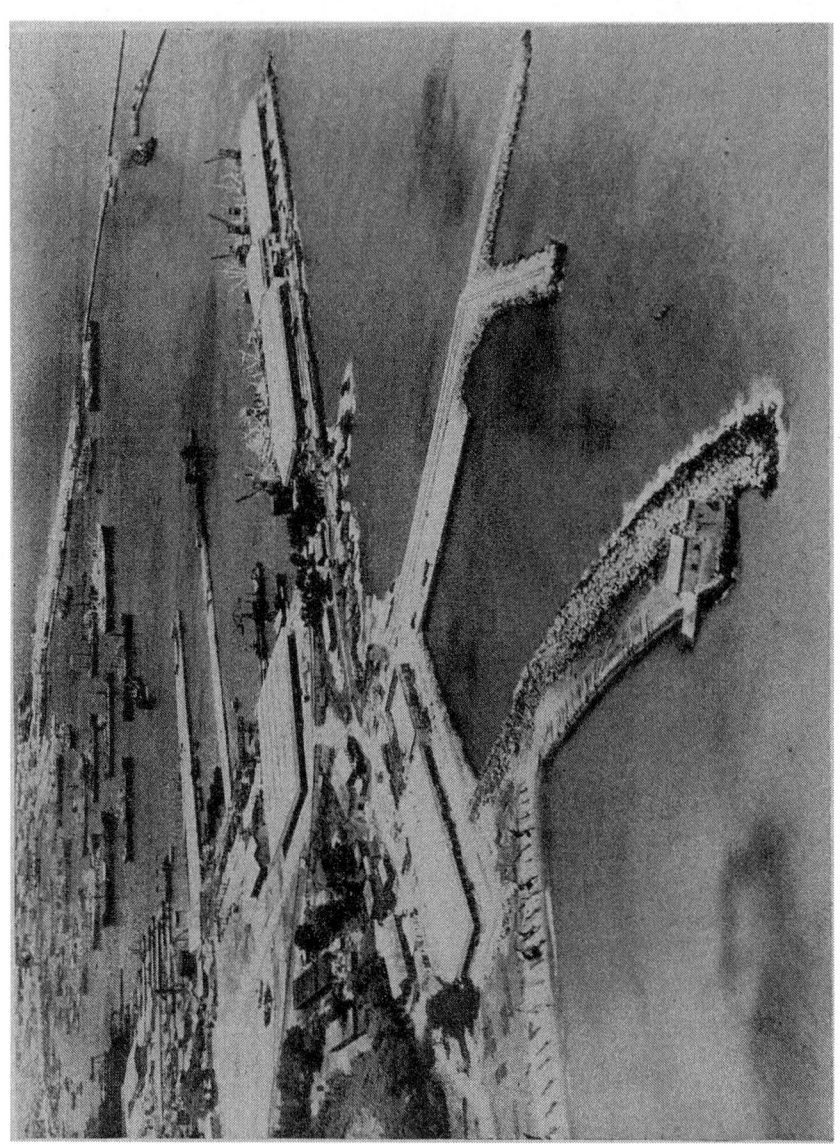

6. Present-day Ceylon—Colombo Harbour

of them being about the most foolish and unjust, and I may add, impracticable, that could well have been hit upon. The most obnoxious of these were the dog and gun taxes, the road, or, as it has been called, the poll tax and the shop tax. The idea of making people in a Buddhist country, where it is contrary to their creed to "drown blind puppies" to take any life at all, pay one shilling per annum for every

> *Mongrel puppy, whelp or hound,*
> *Or cur of low degree*

that might haunt their dwellings was rich in the extreme. But it was also unjust as well as absurd for other reasons than the above. Many of the Kandians in the remote villages live very much by hunting . . . their dogs are often absolutely necessary to scare wild beasts from their patches of cultivation and from their dwellings. . . . Further the tax was impracticable. People would not own the dogs; indeed in most cases they belong to no one and forage where they can. . . . To make firearms a source of revenue . . . when it is considered that these guns were for the most part the commonest Birmingham trash, worth at best twelve or fifteen shillings and they had already paid a considerable export duty. It must not be forgotten either that a gun is an absolute necessity in the jungle. Many of the natives live almost entirely on game or on what they obtain in exchange for it; and without a gun they could neither protect themselves nor their gardens and fields from the ravages of wild beasts. . . . Perhaps the most obnoxious of all the taxes was the road or poll tax. . . . This was really a heavy sum for many of the people to pay (six shillings), and when it is considered that roads are of no service to the Kandians, their jungle paths answering every purpose. They looked upon it as a measure entirely calculated for the benefit of the coffee planter and other Europeans. There was yet another cause of dissatisfaction with the road tax and this was that the Buddhist priests were not exempt. . . . Of the shop tax . . . the people of the maritime districts great numbers of whom keep small shops or boutiques, complained that it was unjust that the man who exposed a few hoppers or a bunch of plantains for sale in a miserable *cajahn* or cocoanut leaf shed, should pay one pound a year for the privilege of doing so, while the rich Moorman in his large shop or warehouse and the Englishman in his counting house or office, should pay no more. Upon the low country people also fell the weight of the cart and the boat taxes while the stamp tax applied to, and was felt by all, Could anything have been more foolish than to promulgate . . . these seven new and direct taxes and that at a time when statistical inquiries were being made in all directions for Sir Emerson's book on Ceylon, thus leading to vague apprehensions of indefinite taxation.' In a footnote Henderson wrote: 'The wildest rumours arose from Sir Emerson's statistical inquiries for his meditated books. Among others that the women were to be taxed in proportion to the girth across their breasts.'

After four days the 'Kandyan Rebellion' was over. But in the meantime martial law had been declared, and Viscount Torrington, the Governor, convinced by his advisers that here was a serious threat to the British power, lost his head. Troops were sent for from India; the Governor's confidential advisers were panicky planters; and for a little over two months troops and volunteers marched through the countryside teaching the 'rebels' a lesson. Colombo had been quiet, except for one demonstration. Soon there was protest against the high-handedness with which the government and the army had been acting. The attack on the Governor begun in Colombo by Elliott of the *Observer* was carried to England.

It may well be that Torrington's opponents in Ceylon found in his conduct over the disturbances just the stick they needed to beat him with. It may well be, too, that the agitation against him in Parliament was helped by political manœuvring against Lord John Russell (whose kinsman he was) and the Whigs, and not by any genuine concern for the ill-used Kandyan peasant. Whatever gave the impetus to the political agitation, it showed two important characteristics of British rule in Ceylon. In the first place not all the autocratic power of the Governor placed him above the reach of outspoken criticism in the island. Secondly, what happened there, even at the highest level, was the concern of a power superior to that of the Colonial Office. Earl Grey, the Secretary of State for the Colonies and Russell, the Prime Minister, both supported the colonial Governor. But Parliament appointed a Commission of Enquiry into the conduct of the government in its handling of the 'revolt'. Among its members were Peel, Gladstone and Disraeli. The Com- mittee issued its report in 1850.

While the debate about his conduct still raged in Parliament Torrington was recalled. He owed his appointment to a Colonial Governorship to his relationship to the Prime Minister. He had to give it up because he had manifestly failed as an administrator. The Queen, who was a remarkable judge of men and had followed the affair, set down her judgement of Torrington as a man whose talents, in her opinion, did not rise much higher than discharging the duties of a Lord of the Bedchamber. To this post which he had vacated when he left for Ceylon he returned. Tennant, his Colonial Secretary, a man of great ability, who was looking forward to a Colonial Governorship himself, was dismissed from the service, but found employment subsequently in the Board of Trade. Woodhouse, his implacable opponent in Ceylon, was dismissed too but was drafted to another part of the empire by Grey. Tennant (Sir Timorsome Emmet as he was dubbed by his fellow civilians in Ceylon on account of his exploit in running away from a crowd in Galle) had been working, with the aid of Ceylonese helpers, on his compendium of all the extant information on Ceylon and used his temporary leisure to complete his work. It was published in 1860. Henderson used an old quip to describe it—'all that is true in it is not new and what is new in it is not true'.

In 1915 things should have been different, for after more than half a century of British law and order, with a more prosperous country and a fair-sized class of educated Ceylonese, some of them sharing in the business of government, the chances of outbreaks of disorder should have been remote. This time the rioting took place mainly in the small towns, and was the result of discontent fanned by religious fanaticism. The trouble arose out of the intransigence of the Coast Moors, as they were called, a group of recent immigrants from the South Indian coast engaged in trade in Ceylon, in objecting to Buddhist processions passing by their mosque in Gampola. These traders, different from the old established Moors in Ceylon, were resented as arrogant intruders by both villagers and town dwellers. The war with its high prices and shortages was imposing greater burdens on the mass of people who were quick to respond to fanatical agitators. The District Judge of Kandy had held that by the terms of the Kandyan Convention of 1815 a Buddhist procession had every right to follow its traditional route, but this judgement was set aside by the Supreme Court and there was growing tension in Gampola and Kandy. Wild rumours were floating about and the civil administration should have either forestalled trouble by dispersing crowds likely to turn excitable or dealt firmly with it at the first sign of its appearance. But it was not ready for anything. On the 28th of May which was Vesak day, the celebration of the birth of the Buddha, sporadic rioting began in Kandy and elsewhere; shops and houses belonging to Moors were looted, and there was mob violence. On the 2nd of June the Governor, Sir Robert Chalmers, declared martial law in the five provinces which had been affected. Thereafter the Brigadier General commanding the troops took over and proceeded to exercise military powers arbitrarily.

Had there been a Senior Civil Servant in Kandy—all of them in key positions were Europeans—anxious to use his authority and the legally constituted forces of the law to maintain order, nothing would have happened. The crowds would have vanished at the first sign of firmness, as they did at the sign of some sixty boys from a secondary school in Kandy in their cadet uniforms and therefore imagined to be representatives of authority. (One of the lessons of 1848 and 1915 was not remembered in 1958, when similar inefficiency on the part of the administration, not now an alien government but one representing the people of the country, allowed lawlessness to become a pogrom.)

What is more, if the senior officers of the Civil Service had been in better contact with the people they were governing and not only with the Mudaliyars they had instituted in office, they would not have misjudged the situation as they did. But Colonial Secretary and Government Agents lived in a world of their own, and the military were called in to deal with a situation which Civil Servants and police had mismanaged.

There was no excuse again for the rigour of military rule and its excesses during the three months of martial law. It is impossible, in the absence of documented evidence, to say how many people lost their lives. A number of prominent Sinhalese, whose work in the temperance movement cast on them the odium of their being anti-government, were arrested, imprisoned, subjected to various humiliations, and later released on the payment of a fine. Among them was D. S. Senanayake, later to be the first Prime Minister of independent Ceylon. The meanest trick of all—as in 1848—as it seemed to the 'Educated Ceylonese', was the Governor's obtaining Privy Council indemnification for 'all the acts done and the proceedings held under Martial Law'.

Sir Robert Chalmers, the Governor, was a Treasury official with a distinguished record of service and a reputation for abstruse and exotic research so often typical of the cultured British Civil Servant. He had accepted a Colonial Governorship when he had reached the heights of Permanent Secretaryship. His reputation as an orientalist (he was a student of Pali and had already begun his translations of the Buddhist Canon) had preceded him to Ceylon. As a young man, fresh from Oxford, he had been interested in welfare work in slum settlements. He was intelligent and he had liberal leanings. He was highly thought of by such an eminent politician as Asquith, and he ought to have been able to rise to this occasion. But he had suffered a grievous personal loss in May 1915, the month in which the trouble began, in the deaths of his two sons on active service. Perhaps this would account for his inability to meet a crisis which he seemed content to leave others to handle.

It is impossible to state who advised him, or what decided him, to read into the situation either a revolt or a conspiracy to embarrass the British in the conduct of the war. In the Legislative Council later he explained that his action in declaring martial law was based on an order in Council of 1896 to safeguard colonies 'against the machinations of a foreign enemy'. Whatever the reasons for his incapacity, Eardley Norton, a barrister from Madras who defended five Sinhalese tried for complicity in the disturbances, was within his rights in declaring: 'Judging the Governor by what he has done in the past, I should expect little from his prescience or his courage. Both were put to the test by the recent riots, and both have broken down.'

As soon as martial law and the censorship were lifted in Ceylon, agitation against the conduct of the government began. It was taken to England by Ceylonese leaders, and had its effect. 'In December 1915 at the urgent request of the Chancellor (Mr. McKenna) Chalmers consented to relinquish the Governorship and return to the Treasury as Additional Joint Permament Secretary.' In 1916 he acted as Under Secretary for Ireland during the time of the Irish troubles, and his later career was as distinguished as that which preceded his governorship of Ceylon. On his retirement from the Treasury he was made a Baron and in 1924 became Master of Peterhouse, Cambridge. The unfounded popular belief in Ceylon—to judge from a ditty sung by schoolboys in which the rhyme-endings were martial law, Bonar Law and mother-in-law—was that his connection with Bonar Law had stood him in good stead.

Chalmers was convinced that in his own words 'a revolt had been put down by rose-water'. Most of the Britishers in the island, however, felt that whips and scorpions should have been employed. The significance of the brief episode—the disturbances began on the 28th of May and were over on June 5th, martial law being lifted on the 30th of August—was the revelation that, in spite of the unity of the country and the efficiency of paternalistic British rule, the rulers were out of touch with the people of the country. But a Governor had had his period of office terminated and this could be regarded as some sort of amends for various sins of omission. Judicious comment on the cause of the riots must be looked for from those who really knew what had happened. C. P. Dias, a member of the Municipal Council of Colombo, a man who could rarely be fooled, wrote: 'The recent riots cannot even by a stretch of imagination be termed "sedition". The disturbances appear to me to have been a sudden burst of resentment on the part of the lower classes of Sinhalese, the artizans, and the unemployed in the villages and towns against the Moslems, particularly the Coast Moors.'

But for these upsets, the sixty-seven years between 1848 and 1915 were a period of peace during which the wealth brought to the island by the development of its plantation economy could be seen in the statistician's survey of the evidence. More than once in his public speeches at the time Ponnambalam Arunachalam (later Sir Ponnambalam), a Tamil who had retired from the Civil Service as Registrar General, referred to the impressive record. He had been Director of the Census of 1901, and since then the Census of 1911 had furnished further proof of 'advancement'. In his lecture on 'Our Political Needs' delivered on 2nd April 1917 at the general meeting of the Ceylon Reform League, Arunachalam paraded his figures. He contrasted 1834, the year of the first Ceylon Blue Book, with 1915, when Ceylon as a Crown Colony was at war with Germany and consequently there was a decline in the volume of imports and exports:

	Population	Revenue	Expenditure	Imports	Exports
1834 ..	1,167,700	3,799,120	3,348,350	3,727,260	1,458,340
1915 ..	4,106,350	51,545,472	50,148,001	168,446,038	273,377,180

As these figures were used as a text on which to hang the discourse on the necessity for reform of the Legislative Council, the speaker was not concerned to work out who chiefly benefited from this great advance. But obviously it was an advance. Colombo had become one of the great harbours of the Indian Ocean, lying strategically between the Near East and Australia. The railway had linked all the major towns of the island with the capital, only Ratnapura and Batticoloa being still without railway connection. Built in 1865 almost exclusively for the purpose of getting the coffee from the hills to the port of Colombo, it surprisingly derived the greater part of its revenue from its passenger traffic, for all Ceylon within easy reach of a railway station seemed to be on the move. In 1905 the extension to Jaffna was ready and the journey there from Colombo, which used to be a safari needing careful planning unless one travelled all the way by sea, was one of travel overnight. In 1902 the first motor-car was imported into Ceylon, and in the 1911 census a new occupation had to be listed for the first time —that of chauffeurs. The gramophone, the sewing-machine and the bicycle were beginning the revolution in the mode of living which the bus completed in the twenties. Over 30,000 persons were enumerated as employed in the service of the state, a very much smaller number than those on the land and in plantations, but here was the beginning of the island's most eminent industry.

Signs of the great advance were to be noticed everywhere— from the bottles of aerated water in the small-town kiosk to the elegant mansions of the wealthy in Cinnamon Gardens. In the figures quoted by Arunachalam in his lecture were those for schools: In 1834 there had been 1,105 schools with 13,891 pupils; in 1915 there were 4,303 schools with 384,533 pupils. In these schools, particularly the secondary schools where English was the medium of instruction, the signs and results of the great advance were most to be observed. These secondary schools, all of them but one managed by Christian missionary bodies until in the eighties the Buddhist Theosophical Society and the Hindus founded their own, had been for many years the subject of attention on the part of various governors and the old Colonial Chaplains. They were all agreed that, as far as the colony's finances permitted, education in English was to be encouraged for both utilitarian and moral reasons. There was bound to be conflict between the two for they are other names for the real and the ideal between which an ancient quarrel subsists. There were practical advantages, not to be disdained, in having 'a number of well-qualified candidates for all the offices which are attainable by Burghers or by natives'. There were equally strong moral imperatives, not to be gainsaid, urging the Christian ruler to the task of spiritual regeneration. The slogan was 'the intellectual and moral improvement of man', and the hope was often expressed that it would be diffused throughout the land. The *locus classicus* is in the comment of Robert Fellows (Philalethes) who wrote in 1817: 'I trust that in the wise councils and magnanimous policy of Great Britain, moral considerations will not be overlooked in the midst of great political views, and that she will make her sovereignty of Ceylon contribute to the increase of civilization, to the encouragement of knowledge, the diffusion of Christian benevolence, and the consequent augmentation of the general happiness.'

Was this, as seen in the work of official and missionary, hypocrisy or self-deception? It was too much an article of faith at the time to have been specially devised to secure through grandiloquent phrases the shoddy design of securing for the rulers a small class through whom they could rule. It is more reasonable to regard it as the contradiction involving all those who isolate the intellectual and moral from the social situation from which they stem. On the vacant stage of history on which the British saw themselves standing in Ceylon in the early decades of the nineteenth century, they could assume that they were free to produce the desirable union of utility and moral good. But soon the stage began to be crowded with a host of figures. There were the consequences of awkward liberal ideas which tended to increase the numbers of native supernumeraries beyond the limits of utility, and the test of profit tended to push moral good into the wings. By 1915 the intellectual and moral improvement of man had become the Cambridge Local examinations and the Intermediate Arts and Science examination of London University, on the results of which two government scholarships were awarded to English universities.

In 1870 a Department of Public Instruction was created, and the number of both vernacular and English schools increased. Utility enjoined on all those who could afford it the duty of qualifying themselves for careers in the newly created government departments. Long before the British decided to finance education from public funds in the United Kingdom, the governments of Ceylon and India were accepting, even in niggardly fashion, financial responsibility for schools. Whether the motives were utilitarian or moral, the government was forced into spending more on schools, and the increasing urban population was drawn into seizing the only place it could occupy in the existing economy, with its lack of alternative industrial or agricultural forms of employment offering similar prospects.

According to the 'utilitarians'—Sendall, the Inspector of Schools in the sixties, must be reckoned among them though his comments were those of a moralist—the schools were not turning out what was wanted. Sendall thought there were too many who were 'shallow, conceited, half-educated youths, who have learned nothing but to look back with contempt upon the condition in which they were born, and from which they conceive that their education has raised them, and who desert the ranks of the industrious classes to become idle, discontented hangers-on of the Courts and Public Offices'. Earlier, Lieutenant-Colonel James Campbell showed exactly where the shoe was pinching: 'Great and important changes have taken place in Ceylon . . . at all events they (the natives) have been taught, whether wisely or not I do not pretend to say, to consider themselves of importance in the state, and, from what I hear, notions of equality with Europeans have been instilled into them, of which many thought formerly they ought neither to be allowed to have an idea, nor was it thought politic that they should ever imagine that they could acquire such equality.'

The missionaries, disappointed in the harvest of conversions which at first had seemed so promising, found that if they could not convert the heathen to Christianity, they could at least improve them by giving them the kind of education Christian youths in the United Kingdom were receiving. There had been conversions of course, but it was doubtful whether conviction about the moral excellence of Christianity had weighed as much in the balance as the practical advantage of being a Christian. The Rev. James Selkirk of the C.M.S. was as ingenuous a missionary as could be found anywhere. He was quite sure that 'the natives love the Missionaries, and the Missionaries love the natives, and look upon them as their sole charge, and it would not excite in me any surprise if they should come over and embrace Christianity in a body'. The first convert at Baddegama was a man 'whose understanding was not very quick and was probably impaired by age . . . he received the name of Edward Bickersteth and is supported by a small monthly allowance'. Edward Bickersteth's understanding was acuter than Selkirk's. Most of these converts were to fall by the wayside. They were Christian so long as there was some 'small monthly allowance' or its equivalent to be hoped for from their faith. Before the British left Ceylon practical advantage again decided their change of faith. Of some of those who still remain Christian it could at least be stated that as yet what they believe means more to them than political expedience. It would seem that Christianity, and more definitely the English education which accompanied it and the way of life the latter assured, came in time to represent values which, apart from the badge of the religion as easily pinned on as discarded, were desirable and therefore to be acquired by those as yet without them.

Education in English flourished in this period. No university or college of university status was founded, though in India the rulers had committed themselves to university education. In the north of the island where American missions had elected to work the Batticotta Seminary might have become the first university of Ceylon. By the end of the period, however, there was a Ceylon University Association organizing meetings, writing memorials and trying to bring pressure upon the administration to found a university in Ceylon. It published its own journal, and prominent among its members were Arunachalam, his brother Ramanathan, S. C. K. Rutnam, who was one of the first Ceylonese to lecture in the U.S.A., and a number of Sinhalese intellectuals.

The principals of these secondary schools were English missionaries; even the Colombo Academy, later Royal College, a state institution, always had a cleric for its principal. There was a wide range of academic distinction and personal ability among these European heads of schools—in the Roman Catholic mission French, Italian and Belgian priests were labouring just as efficiently as the British in the various Protestant schools. The curriculum was quite unsuited to Ceylon, and needless repetition and memory work was resorted to by the pupil in order to grasp the unfamiliar content of what was placed before him. These disqualifications of the schools were noted by principals, government inspectors, and in 1911 by H.M.'s Inspector of Schools from England; and the reports of commissions and committees which reported on education in Ceylon will provide a corpus of intelligent criticism of the content and method of secondary school education. But little change was effected. English was the language of the administration, and the desire of the natives for the only economic security within their reach would have stood in the way of any revolutionary changes. The educational system was part of the political framework.

The receptiveness and the ability of the products of these secondary schools had sooner or later to come up against the limited opportunities offered by the service of the state. In law and in theory there was no bar to their employment in the highest offices, and there had been a few isolated cases of Ceylonese who had been so employed. But in actual fact there was a bar. When Arunachalam, at the end of the period considered here, went carefully through the Civil List and showed how few Ceylonese there were in the highest executive posts, the connection between political agitation and the frustration of the educated Ceylonese at the limits set to their advance in the service of the state was revealed.

The secondary schools, written off though they have been by enlightenment as an outrage to the soul of the nation, were well run, and their products guaranteed the smoothness of the later change in political development. Even those whose early lives were allegedly ruined by them must have felt that the evil they suffered was redeemed by some of the men who taught them. Something more than sentimental attachment to childhood and youth would have to account for the devotion with which for more than half a century the names and examples of the European principals and Ceylonese teachers in secondary schools all over the country have been cherished. Not a secondary school in Ceylon but remembers with lively gratitude men and women whose personal influence on their pupils counted for more than anything in the curriculum or the methodology. In Eastern countries where there is a self-conscious overvaluation of the *guru* (teacher), some traditional emotionalism must have gone into the attitude of pupil to master, but it was the greatest tribute to Europeans like Fraser, Highfield and Hartley that quite naturally they evoked responses which other white men instantaneously inhibited.

English education drove a wedge between the already multifarious groupings of people in nineteenth-century Ceylon. But, for a long time, it united all those who could sink their differences in the common objects they pursued. Into these secondary schools went boys and girls from various communities who up to that time had held aloof from each other. For a time there could be the feeling that, in spite of the difference between English educated and the rest, at least a group on top existed outside the divisions of caste and community.

The great result of English education socially was that it added to older divisions new divisions of cultural differentiation. Not even were the more recent racial groups like the Burghers free from 'caste differences'. Besides the obvious difference between rich and poor, there was also a hypostatized difference between those who chose to regard themselves as Dutch and the rest dubbed 'mechanics' or artisans. On the whole the Burghers benefited most from English education. Their European origins and their work as an urban minority in the Dutch administration secured them British patronage. For a long time they manned the clerical posts in government departments. North drafted them into the beginnings of the police force; Sir Alexander Johnston made use of them in the law courts, and as a Christian community, with English as their home language replacing the Portuguese which most of them spoke, they gained most from English education.

The Sinhalese, differentiated at the beginning of the period into Kandyan and Lowcountry and stratified by caste, were separated by the inventor of a phrase which crept into current usage at the beginning of the twentieth century into the two categories of 'somebodies' and 'nobodies'. This rough and ready but practical distinction is believed to have originated in pique at the forwardness of the new rich who had been content with places lower down the table two generations previously. The 'somebodies' in the group of the English educated were the descendants of the Mudaliyars of Dutch times, a numerous clan whose influence had increased. They were loyal subordinates of the British, and Christian, the more important in the group the godsons and goddaughters of Colonial governors. They were landowning gentry, as they had through a tradition of service with both Dutch and British been acquiring land, most of it coconut plantation and therefore not as profitable as land planted in the new commercial crops. By their official position and their long association with the rulers of the Maritime Provinces, both Dutch and English, they had come to be regarded and to regard themselves as the *crème de la crème* of the Ceylonese. It was with considerable resentment and acrimony that the elevation of a Sinhalese outside their ranks to the dignity of a Mudaliyar of the Governor's Gate was unsuccessfully resisted by them in 1853. Some of them were cultured men and women playing the chief role in the Westernized social life of Colombo and the hill station Nuwara Eliya.

The 'nobodies' were by definition those with money but not 'somebodies'. Some of them, as far as 'caste' in the sense of hereditary social group goes, were not different from the 'somebodies'; but they had made their money only recently. Their English education was more recent too. Their parents had made their way by their own efforts: 'These founders of fortunes were a sturdy type of men, who planted coconuts and rubber and mined plumbago, risking money even when interest rates were high, living frugally, travelling in uncomfortable carts and shivering with malaria in the jungles which they cleared to establish their estates.' (H. A. J. Hulugalle: *The Life and Times of D. R. Wijewardene.*) Their sons, given the best education in English then available, aspired to be 'somebodies' in the first half of the twentieth century. In this group of 'nobodies' were some different in caste but by Ceylon standards very wealthy men. The common possession of both 'somebodies' and 'nobodies' was their English education and English modes of dress, social behaviour and bourgeois culture. Into the ranks of 'nobodies' were pressing those from various caste groups and communities, as more and more opportunities for education in English were provided and more government spending provided work for the products of these schools. All the above were apparently 'the educated Ceylonese Middle Class' referred to in the report of the Soulbury Commission in 1945.

Outside English-educated and English-oriented 'somebodies' and 'nobodies' were those educated in Sinhalese, as well educated in and through it as they could be, belonging to as many caste groups as the 'nobodies', but clearly differentiated from them by their lack of status because of their lack of education in English. They may, for convenience, be called 'anybodies'. They were pressing on the heels of the 'nobodies'.

Beneath 'somebodies', 'nobodies' and 'anybodies'—all of them added together a minority of the total population of the island— were the mass of people, themselves divided by differences of caste, with some rudimentary schooling. These might be called 'everybodies'. The basic unit of this large group is the true *Jedermann*, Everyman as in the Morality divested of all the irrelevant accompaniments of Goods, Kindred and sometimes even Five Wits, the ordinary man symbolized. These last were going to be an imponderable factor in the future.

Among the Kandyan Sinhalese, differentiated from the Lowcountrymen by the circumstances of the political development of the Kandyan Provinces for more than two hundred years, were the chieftains dependent on the British for their official rank, and still traditionally accorded the honour due to their birth by their own people. The same differences between the privileged and the rest to be noted in the Lowcountry Sinhalese would be observable among them. Perhaps they were more strongly marked because the Kandyans had been given the opportunities of English education later than the Lowcountrymen. But they too had been quick to adapt themselves, and

John Bright in the fifties expressed his gratification that the best speech of the evening at a farewell dinner to the Governor, Sir Robert Wilmot-Horton, in 1835, 'remarkable for its appropriate expression, its sound sense and the deliberation and ease which marked the utterance of his feelings' had been made by 'a native nobleman of Kandy'. Bright had never been in Ceylon, but he went on to state, quite truthfully, that the same ability could have been shown by 'numerous others among our native subjects'. There were Kandyans well able to take up naturally the status of a ruling clique now deferring to the British. A few quite early distinguished themselves in the service of the state. Perhaps the most flamboyant was Loku Banda Dunuwille, later a Superintendent of Police, whose ease of manner on horseback, quite uncalled for in a native, appears to have affronted Mrs. Heber, the wife of the Bishop.

The Tamils, concentrated in the Northern and Eastern provinces, were as a result of their geographical separation from the rest of the country, and the industry with which they profited from secondary schooling in English, both more conservative in their life and more forward-looking in their ideas than the Sinhalese. Hinduism, South Indian Hinduism in particular, could apparently present to the new *mores* of English culture a much more solid front than the Buddhism of the Lowcountry-man. There were numerous converts to Christianity in the north too, particularly among the lower castes, but by and large the Hindu had the benefit of a traditional religion with enormous powers of absorption and resilience. No large-scale plantation economy disturbed the holding of land. Tobacco was grown, but on small plots not on wide estates. As a result typical of life in Jaffna was the smallholder, aided by his family in working the land, strongly conservative, but well aware of the advantages of education. It was in the north that the system of mission schools receiving grants for their educational work from the government first developed. There was closer spiritual and cultural contact with South India, and for some time the Jaffna man was regarded as an intruder by the ardent Buddhists of South Ceylon. Of course there were Tamil families in Colombo, but there were differences between them and their Jaffna cousins which must be put down to the less conservative and the cosmopolitan social life of the capital. Caste and religion divided the Tamils every whit as definitely as they divided the Sinhalese, but Tamil culture seemed more resistant to 'anglicization' than Sinhalese.

What was typical of the Tamil then, and is perhaps true even at the present time, was the moral earnestness which comes from a life of constant effort. Nothing happened by chance, the smallest actions had significant moral overtones. Dr. Arnold would have found understanding pupils in most Jaffna Tamils, for, like him, they read sublime significances into every event. A. M. Ferguson relates the following incident: 'So utterly unacquainted were the natives of the north of the island with steam-propelled ships, that when the *Seaforth* visited Point Pedro, with Messrs. Anstruther and Dyke on board in 1841 or 1842, the population crowded to the seashore, and I heard an educated Tamil exclaiming: "Great and marvellous are Thy works, Lord God Almighty." ' Such a remark would scarcely have risen to the lips of a Sinhalese, however astonished he might have been.

The Moors, thanks to Islam, were not divided up by caste, but there were two main divisions among these people, originally Indian and long settled in Ceylon. Most of them were town-dwellers engaged in trade. In the Eastern province was a different element—a peasantry among whom, like the peasantry everywhere, English education had made no inroads. In the major towns there were families of substance who had prospered in their business undertakings, but in general as a community the Moors were still unmoved by the desire for education in English which marked other communities.

There was a small group of Malays resident in Ceylon from Dutch times. North is reported to have divided them into three groups of 'princes, soldiers, and robbers'. He was determined to transfer 'as many as possible from the third sort into the second'. They took kindly to life in barracks, and for a long time there was a Malay regiment in Ceylon.

Birds of passage in Ceylon like the British and, like them, possessed of an important stake in the economy of the island, were the groups of Indian business men. Coast Moors, for the first time enumerated in the Census of 1911, have already been mentioned. There were in addition the Chettiars, the bankers of South India, to whom the Ceylonese landowner was indebted for most of his capital. Tennant in the fifties found that there was not a single Ceylonese capitalist in the sense in which the word would have been used in England; he would have had little reason to change his mind had he been alive in 1915. The few wealthy Ceylonese there were could be described as country gentlemen. The wealth of the country—from its plantations and from its commerce with the rest of the world—was in European and Indian hands.

In the background was the indistinguisable mass of the people of the country. The enterprising few sought their way through education out of occupations which held no promise of improved status, and through newly acquired family names out of positions of reputed inferiority into the lower levels of the 'nobodies'. The increase of money in the island, improved communications, and the growth of small towns aided those with energy enough to leave the village and seek a livelihood elsewhere. But the vast majority were still peasants, tilling their own or working on others' land. And even those who had migrated to towns still kept up their connection with the villages to which they belonged. The condition of the villager at a time when the greater part of the island was malarial and agriculture was a depressed occupation may well be imagined. It was noted by planter, administrator, and by the English educated Ceylonese whose social conscience was awaking at the turn of the century. John Capper, who used to contribute to Dickens's *Household Words*, drew a picture of the state of the poor peasant in Ceylon as it might have been done a hundred years earlier by an eighteenth-century sentimentalist writing about Ireland. In his account the poor, however sore their trials, had, in their virtue, their unaffected simplicity and their possession of land, the advantage of the much better-off reader of their plight: 'Poor to abject misery, in all but rice and a few grains, these people are invariably landholders, some of them on an infinitesimally small scale.'

The condition of the mass of people in the villages—both Sinhalese and Tamil—was doubly depressed. Economically they were outside changes made by capital invested in land, except deleteriously through the encroachment of plantation, both tea and rubber, on the village. The preference of the planter for an easily mobilized labour force with no roots in the country, and therefore manageable, prevented a bigger assimilation of the landless villager in the plantation economy. Socially the villager was depressed too, cut off from the possibilities of education in English which ensured the transformation of the fortunate into minor employees of the public service. The language the villager spoke, whether it was Sinhalese or Tamil, was for all practical purposes of inferior status; the religion he professed was a disadvantage, it was not that of the ruler; and the institutions he knew were being thrown into the discard of the unenlightened and the scorned. He had no vote, so he did not count politically. The well-to-do and the 'great ones' who derived their income from the village had graduated into the ranks of the English educated. Between them and the village there were links, but the differences were much more strongly marked. The 'great one' was going up in the new world; the villager had stuck in the morass of the old.

He really would not have needed his celebrated 'horse sense' —the quality the British writer on Ceylon has loved to extol, most often in instinctive reaction against the educated Ceylonese felt as an aggressive competitor—to see the obvious: that his condition was depressed and if he wanted it changed he would himself have to take a hand in the way he was ruled. That he has taken so long to see this and how he reacted to what he saw and felt throw doubts on the value of 'horse sense'. In any case they belong to a much later stage of the story.

Government Agents and Governors who addressed themselves to the problem felt that something had to be done by improving the irrigation of areas once fertile and now fever-stricken jungle. Work was begun on the restoration of tanks in the Southern and North Central provinces, and in the second half of the nineteenth century, particularly in its last two decades, land was made available for cultivation. The educated Ceylonese who looked at the country tended to see the solution of its inequalities in the provision of more seats for unofficials in the Legislative Council. To him the great evil of the British system lay in its refusal to admit more of the Ceylonese *élite* into its hierarchy.

This opinion could have been justified if the economic basis of colonial rule had been left out of the reckoning. For the superstructure, as the educated Ceylonese of the time viewed it, was a combination of liberal ideas and conservative paternalism.

There were the usual differences between avowed theory and actual practice, and the wise paternalism of the ruler always had the trump card of claiming to know exactly what was good for restive children. The objection being raised by such institutions as the Ceylon National Association, founded by Ramanathan in the eighties, was that the children were growing up.

Another objection, raised not then but later, was that British rule perpetuated itself by its devotion to the maxim 'Divide and Rule'. It would seem, however, that racial divisions had not been created by the British, but that to those existing they added one more—their own caste with its elaborate distinctions and its cohesion in any situations of stress. They did not divide and rule; they ruled because of division with the better justification. They could claim that in view of division their function as rulers was to see fair play all round.

At the head of the British hierarchy was the Governor. The appointment which could be the gift of Prime Minister or some notable in England, despite the arbitrariness of this mode of selection, generally secured men of ability as proconsuls in Ceylon. Torrington was a disastrously bad choice, but Sir William Gregory, who came out to Ceylon as Governor because Countess Waldegrave interested herself in getting him the appointment, was a very good one. He came of an influential Anglo-Irish family, was able, extremely intelligent, and had got into Parliament defeating a noble lord whose cause had been espoused by no less a figure than O'Connell. Had he been a trifle less erratic he might never have taken an appointment in Ceylon, but have done much better for himself in England, for 'he had known everybody who was anybody, both male and female, for the last fifty-five or sixty years', so wrote one of his friends in 1892. 'Even as a Harrow boy he was intimate with illustrious Harrovians like Sir Robert Peel, Lord Palmerston, Lord Aberdeen, and Sir James Graham.'

He had unexpected versatility and a natural superiority of manner. As a young man he had a brief, colourful and disastrous career on the turf. On his death-bed he remembered how he had travelled day and night from Marseilles for Coronation's Derby on which he won a bet of £5,000. This would still be a remarkable *coup* for an undergraduate at Oxford. Gregory was a man of unusual talents, he had a keen intellect and he could

if he had wanted to have written the history of racing in England as no man else could have done. Perhaps it was his knowledge of Ireland which led him to look with understanding on
the plight of the peasant in Ceylon. If he is remembered now
outside Ceylon it is perhaps on account of his second marriage.
His wife was the unusual Augusta Persse, the Lady Gregory of
the Abbey Theatre, the chatelaine of Coole Park, and the friend
of Yeats.

The Governor was the source of all the colony's legislature
and he was the chief executive officer. He was therefore the most
powerful personage in Ceylon, dispensing patronage, and
through the Colonial Secretary, the head of the Civil Service,
keeping in touch with the administration of the whole island.
All official communication with England had to go through
him, and he had the right to make his own observations on
memorials and petitions. He was subject to control from Whitehall and Westminster, but as the representative of the Queen
in the eyes of all persons in Ceylon he was unquestioned ruler,
as his ceremonial 'progresses' through the country proved. By
the end of the nineteenth century the trained administrator
tended to replace the notability chosen on account of his political
influence as Governor.

Immediately below the Governor in the hierarchy was the
Officer Commanding the British troops stationed in Ceylon. He
administered the government during an interregnum or during
the absence of the Governor. His main concern was with problems of imperial defence and the maintenance of order in the
country. Though he sat in both the Executive and the Legislative Council he was not likely to come into much contact with
the people of the country except when he administered the
government.

Though in the world of officialdom the European Civil Servant came next, the European planter and the European head
of the Colombo business house were much more powerful
figures. The tea plantation worker has been described as isolated from the life of the country. The same remark could be
made of the Upcountry tea planter who lived in a wonderful
world of his own creation. By the end of the nineteenth century,
with tea established as the major commercial crop and the early
days of pioneering over, the industry settled down to an era of

prosperity offering golden opportunities to young men from the public schools in the United Kingdom. They came out at the age of seventeen or eighteen, and in the ordinary course of events they could retire after thirty years on a competence which was by any standards extremely handsome. The remoteness of Ceylon from England had been reduced by the steamship, and Englishwomen, whom R. F. Morgan found notably absent in Lindula in the sixties, were coming out to Ceylon in greater numbers. The young man fresh from public school in England would find much to compensate him for his exile in Ceylon. Work was outdoor life in the pleasant climate of the highlands, and play, with club, racecourse, golf links and for a time even riding to hounds, repeated in a transmogrified tropical scene institutions he was accustomed to in England. It was a world closed to all but his kind. There were apparently exquisite social nuances between districts, but these must have given a greater zest to life for those in the know with plenty of time on their hands in the clubs.

The Planter's Raj, as it was known in Ceylon, lasted until World War I, but these years between the turn of the century and the twenties were its halcyon period. There was money in tea; rubber was doing well; the government had not been troubled with conscience about 'trusteeship' in the colonies; agitators were not as yet a nuisance; the labour force was quiet; and the planter was literally monarch of all he surveyed from the eminence of his bungalow. The planting interest and the European commercial interest were almost identical, and by the eighties it was no longer necessary for either to agitate for a greater share in the legislature, for the economic stake of the financial interests represented by tea planter and European business in Colombo was now the major consideration of the government.

The geographical isolation of the Upcountry tea planter from the life of the people of the country repeated more markedly the lack of social contact everywhere between the rulers and the upper classes of the ruled. The majority of Upcountry tea planters were not proprietary planters as most of the coffee planters had been, but the superintendents and assistants on large plantations capitalized in England and owned by limited liability companies. Away from the isolation of the hills, in the south for instance, the European proprietary planter, settled in the island for decades with his children, educated in England, returning to manage the family estates, could be the laird of the village and maintain contact with the people of the country.

What was true of the Britisher in India was largely true of him in Ceylon too. Prejudice, his natural reserve, official attitudes with their own unwritten rules insulated him from educated Ceylonese, and the extreme touchiness of the latter limited what contacts there were. Of course there were unions (legitimate and promiscuous) between white man and native girl. But here, too, unwritten rules were apparently at work. Digby, in the late seventies, noticed that 'The English, Scotch or German mechanical engineer, road officer, or locomotive foreman or plate-layer generally *marries* the native or burgher female with whom he "amalgamates"; the civil servant, the merchant, the planter, and the army officer only keeps her. Planters in the hill country have a class of people only one step removed from the region of the cooly lines, who live to serve their fathers (and masters) in the capacity of conductors.' The last comment was no longer generally true at the end of the period considered here, for Visiting Agents and the Directors of Sterling Companies would have reacted strongly if a planter either blatantly took liberties with his labour force or failed to maintain the unwritten code of conduct.

Occasionally a planter would bundle out of a first-class railway carriage in which he was travelling any Ceylonese—man, woman or child—who dared to intrude. But incidents like that described by G. O. Trevelyan in *The Competition Wallah*, when a planter in South India mercilessly whipped 'respectable' Indians for their temerity in coming too close to the European enclosure at a gymkhana, were unknown in Ceylon. The two peoples, for the most part, lived decently segregated from each other. The effects of this were unfortunate, for they hallowed and sanctified existing caste and racial barriers, even at a time when it seemed that they were being knocked down. Even before the vanguard of middle-class Ceylonese clambered up to the heights previously reserved for the European, caste and race broke up the apparently unwavering front line. It must be a matter for regret that, whatever benefit the Upcountry tea planter might have derived from some contact with educated natives, some of them, accomplished botanists and zoologists interested in the flora and fauna of the land of their sojourn, could not transmit anything of the tradition they brought with them from their homes.

The European business man in Colombo and in provincial towns knew and had some social contact with educated Ceylonese. Some of these business houses had been founded by families long resident in the colony which had become their adopted home.

The most important European in the daily life of the country was the Civil Servant proper, or the highest administrative officer of the state. The term Civil Servant should not be confused with that given in the West to any state employee or functionary. The Civil Servant, after 1880 when open competition and not Governor's nomination became the condition of entry, derived his authority from the Secretary of State and was therefore in the true apostolic succession. Synonymous with the office was immense social prestige and high official rank.

The old class of writer and underwriter, known in Ceylon in the early days of the Madras administration and after, had gone. These officials had been dependent on patronage for their presence in Ceylon, and had been compensated for the inadequacy of their salaries by permission to trade and grow coffee. There were a few distinguished figures among them, but the generality deserved the hard things said about them by Bennett in the early forties. He used the term 'china carriers' of them. This he described as 'a local name, meaning the despicable sycophants, tale-bearers, and toad-eaters who have been too much encouraged by more than one governor; and who, instead of meeting their just deserts, a kicking down the grand staircase, have been appointed to colonial situations'.

The new Civil Servant, the 'competition wallah' as he was known in India, may have cut a poor figure on horseback, but he had been chosen for other abilities than equestrianship. Recruited from England on the results of a competitive examination, the graduate of a British university, he brought to his task no special training such as the Indian Civil Service gave their officers after their selection for the service. But the competitive examination ensured that he belonged to the ablest young men of his year; he had had the benefit of a good education unrestricted to any special field; and he had the prospect of a career round which in India and in the Eastern cadetships, as they were called, legends were growing up. There were misfits among these Civil Servants, there were failures too, but the majority, involved in their work and inspired by the zeal of the conscientious, took a natural pride in seeing that it was well done within the framework of the system to which it and they belonged. Their functions were varied and numerous. They were administrators, magistrates, judges, framers of policy, and institutors of legislation. All the threads of government control of the provinces passed through the hands of Government Agent and his Assistant. Through the ranks of minor official Mudaliyar and other native headmen they were in theory in touch with the people in the provinces. If any European knew the villager, they did, or ought to have done. They were, on the whole, beyond the reach of a bribe, and though there were stories like that of Mrs. Turton's gold sewing machine in *A Passage to India*, their glaring defect was not corruption but favouritism. The best of them were men who would have been notable administrators anywhere.

Many of them, both the old and the new, made good use of opportunities which came their way of conserving and developing a great deal of information on old Ceylon which without their care would have been obliterated. The British Civil Servant's tradition of learned dilettantism had been maintained by people like Hugh Nevill. Even in the bad old days before the competitive examination there were civilians like George Turnour who was both coffee planter and a student of Pali learning. In this tradition of the Civil Servant researcher were H. W. Codrington and L. J. B. Turner. The versatility of the talents which might be found in the Civil Service of this time could be proved by a reference to men like T. W. Rhys Davids, W. T. Stace, and Leonard Woolf, all of whom spent some part of their early working life in Ceylon.

They were on the whole an intelligent, responsible and enlightened body of men. They came closest of all their fellows to knowing and understanding the country where they served. If today an account of the condition of the peasant in the early years of this century were needed, a better rendering of its content, apart from the dry bones of facts and figures, will be found in Leonard Woolf's *The Village in the Jungle* than in any white paper or blue book. He left the service in 1911 after seven years in Ceylon. 'One of my reasons (for resigning)', he wrote quite recently, 'was that I had found that I did not like being an imperialist; by ruling others, I had become convinced that the people of Ceylon ought to be allowed to govern themselves.'

That was not exactly what the educated Ceylonese at the end of the period we have been considering had been asking for. But by 1915 a European war on a world scale had changed many more things than anybody in the various worlds of Ceylon could imagine. One of the issues later given prominence in descriptions of why the war had been fought was the right of self-determination of small nations. This made the greatest difference to relations between England and India, so Ceylon was affected too. The long period of tranquillity marked off by the troubles of 1848 and 1915 was to give place to a less settled era in which troubles of a different kind seemed commoner than before.

CHAPTER 13

From One War to Another

By the beginning of this century the leaders of the group of various Ceylonese united in their common interests were pressing, in the most dignified fashion, not for the right to govern themselves, but for a bigger share in the legislature. In 1907, in a publication *Twentieth Century Impressions of Ceylon*, E. W. Perera, a man of great integrity and respected for his force of character, put the demands of the group with which he was associated in language redolent of the album format of the book in which his article appeared—a leather-bound souvenir illustrating the prosperity and contentment of one of His Majesty's farflung possessions: 'An eminently loyal people, deeply sensible of the benefit of British rule, the Ceylonese are aspiring to win the full measure of British citizenship. A freer constitution, flood relief works, abolition of poll-tax, systematic colonization from the crowded western and southern districts to the restored tank regions, a larger educational vote and a wider field for the people of the country in the higher branches of the public service, are some of the reforms which have been eagerly awaited and are urgently needed, and which alone will crown the splendid monument of administration which a century of British statesmanship has raised in Ceylon.' It was a fair statement of the aims of the lawyers, doctors, business men and country gentlemen now asking for some modification of the existing system.

Those in the forefront drafted memorials, organized protest meetings, sent deputations to the Secretary of State, conferred with Governors, and later boycotted Commissions from England. As the British had done before them, they honestly and sincerely identified the country with themselves. Sir Henry McCallum, the Governor, in his despatch of 1909 to the Earl of

234

Crewe, described the result of one of their proposals as 'of course the establishment, not of representative, but of oligarchical class government'. It was indeed the native counterpart of the oligarchical class rule of the European. But once established it could only imply the demission of British rule and produce conditions far different from those which anyone, even a Colonial Governor, could imagine in 1909.

It has been noted that as early as the 1860s the European commercial and planting interests and the local intelligentzia were insisting on some change in the legislature. They could rightly object that thirty years after the Constitution of 1833 had been framed a completely different economy and a different set of social circumstances demanded some change in the way finances were handled. By this constitution Ceylon was governed by a Governor, who presided over an official Executive Council and also a nominated Legislative Council which could discuss legislation which it had no power to initiate. The Legislative Council, with its three Ceylonese and three European nominated members and its nine officials, could criticize and revise the budget, except for its appropriations on the civil and military establishments. The six nominated members demanded the right to do exactly this, since the planting interest wanted less money spent on an unnecessarily large military force and more on roads, while the rest felt that there should be more room made for them in the higher offices of the civil administration.

The reaction of Governors to demands of this kind was characteristic of the first stage of British objections to any change of the system. It was not permissible; for to alter the constitution was to sacrifice to the self-interest of one section of the community all the others. Sir Hercules Robinson, who had to deal with the political agitation of the sixties, was caustic on the claims of the planting interest to speak for the generality of people in the country. He described the European unofficial nominated member as 'generally a merchant or a planter with little or no knowledge of the island beyond the capital and the coffee district. He is merely a temporary resident, whose sole aim and object is to acquire a competency in the shortest possible time, so as to escape from the island for ever. He is the member of a small but dominant class, whose interests often conflict with those of the majority of the inhabitants, who are life settlers. He has, in the appropriation of the revenue of the colony, objects to advance in which either he himself personally or his class are directly interested'. The sharpness of this observation was no doubt increased by the threat to the policies of the official group.

Sir Henry Ward, at about the same time, was equally stiff in his expression of opinion about the Burghers' claims. He felt it was 'the class which is would be most dangerous to entrust with large powers of legislation. They are good servants but bad masters'. He went so far as to state in his despatch to the Secretary of State: 'If you value the peace of Ceylon, you must never give these gentlemen a preponderance in the Legislative Council.'

The attitude of British Governors like Ward, Robinson, and Sir George Anderson was that the British in Ceylon were there to secure the interests of the people of the country, and that neither the planting interest nor the minority of educated Ceylonese had any claim to speak for anybody but themselves. As Ward put it in 1859, 'in a colony the population of which consists of seven or eight thousand settlers, a small though intelligent class of Burghers, and two million of Sinhalese, Tamils and Moormen, wholly unaccustomed to the working of a constitutional system... the Crown must for many years hold the balance between European and native interests, if it wishes to see order maintained and legislation impartially conducted.'

Except for an increase in the number of officials and of nominated members in the Legislative Council, and certain tactical concessions made to the latter, enabling them to introduce bills without waiting for the Governor's lead and to control supplementary expenditure, there was no change in the way the colony was governed between 1833 and 1910.

Organizations for constitutional reform, as in India, grew out of the social conscience of the educated minority. The Ceylon Agricultural Association, founded by C. H. de Soysa, endeavoured to improve methods of agriculture so that the peasant could benefit from experiments tried out by the well-to-do. The Temperance movement of the eighties combined the militancy of the Buddhist revival of the times with opposition to the government policy on arrack rents and excise, it being difficult to separate one from the other. Groups like these were a focus for all those whose banner was social regeneration. With the later Ceylon Social Reform Society, founded in 1905, 'to encourage and initiate reform in social customs amongst the Ceylonese and to discourage the thoughtless imitation of unsuitable European habits and customs', is connected the name of Ananda Coomaraswamy, the cousin of Ramanathan and Arunachalam. A highly gifted and sensitive soul, with a delicacy of feature and gentleness of manner, he proved in his later development the truth of his belief that 'there is a common universe of discourse transcending the differences of tongues'. For his mother was English, and he was educated in England. He worked a few years in Ceylon in the Mineralogical Survey and then moved away from its uncongenial intellectual climate to his spiritual home in India which he left for the Boston Museum of Fine Arts in the U.S.A. He died there in 1947, soon after his seventieth birthday. Though his own special field became the arts and the philosophy of India, in his years in Ceylon he was social reformer and to that extent politician.

Early in the twentieth century the political colours of all those interested in social reform were hoisted by the Ceylon National Association. Most of its members were drawn from the Temperance movement and from the ranks of the newly formed Low Country Products Association, the Ceylonese counterpart of the Ceylon Planters' Association, still almost entirely European in its membership. In these associations were to be found the well-to-do and the intelligentzia of the English educated. (The expression 'well-to-do' has been used advisedly, for with one or two exceptions, these Ceylonese were not wealthy. They were professional men who had done well in law or medicine—the legal profession had been in existence for nearly eighty years, the Ceylon Medical College was founded in 1870—and had put most of their money into buying coconut land. The rest had made money in rubber, plumbago and real property, but never really had sufficient capital for investment. It is interesting that, according to his biographer, a member of the younger generation drawn into the movement, the biggest newspaper proprietor in Ceylon in the 1920s, had to ask his bank in 1930 for a loan of Rs. 25,000 (less than £2,000). 'This was refused, but the shroff, who played the role of middleman between the bank and its Ceylonese clients, offered to raise the money from a Chettiar money-lender at 12 per cent interest. In such a transaction the shroff would get the money from the bank and lend it to the Chettiar at 6 per cent, and share the difference.' It is necessary to stress this to put into perspective both the financial status of the Ceylonese of this group and some of the drives behind their campaign for more power.

It would be true to say that lack of capital resulted in the restriction of investment. But it should be noted that all the shipping was in foreign hands, so was all banking. Trade in the two biggest money spinners (tea and rubber) was in foreign hands too. The importation of food was in foreign hands. These were all enterprises requiring capital, and providing big returns. The Banking Commission which published its report in 1934 noted that 'the non-Ceylonese element has kept a strong hold on the business, trade and industries of the country, and few opportunities have been allowed to the average Ceylonese to engage in trade and industries either by Government or by business firms'.

If Sir Henry McCallum had had his way he would have given short shrift to the memorials of the Ceylon National Association and all the provincial associations linked with it. He had certainly done his best to short-circuit the discussion in his communications with the Secretary of State. He had in 1907 set up a Finance Committee of the Legislative Council in order to give the nominated members the feeling that they were in touch with the Executive Council and were being kept informed of government policy and its budgetary aims. It was the shadow, not of control but of junior partnership, without any substance. The nominated members, however, once admitted like the camel into the tent from which they had hitherto been excluded, made themselves so much at home that they tended sometimes to edge their hosts out of it. The reality of gubernatorial power was still so dazzling and compelling that, however trenchant members may have been in debate, the Governor's presence at tea after meetings of the Council could be used by him to make up ground seemingly lost in the Chamber.

McCallum's objections to pressure from English educated Ceylonese for change in the constitution were not accepted unquestioningly by the Secretary of State. The Governor had stated that all he wanted an official majority in the Legislative Council for was to protect and safeguard imperial interests. The Under Secretary when he received a deputation from Ceylon could be gracious and unbend to the extent of reducing the official majority to one, and introducing election on a very limited educational and property qualification for four seats in the Council. The Governor's right to nominate members was retained, and six nominated members sat with four elected members and the ten officials in the legislature, over which, as usual, the Governor presided.

This Constitution of 1910 which seriously upset McCallum was very dusty answer indeed to the certainties of the English educated in their schemes of legislative reform. Ramanathan, who had just retired from the office of Solicitor General, was elected to the Council as representative of the new electorate of Educated Ceylonese. With his brother Arunachalam he campaigned for an increase in the number of elected members.

When England went to war in 1914, Ceylon as a Crown Colony was at war with Germany too. Without hesitation the Legislative Council voted money to help the imperial government, and on a very large scale for a poor country money was being raised for war purposes in a variety of ways. Sir Solomon Dias Bandaranaike, the Maha Mudaliyar, was in England at the time, and very characteristically his son, the young S. W. R. D. Bandaranaike, and himself contributed much more than had officially been set down as the limit expected of any Ceylonese. A small contingent of volunteers from Ceylon was drafted overseas, and there was drilling and marching in the local Defence Force.

The four years of war left Ceylon unscarred by any enemy action. In the very first year of the war the exploit of the *Emden* was a godsend to busybodies on the alert to discover German spies and to pester the authorities with stories of suspicious steamer movements along the eastern and southern coasts. Local gossip, never the monopoly of the Ceylonese, had it that the *Emden* had been provisioned by a Boer who had settled down in Ceylon after his period of internment at Diyatalawa was over. This was as far-fetched and unlikely as the suspicions harboured against Sinhalese leaders in 1915. One reason for the circulation of these tales was perhaps the popularity of the large

German colony in Colombo with Ceylonese business men in the decade before the outbreak of war. The German business man was less stiff and more accommodating than his English rivals, and the success of the German export drive into Asia since the eighties helped to develop the myth of the amazing technical superiority of German goods to all others.

Though Ceylon had been spared the ravages of enemy action, soaring prices and some unemployment were among the factors leading to the riots of 1915. The island's crops and plumbago were making money, and throughout the war years and immediately after 1915, when Sir John Anderson who succeeded Chalmers had been able to soothe the wounded feelings of the Sinhalese, the demand for reform of the Legislative Council was increased. In 1917 the Ceylon Reform League was inaugurated. This was the year of the Montagu-Chelmsford statement on the path mapped out by Britain for the development of India. In the same year the first public Conference on Constitutional Reform was presided over by Arunachalam, and in 1918 Ramanathan moved a resolution in the Legislative Council on the necessity for reform of the constitution. A deputation from Ceylon again interviewed the Secretary of State for the Colonies in England. The Colonial Office was awaiting action from Sir John Anderson who was preparing a memorandum on the subject, when he died in March 1918. Though he had been a quiet man who kept his own counsel, he had come out energetically and forcefully on the excesses of his predecessor's government during the riots. British officialdom buried him with maimed rites on account of his alleged partiality for the Ceylonese. At a public meeting after the funeral—described as 'a representative Ceylonese meeting'—a sum of Rs. 200,000 was subscribed on the spot to 'raise in Sir John Anderson's memory a Fund for the promotion of higher education and research in the island'. What became of these high hopes or the promises of money is obscure. No moral could be drawn from these proceedings, for Ceylon either buries the memories of the men it decides to honour or brings them to life again transformed.

Late in 1918 a second Conference met to discuss and press for Reform of the Constitution, and in 1919 the Ceylon National Congress (on the model of the Indian, but more lukewarm in its aims and objects) was founded and held its first session with Arunachalam as President. The demands of the Congress were much the same as those of the Reform League: an enlarged Council with a majority of members elected territorially on a restricted franchise and presided over, not by the Governor, but by an elected member; Ceylonization of the higher branches of the public service.

A new Governor, General Sir William Manning, arrived in Ceylon in 1918. His proposals for a reform of the constitution were proclaimed by an Order in Council in 1920. In the next ten years another Constitution—that of 1924—and the visit of a Parliamentary Commission were the results of continued agitation by the Educated Ceylonese, first given official recognition as a class in the Constitution of 1910, and now with a majority in the Legislative Council, for a larger measure of responsibility.

The constitution mongering of these ten years, with Governor and senior public servants cautious and on the defensive, instinctively feeling that power was slipping out of their hands, is interesting to the compiler of records. That Ceylon was granted 'representative government' in 1924 is meaningful only as a cliché of the colonial historian. Thirty-four members were elected on a franchise which allowed the vote to only 4 per cent of the population. They did not feel themselves unrepresentative of the country and were united in their conviction that they had received a poor substitute for any kind of representative government. The Governor was given wide reserve powers. He could, on any matter judged by him to be of paramount importance, count only the votes of the twelve official members of the Council.

The real centre of gravity in Legislative Council politics had shifted to the Finance Committee and the various Select Committees appointed to review all manner of subjects. Sitting on them the member of the Legislative Council could compensate himself for his lack of power and responsibility in the legislative chamber by investigating, criticizing and prying into all government departments and grilling their august heads, unaccustomed till then to such treatment. Sir Anton Bertram who served as Senior Puisne Justice in Ceylon for many years was very sarcastic about these activities: 'The members of the Legislature have thrown themselves with ardour and enthusiasm into the task of mastering the whole machinery of administration, and have apparently found the subject of administration far more interesting than that of legislation.'

This displacement of the mighty might have seemed a social revolution to those who are always on the look out for its arrival. The 'nobodies' were now 'somebodies', by virtue of the scant respect they could afford to pay to the rulers. This achievement was not part of a plan, but the natural exploitation of the situation. The manifest proof of power—true of Ceylon and of all other countries in the world—lies in the dramatization of superiority. Members of an ineffectual debating society in boarding school could on a committee call the staff to account. That the brass hats of the Ceylon Civil Service were galled was perfectly plain. The resentment came out even in the show kept up (by both the members of the Legislative Council and the bureaucrats) that no knuckle-dusters were used and the most enlightened Queensberry Club rules governed procedure. As Sir Charles Collins put it in his mild words of 1951: 'Unofficial members were not wanting at times in generous recognition of good work by public servants, but the fact remains that the period was one of great difficulty for the services, and the atmosphere created by the attacks on them in Council, and especially in the Finance Committee, was scarcely such as to inspire them to their best endeavours.'

By the end of the twenties a new tradition was in the process of being created: the elected member was going to feel himself free to interfere with the administration. Those bureaucrats who could not acclimatize themselves to the new conditions were, by the next constitution, given the option of retiring with compensation and betaking themselves elsewhere in the colonial service. This tradition of meddling with the administration was fraught with danger, for it had to lead to the sacrifice of efficiency.

In Ceylon, the old administrator may have felt that the deluge was approaching. But the movement, which was being led by the English educated Ceylonese, long before more power (or even the right to superior status) was within its grasp, was no longer a united group of all communities. Fears, not about how power might be wielded but for their very existence, felt by sections in the group, caused a split between the Tamils who had been intellectual leaders of the movement and the Sinhalese. The split came not on a question of a share of the spoils, but over special representation for the Tamils. As early as 1921 Arunachalam and Ponnambalam withdrew from the Ceylon National Congress and founded the Tamil Mahajana Sabha in Jaffna.

Another sign of change with important implications for the future was the opening of the University College, in response to nearly twenty years of agitation, in 1921. This institution, affiliated to London University and preparing students for its degree examinations, successfully implemented that part of the programme of the educated Ceylonese which insisted on 'progressive Ceylonization' of the higher branches of the public service. Twenty-six years after the inauguration of the University College its graduates very nearly manned the whole of the Ceylon Civil Service. They were the products of education in English, graduates of an institution modelled on an English university, and members of an urbanized middle class.

As significant as the creation of the University College in its consequences for the future was the organization of the urban worker in Ceylon. There had been welfare organizations like the Ceylon Social Service League and the Ceylon Workers Welfare League interested in labour conditions, but the political organization of the urban worker began in 1922 with the formation of the Ceylon Labour Union. It was founded by A. E. Goonesinghe, in his day a flamboyant and militant figure who kept the red flag flying on the car which was soon a well-known vehicle on the streets of Colombo. He succeeded in mobilizing the Colombo worker whom up to that time the politician had either lectured or patronized. In 1923 and 1925 Colombo knew its first big strikes. Goonesinghe's militancy, based on his reading of the Irish struggle against the British, did secure various benefits for the cohorts he led. First in the field in organizing the urban worker, Goonesinghe earned his reward in the control of an interest group with voting rights in the next decade. To the credit of his Labour movement must be attributed the demand for manhood suffrage. Its leaders realized what a powerful lever the vote was going to be in the hands of those so far excluded from the franchise. Congress was opposed to these demands and the connection between it and the Ceylon Labour Union did not last very long.

Post-war development and the rubber boom brought prosperity to the middle class in Ceylon in the twenties. It was beginning to be clear that the gradual advance of the educated Ceylonese towards a greater share in the administration could not be checked. The hostile reaction of a Governor of the old school like Sir Hugh Clifford to the 1924 Constitution, and his preference for the less important Governorship of Malaya, showed how the issues had defined themselves. Sir Hugh had had a distinguished record in the Colonial Service; he had a quick mind, an equally quick temper which the mental affliction of his last years drove to exasperation. He had been Colonial Secretary nearly twenty years before and 'possibly could not forget', as an expert has put it, 'that he had the power and was therefore able to pull up and frustrate, during his tenure as Colonial Secretary, many unofficial members whom the government during the later period could not control. Times had changed and there had been a substantial transfer of power by the Imperial Government'. Sir Hugh's denunciation of the constitution called for some reaction from the Colonial Office and a Parliamentary Commission on which all parties were represented visited Ceylon in 1927, under the chairmanship of the Earl of Donoughmore.

Multitudinous deputations, committees and self-constituted spokesmen on diverse subjects poured out evidence before it, making demands, submissions and recriminations, all contained in seven large volumes. The Constitution recommmended for Ceylon—the Donoughmore Constitution—to which a Labour Secretary of State for the Colonies, Lord Passfield (Sidney Webb), added a few touches of his own, set in reverse all previous Colonial Office principles on how a multiracial colony should be governed. The excellence of previous constitutions had been, according to Governor and Secretary of State, their balance of powers so finely contrived that 'no single community can impose its will upon the other communities'. No longer did this seem important. The bar to further progress was not the lack of unity in the country. The Donoughmore Constitution abolished communal electorates and left to the voter above the age of 21, and not to the members of any oligarchy, the duty of deciding how the legislature should be composed. The possibility that he might think communally.was not ignored, and the Governor was left with his old power of nominating to the new State Council representatives of interests neglected in elections.

The stress was laid now on the lack of experience of legislators in assuming responsibility. The 1924 Constitution was condemned out of hand because it divorced power from responsibility, and the Commissioners gave more responsibility over a limited range of subjects to the elected members of the State Council, reserving to three Officers of State—a Chief Secretary, a Financial Secretary and a Legal Secretary—the very important subjects of the public service, foreign affairs, justice and finance. These three—the old Colonial Secretary, the Colonial Treasurer and the Attorney General, all of them metamorphosed—were responsible to the Governor. All other subjects were to be the sphere of seven committees who would choose their Chairmen —the new Ministers.

The important difference made by this constitution, acrimoniously debated in the Legislative Council and accepted at last by a majority of only two votes, was its widening of the electorate. In 1924 only 204,000 people had had the vote; in 1931 at the first elections to the State Council more than seven times that number exercised their new rights. No group or political association had asked for it, and the most influential, the Ceylon National Congress, was opposed to it. But the first political party in Ceylon, the Labour party, had made it an essential part of their programme.

The new constitution repeated most of the main features of the old, stressing and high-lighting them in such a way that in the end a completely new picture was produced. The increase in the number of committees to seven multiplied the old Finance Committee by that number. The Governor had had certain powers reserved in him in the old constitution, these were added to in the new. The powers of Chairmen of Committees—the new Ministers—and of the officials (the three Officers of State) were extended. The ordinary member of the Executive Committee seemed to have been left in much the same position as the member of the old Legislative Council, but he had gained new powers. He was the member of an Executive Committee with some share in shaping the policy of his particular department, and until the war situation intervened, the member of the State Council was not a back-bencher in a parliament with a Cabinet system. Finally, although the key subjects of the public services, finance and justice were the special preserve of the three officials, most of the ordinary business of government departments assigned to Committees overlapped or was linked up with these at various points, so that once again everything under the sun came within the scope of the activities of the member of the new State Council.

Elections to the new Council took place in 1931. Given the ballot, to be marked and put into a coloured box (candidates being identified for the benefit of the voter who could not read by the colours assigned to them), the politically uneducated voter presented it reverently to the great one of his area or the candidate of his caste. Practically all those returned to the two State Councils (of 1931 and 1936) owed their success to their personal and family connections with the constituency rather than to any political considerations. The election of two Europeans to the Council of 1931 was part of the same tendency: a Periya Dorai (big boss) of a tea plantation in Haputale where the majority of voters were plantation workers, and the retired Government Agent of the North Central Province, for many years the great white chief of Anuradhapura, were returned for their respective areas.

No political parties, except for the Labour party, contested the elections of 1931 or 1936. There were none. The Ceylon National Congress had never been a political party, it never based itself on mass support, nor did it attempt to appeal to the country as a party in 1931 now that universal suffrage made such an appeal understandable. The political character of many of its representatives had been expressed with great frankness twenty years earlier by Mr. (later Sir) James Peiris. He had been President of the Cambridge Union Society and a distinguished lawyer. He went on to be a tried politician of the twenties and Vice-President of the Legislative Council of 1924. He was speaking for numerous figures in the group when he said in 1911 at a meeting of the Ceylon Reform Society: 'I do not think a distinction can be made between the members of this Society and those people who are spoken of as the planters. Most of us are planters. Our interests are in many respects identical with those of the planters. It is true that many of them have shown us the way and they deserve the credit for having brought capital into the country and shown us the path along which we may all win prosperity. We have followed in their footsteps and our interests are now the same. The interests of the Ceylonese planters are identical with those of the European planters.'

As for the Labour party, its two successful candidates were the party leader on his way to becoming the Trade Union boss out of touch with the rank and file, and a retired Provincial Engineer whose guilelessness and integrity of character lent the brief distinction of his connection with it to the party of his choice. Of the elder statesmen D. B. Jayatilaka and D. S. Senanayake were the most prominent in the State Council of 1931. Universal suffrage had made no great difference to the composition of the assembly to which much more power and a little more responsibility had been transferred. As a candidate for election to the Council had to be literate in English, by and large the English educated were now going to be in command.

But there were some significant differences. Most politicians of this heterogeneous group of individuals returned to power by a deferential electorate were going to be different from the stereotypes of old. The age of morning suits, of full ceremonial dress, of the turbaned elegance of the Tamil members was going to yield to one of much less carefully garbed legislators. This unimportant sartorial change inside the Council was part of a change in the disposition of forces outside. Universal suffrage brought into the foreground during elections and kept in the background thereafter a nondescript crew of canvassing agents, contact men and public relations specialists without whom elections could not have been successfully managed. These hotel keepers, transport operators, petty traders, because they were apparently successful in helping the candidate whose men they were or in preventing his opponents from getting to the polls, retarded the development of any political organizations in presenting issues to the electorate. It was not the Donoughmore Constitution which discouraged the growth of parties, but the social situation which made them unnecessary. The number of Independents who appeared for election was surprisingly large even when 'parties' had been organized later, because extra-political considerations and the activities of this tribe of 'fixers' were more decisive than party organization.

The heterogeneousness of composition of the Council was reflected in the first Board of Ministers, until in 1936 the astuteness of the Tamil Professor of Mathematics at the University College showed his friends how they could ensure the election of a homogeneous Sinhalese Board of Ministers by disposing their supporters in the various committees according to plan. This manœuvre was instanced as bad faith on the part of the Sinhalese, and later condemned by the Soulbury Commissioners. It was an arrangement enabling a group of persons united for the time being on particular objectives to secure the show of unanimity for their demands: further amendments to the Constitution giving more power to elected representatives and the removal of the awkward control of the three Officers of State.

Proceedings in the State Council set the standard for the subsequent development of the legislature. Most members, and some Ministers, behaved with the utmost individualism towards decisions taken in Committees. In the Council they were addressing themselves not to any specific problems discussed there but to the constituency. Many members had been returned as 'friends of the poor' and pursued policies as vague as that description. It was impossible to hope that procedure of the British House of Commons or the L.C.C., on which the constitution had based its own procedure, could produce a similar atmosphere in Colombo. How could the majority of members of the State Council have behaved differently? They had been drafted, or had chosen to go, into various Executive Committees whose duties and powers had never been defined, in sessions which developed either into duels with the Officers of State or into declamatory protestations of their own devotion to the people of the country. Most members developed a much better sense of aggressive attack than of working out any co-ordinated policies. Jennings and Thambiah in *The Dominion of Ceylon* commented that 'powers were divided among the Executive Committees, the Officers of State, the Board of Ministers, the Governor, and the Secretary of State for the Colonies. Not even the State Council had the power to co-ordinate them all, and actually the Council was a most inefficient instrument of coordination. It consisted not of two or more groups of like-minded politicians but of 58 individuals'. Sometimes the Board of Ministers was not of one mind. The three Officers of States were most often regarded as the Governor's representatives against whom all and sundry could band together.

Despite these unsatisfactory features the new constitution performed a most useful function. It has been praised as 'the constitution that will be placed highest . . . by the constitutional historian and the expert in political institutions . . . as it enshrined certain new and daring changes which have stood the test of time and produced beneficial results'. These were listed as adult franchise, territorial representation instead of communal, and 'the transfer of a considerable measure of executive responsibility to native ministers'. It should be valued much more for the difference it made to the political awareness of the mass of the people and the chance it gave the member of the Executive Committee to make his voice heard in the framing of policy. Both these seemed dangerous possibilities. In the last session of the old Legislative Council E. W. Perera in a seven-point motion on constitutional reform proposed the rejection outright of both the adult franchise and the Executive Committee system. The direction of the current of the thoughts of the old guard was clear.

The Committee system of the Donoughmore Constitution never had a fair trial, for with the outbreak of war emergency regulations, the use of special powers by the Governor, and then the creation of the War Council paralysed it. The State Council continued to meet but in a situation in which decisions were made elsewhere; it no longer had much life. The Ministers were well content arranging things on their own in a 'cabinet'.

Even in the inauspicious period of its early years, with the world depression of the thirties and the severe malaria epidemic of 1934–5, there were marked differences in the tempo of change. They are to be noticed chiefly with regard to the Ceylonization of the higher grades of the public service and the volume of government spending. Ministers and members were united on the first. In March 1933 the Board of Ministers passed a number of resolutions, later accepted by the Secretary of State, governing and regulating the appointment of non-Ceylonese to the public service.

More money was being spent on education, health and agriculture. The Minister of Agriculture, D. S. Senanayake, developed older schemes of tank restoration and inaugurated new projects. Energetic and enthusiastic, he turned his Committee into a well-disciplined unit. Most important were the creation of a State Mortgage Bank and the report of the Commission appointed by the Council in 1934 on Banking in Ceylon. It met at a time when the experience of the depression and the stress placed by it on an economy entirely dependent on world prices for commercial crops were live issues. The founding of the State-aided Bank of Ceylon in 1938, over which Colonial Office authorities dragged their feet, was the first step in a changed financial system.

The depression of the thirties and the malarial epidemic provided both ammunition and a battle-ground for a new generation of politicians who owed allegiance not to nineteenth-century English radical thought, but to European revolutionary Marxism of the twentieth century. Like other political movements in Ceylon this too originated in social service with a definitely local orientation. But the local issue taken up by it could hardly escape antagonizing a government with its attachment to imperial interests. The Suriya Mal (the yellow flower of the Suriya tree) movement was the retort of a few Ceylon ex-servicemen of World War I to what they alleged was the government's lack of concern for them and its whole-hearted support of Earl Haig's Poppy Day Fund collections, the bulk of which was remitted to the United Kingdom. After the protest of its respectable ex-servicemen had been registered and they had given up all connection with it, it continued desultorily, engaging in egalitarian projects and coming to life again only on the anniversary of Armistice Day. In 1933 and 1934 a group of young men, most of them London-trained in Economics and Law, turned it into a political group with a strong revolutionary Marxist programme. One of its earliest associates, a wayward, almost nihilistic schoolmaster who forsook politics for the building up of a school in the slums of North Colombo, first used the expression 'independence for Ceylon'—the *Purna Swaraj* of Nehru in his left period of the twenties—as part of the programme.

This slogan defined the difference between the older generation and the new. These young men of the thirties in Ceylon, at a time when an English poet was confessing to feeling small when seeing a Communist, were politically much more advanced than the generality of English readers nursed on the Left Book Club's pink volumes and the socialism of Laski. Their Penelope was Marx as Lenin and Trotsky had restated his conclusions. Later their Trotskyism led them to affiliation with the Fourth International. First in the field with their principled attack on the existing system in Ceylon which included, in their view both white and brown capitalism, they ensured that Marxism in Ceylon has largely been the impact of the theory of Lenin and Trotsky on colonial problems.

The Lanka Sama Samaja Party (L.S.S.P.) was founded in 1935 under the leadership of this Left intelligentzia. As before, those sufficiently educated to understand the wider political implications of a situation and to give political effect to their reading of it could still be only the English educated. The L.S.S.P. based itself on the urban worker, gradually detaching him from the Labour party and reorganizing him. Apart from the personal connections of its members with some parts of rural Ceylon, the party had no links with the peasantry. Its base was composed of the politically conscious urban workers who, in spite of their political education and their understanding of the value of organization, found it at times difficult to rise above the innate conservatism of their village background. Into the ranks of the L.S.S.P. and out again floated numbers of the disgruntled intelligentzia, giving themselves the delightful thrill of being *avant-garde*, and English-educated adolescents dramatizing in what they imagined to be anti-bourgeois conspiratorial activities personal conflicts of their own.

Of the leaders of this party in the thirties, Philip Gunawardena had already been active in Marxist circles in the U.S.A. A turbulent figure with extraordinary bravura powers of mob oratory, he had a keen mind and very great influence with all sections of the group. N. M. Perera with his much cooler and disciplined mind, his attention to detail, his study of Parliamentary procedure which enabled him to be both effective member of the State Council and leader of a group outside, became much more naturally campaigner and formulator of policy. These two members of a new political party had an influence out of all proportion to its strength either in the Council or in the country. The Executive Committee system enabled them to keep up continual pressure on the Board of Ministers.

The first public success of the LSSP was the episode known as 'The Bracegirdle Case'. A young Australian assistant on a tea estate had appeared on their platforms and had consequently outraged the planting community. He was dismissed, and his deportation arranged between the Inspector General of Police and the Chief Secretary on the basis of an old regulation. The constitutional crisis in the State Council and the action against the Police on the issue of a writ of habeas corpus were clear proof of the political temper of the times. The constitutional implications of the incident, as sketched by Namasivayam in *The Legislatures of Ceylon*, were 'threefold. Firstly, from the point of view of the State Council, it seemed to suggest that an Officer of State was trying to encroach on one of the functions of an elected minister, the Minister of Home Affairs. Secondly, it involved the question of the extent to which an out-of-date Order in Council could be validly used for executive and administrative action by the Governor without the advice of the ministers or in the face of popular opposition. Thirdly, it involved the relations between ministers and heads of departments'.

The legal argument on the validity of the deportation order was argued before the Chief Justice and a Senior Puisne Justice, who held that Bracegirdle could not be deported for exercising his rights of free speech, as in fact he had done. The case was therefore important on several other counts too. It vindicated the rule of law and showed that in a colony the executive could not flout it; the power behind the scenes of the Planters' Raj was shaken; it showed that the Ministers were going to be the dominant figures in the working of the Donoughmore Constitution; through it the LSSP had arrived on the political scene. As for the central figure in the episode, Bracegirdle, he disappeared and was forgotten though the case in which he featured will always secure the attention of students of political and constitutional history.

Two significant events for the future in the thirties were the founding in 1937 of the Sinhala Maha Sabha—an all-Sinhalese political group—by Solomon West Ridgeway Bandaranaike, the Minister for Local Administration and Health, and Nehru's visit to Ceylon in 1939. The name and the family connections of the founder of the Sinhala Maha Sabha proclaimed his connections with the *élite*. He was the godson of a Colonial Governor and the son of the Maha Mudaliyar. He had been Junior Treasurer of the Oxford Union Society, and on his return from England in the twenties he had thrown himself into politics, winning his spurs in a contest for a seat in the Colombo Municipal Council. Clever, far-sighted and a much better judge of political manœuvring than his elders, he saw very early where his future lay. Two possibilities—the staid conservatism of Congress and the demagogy of the Labour movement— could not satisfy his political ambitions. He was perhaps too liberal-minded to be completely at ease in the ranks of the English-educated Ceylonese and he was too well educated to be able to rouse the urban masses as Goonesinghe had done. In either group he would have been a talented junior. He was no revolutionary and therefore unable to rally the young English educated in the thirties. He was a member of the Ceylon National Congress, and in his early years in Congress earned a reputation for radicalism with which its leaders were never sympathetic. Soon after he returned to Ceylon Bandaranaike shed both his Christianity and the conventional garments of the West (trousers and coat) which could be thought of as reprehensible unnational appendages. In so doing he was reminding his elders in Congress of the wave of feeling that had swept the early supporters of the social service movements of the eighties and nineties into organizing themselves. His years of activity as Minister of Local Administration with the contacts he was making with provincial Sinhalese-educated notabilities must have indicated what his sphere really could be, for his creation, the Sinhala Maha Sabha, became the platform of the Sinhalese-speaking lower middle-class man who felt the lack of contact between himself and the upper-class Congressman with his English education and his Western outlook. The Sabha was not a rival to Congress, but a group with objects of its own. It was not a political party, but an organization with stress laid on its Buddhist and Sinhalese programmes.

Nehru visited Ceylon in 1939, at a time when the plantation workers were being organized politically. This very large group, over 100,000 strong, had been exercising the vote as it was entitled to do by the Donoughmore Constitution through the fact that these workers were domiciled in Ceylon. The majority of them had been resident in the island for two generations. Legislation had granted them certain 'rights' of minimum wages, medical attention and housing. Meagre as these were, in relation to the Ceylonese worker the Indian was better protected by the law.

There were Ceylonese unions in existence, and at work in the urban areas. If the plantation worker had thrown in his lot with them, his future would surely have been different. But he, or his advisers, decided otherwise. It was believed that Nehru had suggested the formation of a Ceylon Indian Congress. This was dominated by wealthy Indian planters and business men. The effect of this identification of the plantation worker with an Indian group was disastrous. It was thereby distinguished all the more definitely from the other working-class unions in Ceylon, which created the paradoxical situation of ensuring that the biggest group of workers in the country would be reckoned, with some justice, as non-nationals and therefore moved by interests opposed to those of its nationals.

The plantation worker, separated though he was from the rest of the country, was given the vote by the Donoughmore Constitution. This had a delayed effect on him similar to that which it had on the rural voter. It began even to light up dimly his sense of himself as a person with rights. His vote was the object of respect by people who had hitherto noticed him only as part of the landscape.

The thirties went out in strikes on the plantations, the most serious of which provoked a constitutional crisis. There was shooting by the police on Mooloya Estate in 1940 when a strike was in progress. Left agitation in the Council led to the appointment of a Commission to investigate the circumstances of the shooting. The Council had insisted that prosecutions arising out of the strike should not be proceeded with until the Commission had reported, but the Inspector General of Police refused to carry out the Home Minister's order and was supported in his refusal by the Governor. The Ministers resigned, but the crisis was smoothed over by the Governor's agreement to the appointment of a select committee to report on the constitutional niceties of differences of opinion with regard to procedure. Mooloya was the first of the big plantation strikes. It was a danger signal to the 'nobodies'—the plantation worker was not going to be their man. It showed besides that in an emergency the Governor's hands gripped the reins of power.

In August 1939 the Ribbentrop–Molotov pact had its reverberations in distant Ceylon. It precipitated a clash between the Marxist and Stalinist elements in the LSSP. The Stalinists were expelled—an unusual fate for those who have been uniformly successful in infiltrating organizations they subsequently take over. But these local excitements were completely overshadowed by the war which broke out on 3rd September 1939.

CHAPTER 14

War and Independence

Soon after the declaration of war by His Majesty's Government in London, the Governor of Ceylon convened the State Council and informed it that Ceylon too was at war with Germany. This was accepted by the Board of Ministers and the majority of members of the State Council. The LSSP with its avowed policy of anti-imperialism denounced the war as a struggle between imperialist powers and called upon its supporters to oppose it. The line taken up by the LSSP was based on the Leninist premise that out of the destruction of imperialisms in a world war might be expected the growth of a revolutionary movement in the defeated countries. The party was proscribed and its leaders put in jail. The Stalinist rump ejected by it formed itself into a new party calling itself the United Socialist Party, and tried to enter the Ceylon National Congress. D. S. Senanayake flatly objected to consider such a proposition and resigned from Congress which thereafter subsided. It had fulfilled its function, it had brought together the educated Ceylonese interested in reform of the constitution. In a changed situation, with new groups brought into existence by new persons angling for power, the only hope Congress had of surviving was of being taken up and transformed into a party by a new and dominant personality.

The Ministers, whatever qualms and reservations they may have had about the war and its probable effects on Ceylon, accepted the situation. They were more anxious about running the country in their interests and those of the British, for there was a growing sense of identity between the two. Few people had any attitude to the war in its opening stages, for indeed to all but the far-sighted it could make little difference to the island, except for inconveniences like the black-out and the threat of inflation, noticeable immediately war was declared in the rising prices of food long before stocks were depleted or shipping affected. This war, like the last, it was philosophically accepted, would make the rich richer and the poor poorer. This had been demonstrated to be one of the facts of life beyond human control. Anyhow the war was being waged seven thousand miles away on issues quite unimportant to most people in Ceylon. To the claims and counterclaims of the Allies and the Germans the mass of people were indifferent. The Germans were thought of as uncannily efficient technicians, and there was sufficient ambivalence in the attitude of the educated Ceylonese to the British to turn the increasing tally of reverses in 1940 into cause of satisfaction that the proud had been humbled, and of alarm at the unimagined consequence of a dangerously changed picture of the world.

Militarily the defence of Ceylon in the thirties was unrelated to any reality except perhaps that of World War I. There had always been a garrison in Ceylon, but its Commander no longer as in the twenties sat in the Council or administered the government in the absence of the Governor. His concern was the small Imperial defence force—no more than two detachments of gunners and engineers stationed in Colombo. The Ceylon Volunteer Ordinance of 1861 had led, in the course of time, to the formation of three detachments of Ceylonese Volunteers—of infantry, gunners and engineers. There were also two exclusively European detachments—a Rifle Corps and a Mounted Rifle Corps. But none of these—either Ceylonese or European—could have been considered trained or equipped to meet any front-line wartime demands. The East Indies squadron was based on Trincomalie.

Disarmament, and the failure to work out any scheme of imperial defence in view of German rearmament (particularly the growth of the German navy and submarine fleet), have been unfavourably commented on with regard to England's preparedness for World War II. That the defence of a small colony in the Indian Ocean was neglected does not therefore seem surprising. Trincomalie, in spite of the extravagant claims made for it at the end of the eighteenth century and the beginning of the nineteenth, had not been developed into the naval base it might have been in the twentieth century. The East Indies

R
257

squadron used it, as it used other harbours in the Bay of Bengal. It was equipped with dry docks and naval installations, but it never was, even in the years after the London and Washington naval agreements, more than a station planned and maintained on outmoded naval strategy.

Emergency regulations had the effect of changing procedure. The Governor and the Officers of State, confident that the Ministers would allow nothing to interfere with Ceylon's share in the war effort, allowed much more than previously to be decided by them. The war situation gave the Ministers more power. It took away some of the opportunities for control which sometimes came to the ordinary member of the Council. The eight years between the declaration of war and the Ceylon Independence Act of 1947 could be regarded as the period during which the Ministers proved that the imperial government need have no alarm, even in a situation of war, about the running of the country. The country was quiet, the formation of an Essential Service Labour Corps could deal with any strikes and any interference with Ceylon's supplies of tea and rubber. Relations between the new Officers of State and the Ministers were cordial, for the new Officers were not the Civil Service brass hats of the early thirties who looked coldly down their noses at persons thought to be incapable and self-important. Nothing the Board attempted during these years seemed either beyond the resources of the country or a threat to its economic and financial stability. The most 'revolutionary' of the proposals of any member of the Board was that of 'free education', or the abolition of fees in state-aided schools. This was criticized by a number of the people for its reckless committal of the country to unconscionable expenditure; but it turned out to be, in its initial stages, well within the island's resources.

From the experience of the previous war it was clear that the immediate problems needing attention were the control of food and of prices generally. New government departments came into being, and vigorous plans on paper took up the slogan of 'grow more food in the island'—planters on their undeveloped land, the rice-cultivator on his small holdings, even the urban gardener were urged to help in meeting expected shortages.

The extension of the war in Europe, after the 'phoney' era was over and France fell, made no great difference to the situation in the island. When the Soviet Union was attacked the Stalinists changed their line overnight and interpreted the old imperialist war as a peoples' struggle for liberation. But it was not until 1944 that a Communist Party of Ceylon (CP) was founded. Like the LSSP it was led by intellectuals, among whom the most notable, though he was not the leader, was Pieter Keuneman, a Burgher who belonged to a well-known legal family. His career at Cambridge had been unusually brilliant. He had been President of the Union and Editor of the *Granta*, and an outstanding figure in undergraduate society. He had been trained as a barrister, but gave up the law for journalism. He was the trump card of the CP, a witty speaker in English with the knack of producing a well-turned quip. The regard in which he was held as a person and not support for his political beliefs launched him successfully into municipal politics and later into the House of Representatives.

In 1940 the Ministers, for the first time, were allowed to deal themselves with matters till then considered to be within the sphere of External Affairs controlled by the Chief Secretary. A Ministerial delegation to New Delhi took up with the Indian government the status of Indians resident in Ceylon and their political rights. The bone of contention was the franchise. The majority of Indians resident in Ceylon were the plantation workers, and their conditions of work, housing, medical care and wages were decided by consultation between the Agent for the Government of India and the Ceylon government, and subsequently embodied in legislation. Since the time of the Donoughmore Constitution the plantation worker, or any member of the smaller group of Indian unskilled workers and business men in the towns, who could establish his domicile or the fact of permanent residence in the island was entitled to the vote. The number so enfranchised had risen from 100,000 in 1931 to 225,000 in 1939. Nothing came of the negotiations at New Delhi or of the visit to Ceylon in 1941 of an Indian delegation on the same subject, for a compromise agreed on in 1941 was never ratified by the Indian government. The Ministers were ready to concede domicile of origin to certain classes of Indians long resident in the island, and domicile of choice to those who could, under suitably devised tests, prove their permanent interest in Ceylon; but the Indian government went much further in its demands, seeking considerable modifications in the tests for both qualifications. Though these talks were abortive, the visit of the Ministerial delegation to New Delhi and the subsequent discussions in Ceylon marked a stage in the evolution of Ministerial powers and rights.

With the entry of Japan into the war the situation in Ceylon had to be affected, although, until the defeats in Malaya began to stress the island's changed position in Indian Ocean strategy, little difference was made to either civilian life or military preparations. There was, however, another important landmark in the progress of the educated Ceylonese towards their objective. The Governor appointed a Civil Defence Commissioner to co-ordinate all aspects of the work of government departments dealing with the civilian population in wartime and also to inaugurate a department of Air Raid Precautions. The choice of Mr. (later Sir) Oliver Goonetilleke as Civil Defence Commissioner proved the new orientation in both the Governor's and the government's attitudes to the English educated, for at a time when the island was threatened by war, the choice of the keenest-witted Ceylonese of his generation for a position which normally would have gone to a top-ranking white bureaucrat showed how far things had changed from 1915 and even from 1931. The new Civil Defence Commissioner, as his later career proved, had a flair for the situation calling for a firm grip of the reins, when the stakes were high and the going heavy. 'Somebodies', 'nobodies'—he knew them all, and he could convince all those who crowded round him for favours and advice that for them the red carpet was being unrolled and the bands were playing; a dangerous talent which turned disappointed suitors into critics. But he had undoubtedly better qualities of mind than others of his generation; by any standards at all they were impressive.

The main base of the British forces against any possible attack from the Far East—Japan—was Singapore which had been built up as a great naval bastion. But it turned out in the end that Singapore was in the main a defensive base, that the strategy which would have enabled it to withstand attack from the landward side was put into operation much too late, and that in any case it was based on a deficiency of understanding about the probable course of the war in the Pacific, and a miscalculation of the strength of the British navy in the Atlantic and the Mediterranean. When Japan forced into war by American economic sanctions struck at the U.S. Pacific fleet at Pearl Harbour on 7th December 1941, the efficacy of her main discovery in naval strategy in World War II—that the core of a naval striking force is its carrier—was proved. The huge battleship without air umbrella was going to be a liability and not an asset.

It was inconceivable to the amateur strategists in Ceylon that the British could lose Malaya, even after the Japanese had repeated their Pearl Harbour exploit and sunk the *Prince of Wales* and the *Repulse*. Christmas 1941 and the New Year of 1942 saw much the same kind of activity among the upper strata of Colombo as had by now become regular, even with the restrictions of black-out and wartime regulations. There were as many people shopping in the Fort and the Pettah, as many going through the routine of dancing at the big hotels on New Year's Eve. It is true that they were not representative of the people of Ceylon, but if any persons at all should have been alive to the grave threat now being posed to the Eastern might of the British they should have been. January 1942 was a month in which unknown place-names in Malaya grated on the mind threateningly—Kampar, Kuala Kangaar, Batu Pahat, Slim River. It was impossible even in the face of this evidence to think that Singapore could fall. How that fortress came to capitulate has not been satisfactorily explained as yet. Churchill described it as 'the worst disaster and the largest capitulation in British history'.

Vice-Admiral Sir Geoffrey Layton, second in command of the Eastern fleet, was on his way home when on the death of Sir Tom Phillips he was called back to take up temporary command. He had seen how unpreparedness and lack of planning contributed their quota to the destruction of British power in Malaya. Singapore fell on 15th February 1942; within the next month Rangoon was gone, and soon the Dutch East Indies and the Dutch fleet in Eastern waters went too. The Japanese thrust had brought Ceylon within the front line of the war. A new stress was going to be placed on the strategic value of the naval station of Trincomalie and the harbour of Colombo. As the official historians put it: (There was) 'no base for operations in the Pacific nearer than Ceylon or Australia. Ceylon itself was threatened and the British Eastern fleet was for a period in 1942 forced back to the east coast of Africa. Japanese naval and air power dominated the Bay of Bengal which meant that—again for a period—not only was the great port of Calcutta closed to shipping, but the eastern coast of India was open to invasion.' The Indian Ocean had become vital, not only on account of its importance to British armies fighting in the Middle East, but also to the war in the West for through Persia ran one supply line to the USSR..

Sir Geoffrey Layton arrived in Ceylon on the 5th of March 1942. If Malaya had been unready to play its part in the war, few people in Ceylon had any conception of what readiness meant. The same air of uncertainty and irresolution hung over everything. The directive given Sir Geoffrey Layton was perfectly explicit: 'You are appointed Commander in Chief, Ceylon. All naval, military, air and civil authorities in the area, including the Governor and the Civil administration will be subject to your direction. Your immediate task is to ensure that all the measures necessary for the defence of Ceylon are taken forthwith and that the military and civil measures are properly co-ordinated. The Governor has emergency powers under the constitution and the power to issue defence regulations which he can use to the extent you may require for any such measures. ... In the exercise of your authority in civil affairs you will have regard to the importance and value of the maintenance of the services of the civil government as long as they can operate efficiently in the prevailing conditions.' He was given almost dictatorial powers; he had no need to use them because he had a Governor and a Board of Ministers only too ready to co-operate.

Sir Geoffrey was forthright in his demands and he had his way. If Ministers then in power related much later after the event how they had stood up to the doughty Commander-in-Chief, this could be regarded as retrospective support administered to severely deflated egos. Actually Sir Geoffrey had too much on his hands to have had time to bother about the figure cut by the champions of civil rights. Defences had hastily to be assembled and Ceylon had to be made ready to meet a Japanese attack which could be expected at any time.

In 1941 the only aircraft in Ceylon were those of a Vildebeeste

Bomber Squadron, popularly known as 'flying coffins', and a
Catalina Flying Boat squadron. Against Japanese Zero fighters
neither was likely to be of much use. The defences were now
strengthened with the accession of four fighter squadrons, including one of Hurricanes, a Bomber squadron of Blenheims
and three Fleet Air Arm squadrons. A new airstrip on the racecourse at Colombo was prepared and anti-aircraft guns and
radar equipment were installed. As the war visibly moved closer
to Ceylon there was growing uneasiness.

From the middle of March the number of residents leaving
Colombo for the hills increased. In the newspapers the rents of
houses in provincial towns inland rocketed. But there was as yet
no general exodus from the capital. It was noticeable, however,
that at this time of the year when the heat of the coastal plain
generally sets in motion the trek of the well-to-do to the hills
more people of all classes were on the move than before.

The attack, even invasion of the island expected by the Allied
forces was announced by a lone Catalina on reconnaissance on
April 4th. It began on the morning of Sunday, April 5th, when
a force of carrier-based bombers of Vice-Admiral Nagumo's task
force raided Colombo from a position about 150 miles south of
Dondra. It was this First Air Fleet which had crippled American
shipping at Pearl Harbour. The air-raid sirens had been wailing
for a few minutes only when the first bombs fell. It was not a
heavy raid, but it struck two merchant ships in the harbour,
destroyed some part of the fish market in St. John's Road and
a few buildings in Ratmalana. A block in the Lunatic Asylum
a few miles away from the town was hit too.

The defences had not done badly and the fighters had brought
a few raiders down. But ignorant of either the extent of damage
inflicted on the town and harbour or the intentions of the
Japanese, the majority of people in Colombo panicked and
streamed out of the city, using any method of transport available. It was a dismal, wet, April day; the monsoon had not yet
broken but there was thunder in the air and the atmosphere
was full of steamy heat. By evening Colombo was silent and
dead. Few people were about in the best residential quarters,
except for the services and a few civilians, to read the posters
in large type warning prospective looters that the penalty for
looting was death.

Four days later Trincomalie was raided and oil installations in China Bay set on fire. The *Hermes*, a small carrier, and a destroyer *Vampire* were sunk. The other Japanese task force under command of Admiral Ozawa had in the meantime been engaged in sinking shipping in the Bay of Bengal. To their large score were added the cruisers *Dorsetshire* and *Cornwall*.

. The civilian population had run away; but the administration, in spite of numerous absentees, contrived to function and the forces were temporarily in command of the situation. By contrast with the Madras government which panicked after the raids on Vizagapatam and Coconada, Colombo and Ceylon were normal. Fortunately nothing happened after the raid on Trincomalie on the 9th of April. It is now known that the Japanese had failed in the major objective—to destroy Admiral Sir James Somerville's Eastern fleet. This had kept out of the way in Addu Atoll in the Maldive Islands. The threat to it was so great, however, that in view of the presence of Japanese carriers in the Indian Ocean it was decided to withdraw it to East Africa. One part of the Japanese plan had been fulfilled— the demonstration of their strength to the civilian population. Vice-Admiral Ruge, reviewing the war at sea from the German point of view, wrote in 1954: 'The British were lucky to escape a catastrophe. After the loss of their two battleships off Malaya, they had sent Admiral Somerville to the Indian Ocean with a fleet consisting of two carriers and five older battleships. On receiving a report of the appearance of the Japanese squadron the British ships steamed from the Maldive Islands to meet it, but turned back again without seeking battle. The Japanese air reconnaissance, working without radar, did not spot the British ships, whereas the latter had picked up the aircraft on their own radar screens. The British carrier-borne aircraft were anti-quated; the excellent Japanese air squadrons would have wrought havoc among the British ships. It is doubtful whether Churchill's Government could have survived such a disaster.'

In the final analysis therefore the raids on Ceylon, either through strategic deficiency or the superiority of British equipment, had failed to bring off the grand Japanese design. Satisfied though the Japanese must have been with what they had achieved by them, they had in the end done no more than strike terror into the mass of the civilian population, cause some damage in Trincomalie and destroy nearly 100,000 tons of shipping in the Bay of Bengal. But they had failed to get the Eastern fleet, they were not even aware of its location. The inadequate defences of Ceylon, soon to be greatly strengthened, had escaped the strong pressure which might easily have been kept up. The expected invasion which the bulk of the population expected never took place, and by the end of May those who had fled from Colombo streamed back. Later in the year the battles of the Coral Sea and of Midway in the Pacific made it plain that American naval power, having recovered from the shock of Pearl Harbour and destroyed Nagumo's carrier force, was going to keep the Japanese fully occupied. The Indian Ocean was unvisited by their fleet. Wavell had in the end been proved right. The Japanese attack on India was going to be a land operation based on the Burmese frontier.

To most amateur strategists at the time the failure of the Japanese to capture Ceylon had been due to the dramatic suddenness of their successes and their consequent inability to profit from them. Had they been less successful at first, it was argued, they would ultimately have triumphed. Actually the capture of Ceylon had never been envisaged as necessary to their schemes of economic self-sufficiency—the Great Eastern Co-Prosperity Sphere they planned. These demanded the capture of Malaya, the Philippines, the Dutch East Indies and New Guinea, which would have given Japan the raw materials she needed and would have ringed her with a circle of defence she could have maintained.

No invasion took place. More and more men and materials were arriving in the island, and by November 1942, with the German disaster at Stalingrad and the beginning of Montgomery's successful North African campaign, a different complexion began to bloom on the face of the war. In 1943 a co-ordinated South East Asian Command was set up under Lord Mountbatten, with his Ceylon headquarters at Peradeniya. By this time Ceylon was being prepared as the bridgehead of invasions of Malaya, Sumatra and Burma. Airstrips were being built all over the country—one near Sigiriya produced a Heath Robinson contraption of bamboo with wads of cotton pressed up against the painted face of the fresco pocket to prevent damage to the paintings from the vibration of the aero engines.

Soldiers, sailors and airmen of all nations were pouring into the island; the Allied governments were pouring money into preparations for the SEAC thrust, spending in these years Rs. 400 million annually—more than the annual revenue of the island. So far as Ceylon was concerned the war with Japan had receded into the comfortable distance of bulletins announcing the successes of the American navy and marines on islands and beaches once thought of as the setting for Somerset Maugham stories or the researches of anthropologists.

It was a good war for practically everybody in Ceylon who had anything to sell or could undertake to supply the forces with anything at all. Fortunes were made by hundreds of people—the honest, the cheats, the enterprising and even the slack. With Malaya and the Dutch East Indies in Japanese hands, Ceylon was the largest supplier of rubber for Allied war demands, and plantations were being 'slaughter-tapped'. Unskilled labour all over the island found unexpected sources of money in the work provided by forces' installations. Only those with fixed incomes—the urban clerk and the public servant—found the war ruinous. Inflation and wartime shortages increased the cost of living intolerably. No part of Ceylon seemed to be out of range of a day's walk of some forces' camp. Even on remote beaches on the eastern coast sooner or later some coast-watching unit was to be met with.

It was a good war for Ceylon. The raids of April were soon forgotten. The forces got on well with the civilian population. They were welcome in their homes and made much of, not because they were regarded as defenders of the island, but as interesting people with whom there was much in common. The forces appreciated the friendliness and the genuine hospitality of the Ceylonese, and even now, nearly twenty years after these events, recollect with pleasure the mention of places as different from each other as Bandarawela, Trinco and Galle.

The meeting of West and East during these years made a difference to the attitudes of most people in Ceylon. It might even have made some difference to the future of the island. For the first time Ceylonese came in contact with the white man as an ordinary human being, a person like themselves in fact, stripped to the waist in tropical heat and working on the same laborious tasks they knew only too well—road-making, clear-

266

ing the jungle and moving heavy loads from place to place. He was no superman isolated from themselves by differences of status and caste, but a person separated from them by the easily surmountable barrier of language. Not for a moment is it possible to describe their raction as a recent writer has done: 'During World War II British and American troops stationed in Ceylon daily demonstrated that even manual labourers, mechanics and drivers for the Allied forces lived a life of plenitude hitherto unimagined by the average Ceylonese.' On the contrary, the attitude of most Ceylonese must have been: 'What bad luck—to have to do such work and to eat such food.' The canned food and the beer would not have been envied as indices of a 'life of plenitude'. Perhaps there might have been a tinge of some tragic catharsis in seeing the white man labouring with the sweat of his brow at tasks believed to be impossible to a man of such high estate. The Chinese and Malays reacted to the spectacle of British soldiers to whom Yamashita gave the job of sweeping the streets of Singapore after the capitulation in much the same way.

On the part of the ordinary ranker, though the politicians and not he made the decision, there was genuine good feeling and interest in the people he met, and the certainty too that, however undeveloped they might have been, they had a good right to rule themselves if they wanted to. Many Ceylonese given the opportunity had shown their skill as mechanics and drivers. They were in addition warm-hearted and demonstrative, and as the soldier reflected on the shape of the post-war world he could give it meaning and coherence without forcing into it any pattern of colonial empires for which he and his comrades had been fighting in the torrid jungles of the East. The mood which went into the British election of 1945 and gave the cue to the Labour Party of the role it had to play was largely generated by the feelings of common soldiers all over the world who had had enough of shouldering the white man's burden. The independence of Ceylon was not won in any of these forces' camps about the island, but it would not have seemed strange or dangerous to those who manned them in the years between 1942 and 1946. Those higher up who could have influenced political decisions would perhaps have agreed that the Ministers and the 'English-speaking natives' were educated and well-meaning people, well able to look after themselves.

. The old State Council given another lease of life in 1942, though elections were due in 1941, continued. After the excitements of the first few months of 1942 there was a change in the composition of the Board of Ministers. The Minister of Home Affairs and the Leader of the State Council since 1931, Sir Baron Jayatilaka, was, in the inelegant contemporary phrase, 'kicked upstairs' and proceeded to India as Ceylon's representative. D. S. Senanayake succeeded him as Leader of the House, and A. (later Sir Arunachalam) Mahadeva—the son of Sir Ponnambalam Arunachalam—joined the Cabinet as Minister of Home Affairs. One part of the manœuvre is related in *An Asian Prime Minister's Story*.

The change placed leadership in the hands of D. S. Senanayake, a better representative of the group than the scholarly Sir Baron. It removed from the Board of Ministers the unfortunate liability of being 'pan-Sinhalese' as it was called. The inclusion of a Tamil was an accession of strength. It was still a homogeneous Board, but it did not exclude a minority community.

. In May 1943 with the threat to Ceylon over and the final struggle for victory ahead, the Secretary of State for the Colonies issued a declaration that 'the post-war re-examination of the reform of the Ceylon Constitution, to which His Majesty's government stands pledged, will be directed towards the grant to Ceylon of full responsible government under the Crown in all matters of internal civil administration, subject to certain conditions relating mainly to defence and external affairs'. Once victory was achieved His Majesty's government would 'proceed to examine by suitable Commission or Conference such detailed proposals as the Ministers may in the meantime have been able to formulate'.

The readiness of the Ministers to take up this proposal was, according to Sir Ivor Jennings's account of the constitutional history of these years, due 'to a significant change of personalities'. He was referring to the fact that D. S. Senanayake was now leader of the State Council and Vice-Chairman of the Board of Ministers. Equally important for the future, and understandably insufficiently weighted in Sir Ivor's account, was his own part in making it possible for D. S. Senanayake to put forward that kind of proposal which would make compromise between the Colonial Office and the Ministers certain. Sir Ivor had been in Ceylon as Principal of the University College since 1940. In 1942 he effected the long-overdue transformation of the College into the University of Ceylon. He had been appointed Assistant Civil Defence Commissioner, was trusted by D. S. Senanayake and his confidant Oliver Goonetilleke. The constitution he drafted for the Board of Ministers was the first of the many for which he was responsible in various parts of the British Commonwealth. He was a shrewd judge of what the Colonial Office would appreciate, and the Ministers' Draft with its stress on a system of weighting looked after communal representation in a way which would have been acceptable to Whitehall. In 1944 the British government announced that a Commission would be sent to Ceylon to report on the draft and also to get the views of the various communities in Ceylon. The Board of Ministers considered that this contravened the spirit of the declaration of the previous year, withdrew its draft and refused to co-operate with the Commission.

The Commission headed by Lord Soulbury arrived in Ceylon in December 1944. Its other two members were Mr. (later Sir) Frederick Rees and Mr. (later Sir) Frederick Burrows. As in 1927, multifarious groups and associations as well as a number of lone fighters for one cause or the other gave evidence before them. The leader of the Tamil Congress, now arguing for a scheme of balanced representation which would give the Sinhalese fifty seats in the Council or legislative chamber, as well as equal representation in a Cabinet, was responsible for a virtuoso performance of several hours of impassioned oratory which enthused his supporters but failed to persuade the tribunal he exhorted. The Commission was in contact privately with the Ministers: 'The Honourable Mr. D. S. Senanayake, Minister for Agriculture and Lands, Vice-Chairman of the Board of Ministers and Leader of the State Council, had an opportunity of expressing his views to us in a series of most valuable private discussions.' Other unofficial leaders of the group, notably D. R. Wijewardene, the owner of the influential Lake House group of newspapers, were in touch with the Commissioners. In a letter to him, quoted by his biographer, Lord Soulbury wrote: 'The advice and assistance you have given to us will prove invaluable and will materially help us in solving a difficult problem.'

The Soulbury Commission therefore could not do other than recognize the rights of those who had come to be in the course of the last ten years the leaders of the State Council and of political opinion in the island. They were the representatives of the heterogeneous group of the English educated, with differences of religion, caste and community unseen in the close array of the ranks now that the prize seemed within sight. That power was very close seemed to be indicated by the appointment of Oliver Goonetilleke to the post of Financial Secretary in 1945. This could be reckoned as the fall of the citadel of European bureaucracy and the triumph of the campaign for the Ceylonization of the higher grades of the public service. There were discordant voices heard in the evidence given before the Commision—notes of that 'abundant evidence to show that the hopes of the Donoughmore Commission that communal tension would eventually disappear as a result of territorial representation have so far not been realized'.

The Commission's report was published in October 1945. It 'accepted the Ministers' draft as a basis, added a Second Chamber on the Burmese model, made more flexible the powers of the Delimitation Commission . . . enlarged the powers of the Public Service Commission, and added qualifications and exceptions to the limitations on the Governor's powers inserted in the draft'. The Commission rejected communal representation. The Executive Committees disappeared. A Cabinet system, as the Ministers' draft had suggested, was approved. It did not recommend Dominion Status—'the goal of the people of Ceylon'—because 'for reasons given in various sections of our Report, it is clearly not possible to reach the goal in a single step'. A Cabinet system, it was hoped, would produce political parties and a party system which would be another stage in the progress towards the goal.

The State Council accepted the new constitution, but there had been further discussions between D. S. Senanayake and His Majesty's Government, and as a result 'the Government of the United Kingdom, at Mr. Senanayake's request, agreed to the conferment of "fully responsible status", a new term for Dominion status. Heads of agreement relating to defence, external relations and the status of public officers were settled in July. . . . In December the Ceylon Independence Act, 1947, was passed by the Parliament of the United Kingdom'. (Jennings & Thambiah: *The Dominion of Ceylon.*) The 4th of February 1948 was to be the appointed day on which Ceylon would achieve independence and become a self-governing Dominion in the British Commonwealth.

What won independence for Ceylon and gave the English educated more than they originally set out to gain in the twenties? Was it, as has been suggested, a reward for the impeccable behaviour of the Ministers during the war; the good impression made on the Colonial Office by D. S. Senanayake; or the excellence of O. E. Goonetilleke in the role of 'the servant of two masters', improvising in true Commedia dell'.Arte style on a libretto furnished by the Civil Defence Department, which captivated the Soulbury Commission and brought everything to a happy conclusion?

To frame the question in terms of who or what won independence for Ceylon is wrong. His Majesty's Government could not help giving Ceylon independence now that a certain stage in world affairs had been reached. England had won the war, but it had been a disastrous war; and England had been beaten by the Japanese in Hongkong, in Malaya and in Burma. And now that the war was over, England and the U.S.A. were assisting in the break-up of the former colonial possessions of the French and the Dutch in Asia. It should not be forgotten, too, that the policy of the Labour Party long before the war favoured self-government for India, and that the history of the Indian mass movement had made it clear to all but the most conservative politicians in England that Empire on the old style could not be maintained. Indeed Asiatics were no longer ready to accept the overlordship of Western nations when twice in the previous half-century an Oriental people had worsted a European power. The example of Japan—not as the conqueror of Russia, but as an Oriental country which had done as well as any European power—was often quoted by politicians in Asia. (Sir Ponnambalam Arunachalam made a stock point of it in his speeches.)

In this context the disposition of His Majesty's Government to grant Ceylon self-government was helped by the feeling that in handing over to the Ministers they were dealing with persons whose political and economic interests did not differ very greatly from theirs. The personality of D. S. Senanayake or of O. E. Goonetilleke possibly turned the scale already trembling in the balance. What was obscured in 1947–8 in the paean of self-gratulation by His Majesty's Government, the Colonial Governor and the Ministers in Ceylon, was that the island had been identified with the Ministers. The corollary of this was the suspicion of a large number of people outside the charmed circles of power that independence was a private negotiation between the British and the 'nobodies', in which the high contracting parties arranged things to their own satisfaction. It was therefore impossible that there should have been much enthusiasm about it apart from the ranks of those who brought it off.

Though there was no great popular acclaim for independence the reputation of D. S. Senanayake stood high in 1947. In the group he led in the days of the State Council, whatever hidden stresses there may have been, his personal qualities enforced respect and submission to him. He had been nicknamed 'Jungle John' in Ceylon, for in contrast to his elder brother F. R. Senanayake he had not been to Cambridge, nor was he in contact with statesmen in England. He had started life managing the large family estates. He was wise enough to use the purchase this reputation gave him to pull roughly into line any stragglers on the march. Actually he was no 'Jungle John', but an experienced tactician so long as he had to deal with persons of his group. He had all their biases and prejudices, so he knew his men. He had in addition a great fund of good sense which was denied to many of them, and devotion to his plans for the country. He was a better representative of the 'nobodies' and paradoxically of the 'somebodies' too—of all the English educated in fact—than most others of his group in the years between 1947 and his death, the brief interlude in which they were Ceylon.

As leader of the State Council in 1947 he had to bring a party into being to work the new constitution. This he proceeded to do. On July 4th the State Council was dissolved, and the general election to the new House of Representatives fixed for August.

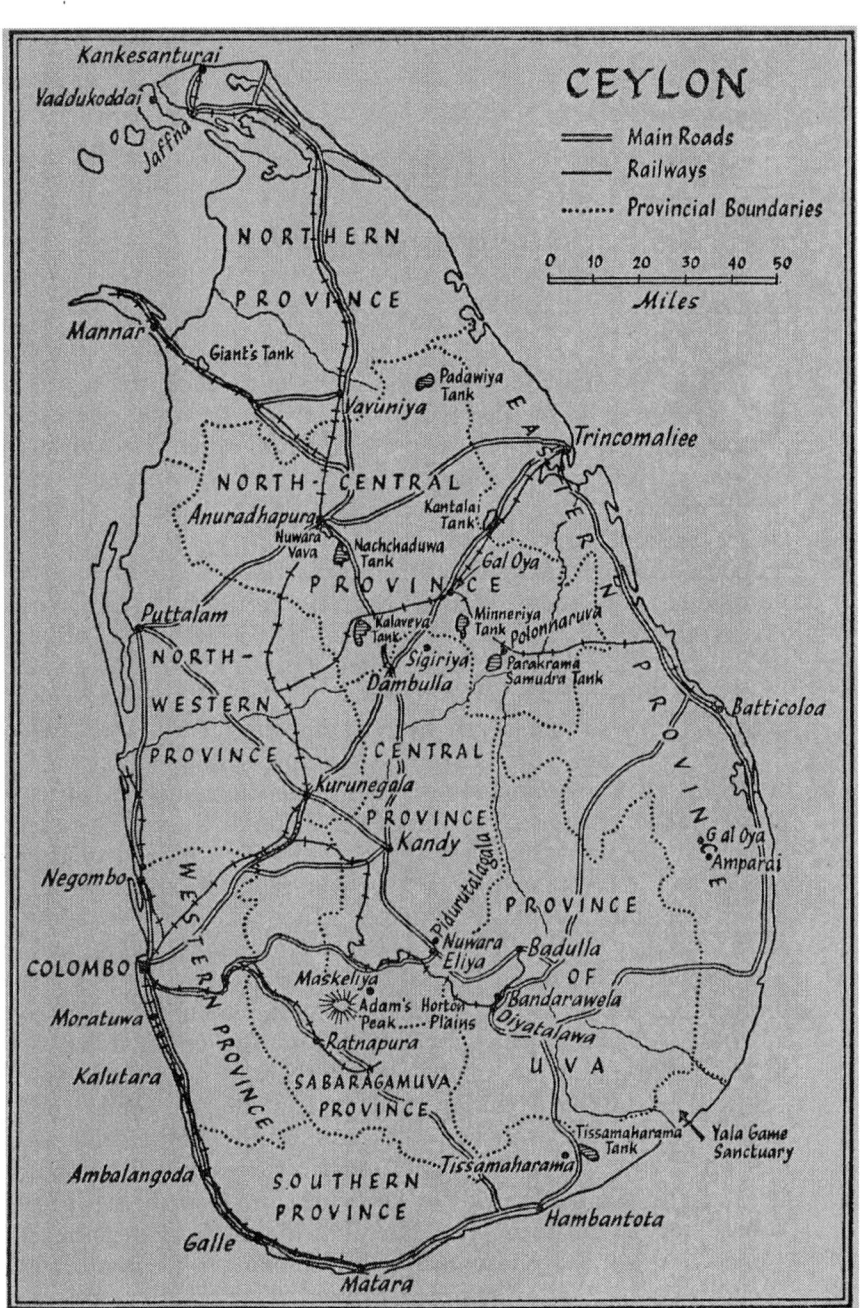

CEYLON

━━━ Main Roads
── Railways
······· Provincial Boundaries

0   10   20   30   40   50
━━━━━━━━━━━━━━━━━━━━━━
Miles

Kankesanturai

Vaddukoddai

Jaffna

NORTHERN

PROVINCE

Mannar

Giant's Tank

Vavuniya

Padawiya
Tank

Trincomaliee

NORTH-CENTRAL

Anuradhapura

Kantalai
Tank

Nuwara
Vava

Nachchaduwa
Tank

Gal Oya

PROVINCE

Puttalam

Kalaveva
Tank

Minneriya
Tank

Polonnaruva

NORTH-

Sigiriya

Parakrama
Samudra Tank

WESTERN

Dambulla

Batticoloa

PROVINCE

CENTRAL

Kurunegala

PROVINCE

Kandy

Gal Oya
Amparai

Negombo

Pidurutalagala

PROVINCE

WESTERN

Nuwara
Eliya

Badulla

COLOMBO

Maskeliya

Adam's
Peak

Horton
Plains

Bandarawela

OF

Moratuwa

Diyatalawa

Ratnapura

UVA

Kalutara

SABARAGAMUVA

PROVINCE

Tissamaharama
Tank

Yala Game
Sanctuary

Ambalangoda

SOUTHERN

Tissamaharama

Galle

PROVINCE

Hambantota

Matara

MODERN CEYLON

CHAPTER 15

Sturm und Drang

On 4th February 1948 the Duke of Gloucester, representing H.M. the King of England, formally opened the first Parliament of independent Ceylon. The 4th of February, Independence Day, has since been celebrated as a public holiday. The new Constitution of 1948 brought into power as constitutional rulers of the country the cohort of 'nobodies', their ranks swelled now that victory was theirs by accretions from above and below. The members of the old Board of Ministers and their supporters now handled the prize which was at last in their grasp. They stepped into the shoes of the white bureaucrats who accepted the new situation with grace. There was no hasty flight from the top grades of the Civil Service. In the new administration a number of older Europeans remained as new Permanent Secretaries to the Ministers, or as Heads of Departments. The last of the Colonial Governors continued as the new Governor General—the figure-head of the new state, the ceremonial personage who reads the speech from the throne and accepts the advice of 'my ministers'. In 1948 Lord Soulbury was invited to Ceylon as Governor General, and his presence set the seal of official British approval at the highest level on the new order. The Planters' Association and the Ceylon Chamber of Commerce were cordial, and the political barometer in those quarters read Fair Weather.

But the winning of independence, and all the pomp and circumstance associated with the visit of the royal duke to Ceylon, did not mark the conclusion of a fairy tale for anyone, not even for the leaders of the 'nobodies' and 'somebodies'. In actual fact the fourteen years since His Majesty's Government agreed to grant 'fully responsible government' to Ceylon have been, by contrast with the previous hundred years of its story, a

274

period of storm and stress. The twelve years (1947–59) considered in this chapter begin with a large-scale strike by the lower grades of the public service which might have developed into a general strike; they end with the assassination of the Prime Minister. In addition they include the creation and collapse of the party brought into being to run the new constitution; a civil disobedience movement and disturbances which led to the resignation of one Prime Minister; a catastrophic general election which eclipsed another; two short episodes of communal rioting, sharper and bitterer than any known before; the declaration of a state of emergency three times; and continual labour unrest and strikes which have added to the difficulties of an economy already in trouble with post-war inflation.

It is tempting now with the hindsight provided by fourteen years of the development of events to read into the situation in 1947 much more than was manifest then. But there were clear signs in 1946, and more definitely in 1947, that everybody was not going to be happy ever after, for the 'nobodies' were not regarded as the saviours of the country or the architects of a new order. Continual labour unrest and the difficulties of an economy in trouble with post-war inflation have already been referred to. They were not the machinations of Left agitators determined on selling the country to the Communists—as so often made out by propaganda. Left agitation canalized genuine economic grievances among the urban workers into a Left movement led by the LSSP whose leaders returned to public life in 1946, and the Communist party, and away from the old Labour party, too much identified now with the ruling class to rally its supporters into action. The cost of living, always soaring above the government's Cost of Living Index, and the housing shortage which followed on the war with its shortages everywhere forced the lower grades of the public servants—the clerical workers—into a new and strange militancy. They too were 'nobodies'. But they were feeling the pinch while others had prospered.

A few of the strikes may certainly have been tactical moves in the war of various Left groups to capture union support. But it would be fair to state that the new ruling class could expect little but hostility from the urban worker, now for the first time

275

joined by the white collar worker. Strikes on the plantations in the late thirties showed that little could be expected from the plantation worker either. He was going to be much more sensitive to Left organization than to any pleas from the Board of Ministers.

The war situation had forced upon the Board of Ministers the state control of the importation of rice, flour and sugar. On the one hand the government through its food subsidies seemed committed to providing the welfare state, on the other it represented interests anxious to stabilize the economy as it existed and to enable the new Ceylonese business man to enjoy his share of the cake. That a great deal of money had been made in wartime by the old and the new rich was an open secret. How it had sometimes been made caused a slump in the reputations of the mighty in a country appreciative of rumour.

Ceylon had come out of World War II with the very large sum of Rs. 1,260 million in blocked sterling balances. More important, the greatest profit of the war in human terms had been the success of the forces' campaign against malaria. Massive use of DDT by the imperial government, on a scale no colonial government could either have afforded or contemplated, had brought down the number of cases of malaria from 3,225,477 in 1942 to 1,350,521 in 1947. With malaria and its attendant ills curbed there was a spectacular fall in the death-rate. This more than anything else accounted for the growth of population and the rate of population increase. This rate of 2·8 per cent per annum is one of the highest in the world. The sharp edge of economic distress given by this increase of population without a corresponding increase in the productivity of the country could in a tropical country with its family institutions be blunted by physical conditions and social custom. But even in under-developed countries the gap between the increase of population and stationary productivity does lead to manifest economic distress. It was noticeable in Ceylon—in towns as well as in the countryside—in the endemic underemployment. That there were people who seemed to be content to stand and stare by the roadside was due in many cases not to choice or to the custom of the country, but to necessity.

To the mass of people in the country—the 'everybodies'—independence conjured up no pleasurable vision. It had not altered their status or their standard of living. Independence, the British Commonwealth of Nations, Freedom, were sounds with little meaning. Their immediate concerns were the drying up of wartime employment, the demand that the standard of living kept up on government subsidies should be maintained, and the increasing number of school-leavers, particularly from the Sinhalese and Tamil schools, absorbed in gainful work. The United National Party with its advertised reliance on England —one of its ministers described Ceylon at the time as 'a little bit of England'—was too much committed to the brave new world of its own planning to rouse enthusiasm in the country. The urban worker under the tutelage of the LSSP was pressing for a different sort of world. On the other hand the educated who did not belong to the oligarchy, particularly those educated in Sinhalese, to whom independence could have had some charismatic meaning apart from its political significance, looked at it not as the happy condition of absence of political restraint from the old rulers, but as the opportunity and the necessity to revive the spirit of the ancient kingdom about which there were hazy ideas but strong emotional drives.

There had been a revival of Oriental learning and an interest in the culture of Buddhism in the last three decades of the nineteenth century. Like the cultural reform movement which followed it on a higher social level and was derived from it, it had political implications. It was uninterested in the goals of successful Anglicization and the case for constitutional reform shortly to be set before the 'nobodies' by their leaders. Since 1873, when a learned *bhikkhu* had worsted some Roman Catholic missionaries in a controversy, there had been a tradition of educated Buddhist militancy *vis-à-vis* Christianity and the West. Though the controversy could not be understood by the masses, the names of the *bhikkhu* prominent in it and of the scholar Sri Sumangala Thera were known and respected by them. A philosophical direction was given the movement among the English educated by Buddhist pioneers from the West—particularly the Theosophists like Olcott and Annie Besant. Later the Anagarika Dharmapala, the son of a wealthy Sinhalese family, in his rejection of the conventional opportunities of material advancement eagerly grasped at by others of his generation, symbolized the efficacy of Buddhist and Oriental values—

national values in fact—in contrast to the dubiousness of those of the West. There was a difference between these pioneers and their latter-day spokesmen, but their tradition of Buddhist nationalism could be invoked by the self-conscious Puritans of the forties to throw into the discard what was quite immaterial to them in the new dispensation. They were Puritans with Cavalier ambitions—Puritan in their opposition to the degenerate West with its cocktail parties, race meetings, various articles of dress (from trousers for men to housecoats for women), but Cavalier in their determination to improve their own standard of living and comfort with its cars, refrigerators and so forth. They could honestly believe in the superiority of *Ayurveda* to any medical knowledge the West had developed, but they would not have abjured the ministrations of an M.D.(Lond.) whenever the need arose. In neither of the worlds in which they lived was Free Lanka in the British Commonwealth of Nations meaningful. It turned out therefore that both the party in power and the Left opposition were discredited by those who identified the good life with the great renunciation of the present and the pilgrimage into the past. They waited with growing impatience for some opportunity to make themselves heard.

To the new ruling class and its supporters the omens were propitious. Political control and fiscal autonomy had passed into their hands. Though the figures had changed, the scene remained much the same. Sir Ivor Jennings noted in 1948 that all those who voted for the candidates put up in the general election of 1947 by the new party formed by the oligarchy 'knew, or ought to have known, that they were voting for the present economic system with an ample measure of progressive social reform'. The new age was going to be the old Donoughmore age writ large. Its personalities and policies were going to be of the thirties, at least on the government side of the House. Its vision of the future was to be the re-drawing of the old picture as the Board of Ministers envisaged it. But, however much it might have seemed the same old thing, it could not quite have been the same.

The Soulbury Commissioners in their report described the problem of devising a constitution for Ceylon as 'essentially the problem of reconciling the demands of the minorities for an adequate voice in the conduct of affairs . . . with the obvious fact that the constitution must preserve for the majority that proportionate share in all spheres of Government activity to which their numbers and influence entitle them'. They were clear that control had to pass into the hands of the Ceylonese. They were certain, too, that without a government convinced 'that the contentment of minorities is essential to the well-being of the island . . . no safeguards that we could devise would in the long run be of much avail'. It was on this last account that they were not in favour of granting complete self-government to Ceylon. They were uncertain about the effects of communal differences in the island: 'When political issues arise, the populace as a whole tends to divide, not according to the economic and social issues which in the West would ordinarily unite individuals belonging to a particular class, but on communal lines. It is this factor more than any other which makes difficult the application of the principles of Western Democracy to Ceylon.' They noted again that 'the hopes of the Donoughmore Commission that communal tension would eventually disappear as a result of territorial representation, have so far not been realized'. Yet they could not do other than recommend a constitution modelled on the British Constitution—one that had been evolved by a country with a very different history from that of Ceylon, with a different economic and social structure. It was impossible for them to have done otherwise for the politically conscious sector in the island was the oligarchy, the English educated, knowledgeable about English institutions, valuing them, and confident that they would run them themselves. Communal rifts were plastered over by the oligarchy in its anxiety to persuade the Soulbury Commissioners that it spoke for the whole country. The most that could be said in extenuation of the conduct of the leaders is that they honestly believed that there never would be a time when it would be necessary to reflect on communal differences to which they now turned a blind eye. It would perhaps have been different if the British had begun training for political responsibility much earlier. Lord Hailey, writing in 1946 on Colonial Administration by European Powers, thought that 'if we (the British) had at a much earlier date recognized self-government as our objective and had adjusted our administrative system accordingly, self-government would have a much greater chance of success than it seems to have today'. But in Ceylon, in 1946 and for some years after, there seemed to be no doubt that the skies would continue to be blue. The chorus of praise for the absence of communal strife at the change-over from British rule is the burden of all foreign comment on Ceylon at this time. It reached a high C in the report of the International Bank for Reconstruction and Development in 1952—the people of Ceylon were 'dedicated to parliamentary government and democratic methods'.

The Donoughmore Commission had, according to the Soulbury Commissioners, given the members of the State Council experience of some share in the administration 'owing to the absence of political parties'. On this account, apparently, Executive Committees had come into being. Now that experience in administration had been provided, a Cabinet system was asked for by the Ministers. This the Soulbury Commissioners were only too ready to grant, in the hope that political parties would come into being. In 1946 the Board of Ministers appointed a Delimitation Commission to demonstrate the seriousness of their intention that all communities in the island should have a share in representation in the new legislature. Sir Ivor Jennings described the success of the scheme of the Commission which 'by a system of weighting for sparsely populated Provinces enabled the minorities to obtain higher representation than they could have obtained had all constituencies been of equal size'. Its scheme, it should be noted, was based on 'the assumption that race, religion and caste were the main factors'.

The elections of 1947 should be placed in the context of the Minister's demand for Cabinet government and the report of the Delimitation Commission. There were at that time three parties in existence: the debilitated Labour party; the LSSP, now split into two groups; and the CP. But these were not the representatives of the Board of Ministers and two of them would certainly have been opposed to the Board. To work the constitution a new party had to be brought into being. This was the United National Party (UNP) of 1947 under the leadership of D. S. Senanayake, supported by various political organizations like the Sinhala Maha Sabha and the Muslim League. Its deficiency was not the popular gibe at its expense that it was an 'Uncle Nephews party'. If the innuendo was nepotism it is known in political parties all over the world; if it objected to the close relationship of the leaders of a political group to each other, this was true of most parties, particularly in under-developed countries.

The trouble with the UNP was that it was not a party at all. It was a group of personages brought together by the dominant personality of D. S. Senanayake, for the *ad hoc* purpose of providing a mode by which the Soulbury Constitution could be operated. According to authority, in 1947, 'the UNP had no very positive policy to offer, nor was it well organized'. Its lack of policy was not of much consequence to its leaders for the elections were presumably going to be decided as they had been in the past—by voters expected to choose the right man according to considerations more important than those of party programmes: those of caste, religion and community.

The prelude to the elections was the strike of government clerks for full Trade Union rights. Here was an indication that an important sector of the English educated (for it was not possible to enter the clerical service without a knowledge of English and secondary school education) differed basically from the 'nobodies' to which they belonged. The clerk in the lower grades of the public service came out into the open on a political issue. The strike was supported by members of all communities, and when the Police opened fire on the strikers and killed one of them, a Tamil, he was regarded as the martyr of the movement. After a few weeks the strike was broken, but it was a symptom of the changed political situation.

In opposition to the UNP which put forward the largest group of candidates were the two units of the LSSP; the CP; the Tamil Congress (TC), which contested seats in predominantly Tamil areas only; the Ceylon Indian Congress (CIC), like the TC contesting areas where the Tamil plantation worker was well represented; and 196 Independents. The last were all, to a man, 'friends of the poor', and anxious to propagate universal benevolence. They offered themselves for election on the same good principle which swayed all parties in their choice of candidates: 'the right race, religion and caste'. The UNP received its most consistent support from the newspapers of the Lake House group which had almost a proprietary interest in the future of the old group and the new party. *The Times of*

Ceylon, not involved on the level of personal attachment to any group, was more cautious and critical. Instead of the ballot boxes, each in the colour assigned to the candidate (which would have stretched the range of easily obtainable colours in some constituencies where more than ten candidates appeared for election), candidates were assigned symbols. There were allegations and counter-allegations of election malpractices and no less than nineteen election petitions, caused not by the inability of the Ceylonese to take defeat gracefully, but by the way in which victory seemed to depend on corrupt practices.

The UNP secured 46 seats, obtained the support of quite a few Independents and so formed the government. In the opposition were 20 Left candidates, 7 CIC and 7 TC candidates. Barely half the electorate had voted, the voter in the rural areas being more ready to go to the polls than the urban voter. This was significant for the future.

When the new House of Representatives met in October 1947, it was not quite the old State Council, but included a large number of its personalities in the new government and a strong element representing the Marxist Left in the opposition: the two LSSP groups, both Trotskyist but divided on personal grounds, and the CP labouring under the double disadvantage of having supported the war effort of 'imperialism' and being more devoted to the Soviet fatherland than to anything else. The Soulbury Commissioners had been correct in their estimate that there were 'definite indications of a Left Wing movement more disposed to concentrate on social and economic than on communal issues'.

The government had a plan—the Post-War Development Plans of the Board of Ministers of 1946 in a new guise. But it was based on the existing economic structure, it was neither bold nor imaginative enough to do more than help the country to lag haltingly behind the demands of natural growth of population. Money was being spent, however—on agriculture, on schooling, on health, and on various uncoordinated projects of the Department of Industries.

The show-piece of the government's schemes was the completion of the first stages of the multipurpose Gal Oya project—damming the waters of the Gal Oya river in the Eastern province for irrigation and the development of electric power. A

Board on the lines of the TVA was constituted in 1949 to assume responsibility for the colonization and industrial projects covered by the scheme. As the brain child of the Prime Minister it was used both by its proponents and critics as index of practically all the UNP government's planning. This and the other schemes of the First Six Year Plan (1947–53) were naturally an extension of the old proposals for post-war development —the improvement of the port of Colombo; the development of the hydro-electric scheme at Norton Bridge; expansion of health and education services, and a continuation of the Department of Commerce and Industry's wartime attempts at small-scale manufacture of some consumer goods. The stress was definitely to be laid on agriculture. This was the sphere in which there had been the greatest activity and the most consistent effort.

All these several parts of government policy, on which attention was focused daily in the House and in newspaper discussion, maintained as heretofore the public interest of the English educated as well as the growing class of newspaper readers in Sinhalese and Tamil. Newspapers in Sinhalese had a bigger circulation than those in English. As in the thirties attention had been concentrated on the duel between the Ministers and the Officers of State and the Governor with his powers of certification, so now it was directed on that between the government and the opposition. The first subject on which the government had to defend itself was the Defence and External Affairs Agreements which were part of the Constitution of 1948. They had been negotiated by the Prime Minister and His Majesty's Government. It is significant that there was so much suspicion of them that, in spite of public assurances, it was popularly believed that there were some secret undertakings which reduced the quality of the independence of the country. The presence of the British navy at Trincomalie, of the R.A.F. at Katunayake, and of wireless stations manned by Imperial services personnel were adduced as proofs of spurious independence. In addition there was a growing demand that Ceylon should keep clear of any involvement in the power politics of the two blocs in the world. Even if there had been no secret undertakings, British bases on the island could be a threat to the integrity of the country.

The inordinate attention given to unending debates in the

House of Representatives was a disservice to both government
and opposition, for it protracted issues and used energies which
seemed irrelevant except to Parliamentarians. Public attention,
through the newspapers, continued to spread itself wide over
all the activities of the new class in power. With Dominion
status Ceylon had to take up the official duties of representation
at international conferences, and establish missions abroad. In
1949 Mr. Senanayake attended the conference of Dominion
Prime Ministers held in London. Whatever the interest or the
success of the government might have been in running the
country or dealing with its problems, what the public heard of
and could see was what an American writer has called 'the
generous bonanza' to reward the faithful and to enlist support
among key groups of voters. More money was being spent, now
that Britain and the U.S.A. could export them, on consumer
goods of all kinds. It was an era of conspicuous private spending
by the rich—the bus tycoons in their preposterous American
cars with pennants flying; the war profiteers buying and taking
over anything which could still be turned to profit. In Colombo
a new type of social life for the oligarchy with cocktail parties
and receptions produced a gilded swarm whose doings the
English newspaper doted on. It was a brash and brittle era that
the 'nobodies' had inaugurated, with its synthetic culture as
bright and lifeless as the artificial lights which made the night
hideous at the wedding receptions of the new rich.

The energies of the Prime Minister, which had to be hus-
banded on account of his ill-health, were too much taxed by
public life and a Cabinet which had sometimes to be kept in
order.

In 1950 the Commonwealth Prime Ministers met in Colombo.
Out of their discussions came the Colombo Plan to help the
under-developed countries of Asia. It was formally launched in
the following year, membership not being restricted to Commonwealth countries. An army of experts of various kinds had
already been descending on the country at the request of Ministers and Heads of Departments. Their number was now
increased. Their extensive view surveyed all manner of schemes,
and they were off—having praised the country, the Minister
with whose department they had worked, and the people—to
similar episodes elsewhere or to well-merited obscurity. Though

there had been some fall in foreign assets, the Korean war and the rise in the price of rubber and stockpiling of raw materials came to the rescue, and the financial position remained much the same as before. Government projects were being paid for by budget surpluses and disinflationary financial policies.

Early in the UNP government's tenure of office the Prime Minister met Nehru to discuss the franchise rights of Indian Tamils. But once again no change occurred in the existing situation. Since independence the Indian government had formulated its own definitions of Indian citizenship, and those whom the Ceylon government had so far treated as Indian nationals were by Indian law unrecognized as such. In 1948 and 1949 the Ceylon government decided who were to be regarded as citizens of the country and entitled to the franchise. The effect of the new Indian and Pakistani (Citizenship) Act of 1949 was to disfranchise the majority of the plantation workers and turn them into stateless persons. By 1943, 168,000 'Indians' had secured the franchise on the test of domicile. The new tests applied to a barely literate population group made citizenship by registration an exacting process and deprived those on the registers of the vote. The Ceylon government acted on the assumption that it was excluding the nationals of a foreign country from voting in its elections; to the Indian government whoever these persons were they were not the nationals of India. So far as future elections were concerned the new Act removed from the register a body of voters likely to be hostile to the UNP, for the plantation voters had behaved as other voters had done, supporting the men of their own religion and race. Most of their candidates were closer to the Left politically than to any other group. Besides the plantation strikes in 1939–40, notably the Mooloya strike, had convinced the leaders of the oligarchy that they had no power to influence the plantation worker.

The elaborate precautions of the Delimitation Commission in 1946 to show that minorities would be considered by the weightage given to sparsely populated provinces, etc., could now be dropped. The action of the UNP government in sponsoring the new citizenship Act has been defended. It is difficult, however, not to convict the old Board of Ministers of disingenuousness in making use of the Delimitation Committee's scheme only so long as it had served its turn.

The Minister of Commerce, a Tamil, resigned from the Cabinet on the issue of the exclusion of the plantation worker from the franchise, but in his place appeared the leader of the TC. The appearance of communal unity within the Cabinet had been preserved. The militant section of the TC went out of it to form the Federal Party (FP) under the leadership of an earnest Christian lawyer. It stood for a federal constitution for Ceylon with some degree of provincial autonomy for predominantly Tamil provinces in which it was interested. It was never clear whether its Federalism was born out of the wish to unite with the rest of the country or to separate from it.

In 1951 an already weakened Cabinet received its second shock when S. W. R. D. Bandaranaike, the Minister of Local Administration resigned because he could not find himself in agreement with its policies. As Minister of Local Administration he had been in touch with the ramifications of local government all over the island and was aware of feeling in the provinces. He must have realized how strong, in spite of the prestige of the Prime Minister, the mood of the minor figures in the country was against the ruling class. His decision to resign from the government has been put down to personal ambition, so far unsatisfied and unlikely to be gratified in the near future, for he was not even Leader of the House. But his ambitions, whatever they were, could scarcely have been made up of any stern stuff at all, for the latter was so noticeably lacking in his constitution. As a 'somebody' and an able politician S. W. R. D. Bandaranaike could appeal to the 'everybodies'. On the day of his return to Ceylon from England in 1925 he told the residents of Udugaha Pattu in Siyane Korle who welcomed him home: 'I can assure you that my heart is Sinhalese to the core.' Twenty-six years later the appositeness of that remark was to be realized.

He founded the Sri Lanka Freedom Party (SLFP)—Sri Lanka evoking the national past, and Freedom aimed at the unsatisfactory independence the UNP had gained for the country. Bandaranaike's crossing over to the ranks of the opposition was expected to place the government in jeopardy, but the support promised to him in the House failed to declare itself, and the UNP continued on its way.

In 1952 a Colombo Plan exhibition held at Colombo was due to be opened by the Princess Elizabeth, but the sudden death

286

of King George VI prevented her and the Duke of Edinburgh
from fulfilling their engagement. The Exhibition, an immense
public spectacle, was opened with much *éclat* in March 1952.
In the same month D. S. Senanayake, exercising his horse on
Galle Face, was thrown heavily and died two days later. In his
endowments and his limitations he had been an outstanding
representative of his class, and the grief expressed throughout
the country was a tribute to a familiar figure passing away from
the political scene.

The Governor General, out of the island when the Prime
Minister met with his accident, flew back from London, and
after a few days of rumours it was announced that the late
Prime Minister's son, Dudley, the Minister of Agriculture and
Lands in the Cabinet, had been persuaded to become the new
Prime Minister. Sir John Kotelawala, the Leader of the House,
Senior Vice-President of the UNP, its Propaganda Chief and
Treasurer of the party with over a million rupees in its chest,
was, in his own account of the story, kept out of office by 'a
masterpiece of strategy'. He threatened to resign and to leave
the country, but was prevailed upon to accept the situation and
to continue as Minister of Transport and Works. A few days
later the new Prime Minister decided to dissolve parliament
and to appeal to the country for a mandate.

Dudley Senanayake was now in his early forties. Naturally
modest and open, he was respected and liked. In his youth he
had been a sportsman, good at cricket and boxing; he had a
scholarly mind and had taken a good degree at Cambridge. His
entry into politics in the early thirties seemed so far from the
predilections of the young man he was that it was probably the
result of that mixture of impressionability and conscientiousness
so characteristic of him. What brought him into politics in 1936
and persuaded him later to accept the Premiership, probably
took him out of politics in 1953.

The election of May 1952 which the UNP won with a handsome majority was decided really by the wave of popular feeling
caused by the death of D. S. Senanayake and the appeal of his
son. As Sir Ivor Jennings pointed out: 'The death of Mr. D. S.
Senanayake drew attention to the fact that the leader of the
UNP had been a statesman of international reputation. The
succession of his son gave opportunity for the display of that

peculiar Ceylon characteristic, that the newcomer to any post is given an enthusiastic welcome and has at least a year before the ants begin swarming over him.' As positive factors in the campaign which helped the government should be noted 'the removal of the Indian vote', 'the election was so organized as to favour the UNP', and 'the UNP was well supplied with transport'.

In a contest which brought 70 per cent of the electorate to the polls the UNP won 54 seats. In the opposition were the SLFP with 9 seats; the LSSP 9; a coalition of the CP and Philip Gunawardena's splinter group of the LSSP 4. The Tamil Congress which supported the UNP won 4 seats, and there was a small bag of mixed Independents.

The issues raised by the centrist SLFP with its programme of a republican constitution and the national languages had not as yet either the time to secure the backing of the 'anybodies' nor the opportunity presented it four years later. The Fourteen Point Programme of the LSSP—clear and unambiguous as a political document—made little difference to its showing in the election. All Left parties suffered from the label fastened upon them of being supporters of the plantation worker and being therefore not truly national.

In 1952 under continuing Left agitation the UNP government, faced with a difficult financial situation, began trade talks with Communist China to exchange Ceylon's rubber for Chinese rice. Strong U.S.A. pressure was brought to bear on the government through sections in the Cabinet ostentatiously hostile to Communism, and in official pronunciamentos from Washington and the U.S. Embassy in Colombo. But since the Chinese government offered better terms than those suggested by the U.S.A. which refused to remit any of its demands, the Ceylon government had no alternative but to sign the agreement negotiated in Peking by the Prime Minister's cousin, the Minister for Commerce. China paid a higher price for Ceylon's rubber than that obtaining on the world market, and sold its rice again at more favourable rates to Ceylon than those offered by other producers.

The Trade Agreement—its terms to be ratified annually—has benefited Ceylon. It gave stability to the rubber producer, and it helped the government over an awkward hurdle. U.S.A.

hostility to Ceylon's trade with China, its clumsy manœuvres to interfere with shipping and prevent it from handling the rubber and the rice, provoked a quick and angry reaction both from the Opposition and from the nationalist in the country. If Washington had intended to win friends it had set about it most inauspiciously. Wriggins's comment: 'From the specifically Ceylonese point of view, Washington's policies that preceded and followed Ceylon's economic agreement with China left a most unsavory recollection' is appropriate.

In 1952 the report of the International Bank for Reconstruction and Development, whose mission had visited Ceylon in 1951 after the death of D. S. Senanayake, was published. In a very conservative prognosis of the state of the nation, it drew attention to the need for caution and expressed doubts 'whether increasing production in the old patterns can any longer keep up with a greatly accelerated population growth'. It had only cold comfort to administer. However, it praised the 'sound policies pursued by the Central Bank in the monetary field and the prudent and skilful handling of the Government budget by the Minister of Finance'.

It was precisely this sound policy which precipitated the crisis of 1953, when on the advice of the Central Bank the Prime Minister decided to reduce the subsidy on imported rice and so increase the price of rationed rice. He conscientiously accepted the advice of his financial advisers and undeterred by the opposition decided to press on with his unpopular measures. The Left opposition, led by the LSSP, called for a *hartal* (a complete stoppage of work together with passive resistance) for August 12th. It was so successful in the urban areas in the Western province and in the south of Colombo that there were incidents between police and workers. In the shooting ten people were killed. A state of emergency was declared, and a curfew ordered.

The *hartal* with its consequences led to the Prime Minister's resignation, in spite of the advice and pleadings of his friends, in October 1953. The Leader of the House, Sir John Kotelawala, was the new Prime Minister.

If the first few years of UNP rule had been a 'bonanza period', the Kotelawala administration might be described as the period of the Saturnalia, in the sense that it gave itself up to spectacles which diverted its admiring friends and which the section of the press devoted to the Prime Minister inflated into a Roman holiday. The new Prime Minister was over-confident and hasty in speech. Played up by a sycophantic press he apparently enjoyed the new platform on which he strode, unaware of the strength of the opposition being built up against him in the country. His *An Asian Prime Minister's Story* provides a good impression of the man he was. The picture that emerges is not of 'a playboy of Western European capitals' (in a recent American description), but of a Prime Minister who did not feel that his title hung loosely about him.

In April 1954 the Queen and the Duke of Edinburgh, who had to postpone their visit to Ceylon in 1952, kept the promise made then to visit the island at the first opportunity. Their short stay in the country in the heat of April brought immense crowds on the streets of Colombo and on the royal route to Kandy and Polonnaruva to demonstrate the friendliness and interest of the ordinary people in their visitors.

The centre of gravity in the two and a half years of the Kotelawala régime was not in the events recorded in *An Asian Prime Minister's Story*—the meetings with Heads of States, the Conference of the five South East Asian Prime Ministers in Colombo in 1954, the girdles thrown round the world by the Prime Minister on tour, the Bandung Conference or Ceylon's admission in 1955 to membership of the United Nations Organization. Nor was it in Colombo—neither in the Cabinet from which the Prime Minister's cousin, the Minister for Commerce and Trade, resigned in 1954, nor in the UNP from which Dudley Senanayake withdrew in the following year. It was in the provinces, where the campaign of the SLFP for the establishment of Sinhalese as the official language led by the Sinhalese educated—the teacher and the practitioner of Eastern medicine or *Ayurveda* (the 'anybodies' as they were for convenience called earlier)—was receiving the strong support of the younger *bhikkhus*. On a higher level than this, that sector among the 'nobodies' which counted itself Buddhist-nationalist had organized the All Ceylon Buddhist Congress, and in preparation for the celebrations of Buddha Jayanti year (1956 which was officially reckoned as marking the 2,500th anniversary of the Buddha's attainment of Nirvana) appointed a Committee of

Inquiry to investigate 'the present state of Buddhism in Ceylon and to report on the conditions necessary to improve and strengthen the position of Buddhism and the means whereby those conditions may be fulfilled'. The government was attacked because the historic role of Buddhism in Ceylon had been insufficiently appreciated by it. By its patronage of English education given by Christian missionaries it had betrayed Buddhism.

The Leader of the Opposition in Parliament, S. W. R. D. Bandaranaike, kept baiting the government about its policy on the national languages. It was the feeling sparked off by the popular enthusiasm for Sinhalese alone, and not for the two languages Sinhalese and Tamil, which eventually spelt the ruin of the UNP. No one who heard the crowds of young students in the provinces who had had an education in Sinhalese, and now having sat for their GCE or school-leaving examination had nothing to do, could doubt the vigour of their protest that they did not want two languages. The SLFP in its election manifesto of 1952 had undertaken to make Sinhalese and Tamil the official languages, but policy was taken out of the hands of the party leadership by the enthusiasm of its supporters for a cause they could understand and to which they could respond. The government if it wished to survive the storm had to trim its sails to the wind.

As communal feelings were being roused, the Tamil leaders in the UNP grew more alarmed and asked for some pledge. The Prime Minister visited Jaffna early in 1956 and was reported to have promised 'parity' of Sinhalese and Tamil. This was taken up in South Ceylon with aggressiveness. The UNP changed its line in February 1956, declared itself for Sinhalese only and lost all its Tamil support immediately. The Federal party remained the last resort of the Tamil reacting communally against Sinhalese communalism. In 1956 the government had yet another year before the next general election, but unaccountably the Prime Minister decided to appeal to the country at once. Parliament was dissolved and the elections fixed for April 1956.

A merger of the SLFP, a recent organization of *bhikkhus* called the *Eksath Bhikkshu Peramuna* (United Front of the *Bhikkhus*) and Philip Gunawardena's splinter group, now coupling

Marxism with communalism, produced the *Mahajana Eksath Peramuna* (MEP)—the People's United Front. The two Left parties—the LSSP and the CP—made an election agreement with the MEP to prevent rival candidates from splitting the anti-UNP vote.

The election was an MEP avalanche which swept away 48 of the 56 UNP seats in the House. If this was the first election which had been fought on a programme, it was curious that its most important item—Sinhalese as the official language—was common to the two main contenders. Stronger than the appeal of the leader of the SLFP and the disastrous effect of the 'image' of the leader of the UNP was the surge of feeling that demonstrated that what the voter wanted was nothing which the UNP could offer. Though the UNP lost the election they still polled over 700,000 votes.

The Left (if Philip Gunawardena's section which went into the government is taken into consideration) increased its strength. It must have benefited from the popular swing against the UNP. The LSSP, however, kept itself clear of communal politics.

The election did not shift the control of political power from one segment of the population to the other. That would have remained with the 'nobodies' whatever the result. But now it was going to be directed towards ends different from those set out by the previous government. The voter thought he had won the election and that the government which came into power was his. After the first night of the election when the UNP heads began to roll, the results of the remaining three days were received with increasing acclaim by the ordinary voter in the provinces. When Parliament was due to assemble, popular excitement already raised by the costume worn by the members of the Cabinet introduced by the Prime Minister to the Governor General, now Sir Oliver Goonetilleke who had replaced Lord Soulbury in 1954—the cloth and loose white shirt associated with the Sinhalese nationalist teacher—rose to such a pitch that the crowd rushed into the chamber and took possession of it. It was their government and their House.

The FP had become the sole representative of the Tamils of the north and the south. They had secured 10 seats, more than the 8 the UNP had succeeded in gaining. Behind the Prime

Minister were the Buddhist fringe of the 'nobodies' and the 'anybodies'—the latter an authentic indigenous middle class, alive to its lack of status *vis-à-vis* its English-educated counterpart. Both groups united in their distrust and dislike of the defeated oligarchy and its friends, and were a little restive under the control of S. W. R. D. Bandaranaike. Between them and him there was a difference, for he was, in spite of irresolution, in spite of ambition, liberal-minded and cultivated. He could have worked out a settlement with the Tamils; he might have controlled his rank and file, but racial forces unleased by the election campaign, were too strong to be brought to heel, and besides the defeated party was now professing a programme of violent communalism.

The task before the new Prime Minister was a sombre one. First of all, he had in the Cabinet to make good out of his own powers of mind and political abilities the deficiencies of his party personnel, and to prevent an open breach between the conservative elements in his party and the Left sector of the MEP in the person of the ebullient Philip Gunawardena; in the House to deal with an able opposition led by the LSSP, ready to support him, but determined to move him to positions much more to the left of those of his colleagues. Most important was the task in the country—to prevent the strong desire for change of the existing social order which put him into power from being diverted into communal forms.

Within three months of the MEP's accession to power the Sinhalese Only Bill came before the House. All the strong feeling which swept the UNP from power demanded Sinhalese only for a mixture of reasons. In the demand were invested national feeling; frustrations of a hundred and fifty years that ideas and ideals foreign, and therefore unacceptable, to the majority of people had been forced upon them; longing for a way of life markedly different from the unsatisfying contemporary; the economic distress of young men and women flowing almost ceaselessly through the millrace of the new Sinhalese schools and in danger of stagnating in idleness; strong prejudices only too easily worked up into aggressiveness against anything which seemed to stand in the way of the promised cultural regeneration.

The demand for the official recognition of Sinhalese was

rational and healthy. It was intolerable that the majority of
people who did not know English should have been penalized
on this account. But campaigning for Sinhalese only were
extremists who distorted the case they presented. The possession
of Sinhalese as the official language was no quick cure for the
ills of the state. It would not solve unemployment, nor would it
at the wave of the wand change the pumpkin into a gilded
coach.

The situation got out of hand because of these small groups.
And as the election had been fought it was easy to see how thin
were the partitions dividing rational demands from irrational
fears. Both the MEP and the UNP did not scruple to break
through them to secure political advantage. Of the numerous
things which could possibly have saved, quickness of decision
and decisiveness in action were most necessary. These, unfortunately for himself and for the country, the Prime Minister
did not possess.

A peaceful demonstration of the FP against the introduction
of the Sinhalese Only Bill caused a disturbance on the Galle
Face Green in Colombo. There was much more serious trouble
in Gal Oya where Tamil colonists were attacked, and only the
timeliness of the intervention of a senior Police officer saved
the situation.

The next two and a half years were marked by labour unrest
in Colombo, particularly in the port. In its legislative programme the main feature of the three and a half years of MEP
rule was the trend towards welfare socialism, which kept widening the rift between the conservative and Marxist elements in
the Cabinet. The SLFP programme had been vague in its
definition of its plans and the stages of their fulfilment. It was
easy enough to abrogate the Defence Agreement of the 1948
Constitution. The British navy moved out of Trincomalie, and
R.A.F. personnel out of Katunayake. The nationalization of
transport had the immediate appeal of a measure which would
deprive a small section of the very rich, deeply pledged to the
UNP, of money and influence. But it was so well advertised and
so ill carried out that it turned out to be a poor sort of nationalization. That of the Port of Colombo followed in 1958.
Colombo handles more shipping than any other South Asian
port; though traditional modes of unloading cargoes still cause

wastage of manpower, its modern warehouses and equipment must bring costs down. Since the nationalization of the port there has been less labour trouble among harbour workers.

Throughout this period the Prime Minister and his Cabinet had been subject to cross-fire from various pressure groups now determined that their demands should be met by the men they believed they had put into power. The economic insecurity which underlay communal feeling was being distorted into fantastic apprehensions. That talks were going on between the Prime Minister and the leader of the FP, Chelvanayagam, only served to heighten the intransigence of the racialists exerting pressure on the government through a few Members of Parliament and the masses in the south. The FP programme of a separate state alluded to by some of their supporters was equally fantastic. But it was the demand for regional autonomy—which had some likelihood of succeeding—which aroused their opponents to greater fury. Some agreement had been reached between the Prime Minister and the Tamil leader, but what its substance was is still not clear. But it was referred to on both sides as the Bandaranaike–Chelvanayagam Pact, and described by Sinhalese extremists as a betrayal of the nation.

A government weakened by the lawlessness of its supporters and the paralysis of the administration through continued interference by Members of Parliament, could deal with no situation at all. Strikes in Colombo in May 1958 threw the Police into confusion, because orders given and as frequently countermanded over the previous two years left them bewildered as to where they stood. Earlier, *bhikkhus* in the south of the island had been organizing a campaign of boycotting Tamil shops as retaliation in advance for the Federal party's threat of a *satyagraha* campaign if the Bandaranaike–Chelvanayagam Pact was not honoured. It was obvious that a dangerous situation was being created. Communal violence began on Thursday, May 22nd at Polonnaruva, and in Colombo on Monday, May 26th when the racialists were convinced that the police were powerless to take action against supporters of the government.

All over the Southern, Western, and North Central provinces there were lootings, burnings and savagery on such a scale as had not been known before. On the night of May 26th the LSSP informed the government that if it could not bring the

295

situation under control the party would be compelled to call out its organizations to make their own arrangements for defence. This statement was given prominence in the newspapers on Tuesday morning, May 27th. Later that same day—at 12.15 p.m.—a state of emergency and a curfew were declared throughout the island and the army was placed in control by the Governor General. By Tuesday evening the situation was quiet, though in some areas, notably in Ratmalana and in Polonnaruva, there were sporadic outbreaks of violence on Wednesday, May 28th.

With the declaration of the state of emergency the Governor General took over. He administered the country, while the military maintained order. That he had risen to the occasion and run a more practical and efficient Civil Defence organization than was ever needed in 1942, was clear only to those who at a time of press censorship knew what was happening in the country. Rumours and counter-rumours were flying about during the three days of terror.

The Tamils were the sufferers in loss of life and property. Jaffna was relatively quiet. Ceylon had regressed to the days when the wilderness separated Jaffna from Colombo and the only easy mode of access was by sea. Tamil refugees were evacuated by ship from Colombo to Jaffna, and armed convoys had to be used to bring to safety those threatened in the south. By the middle of June there were few Tamils left in Colombo and in the south, and practically all Sinhalese in the Northern and in the Eastern province (except in Gal Oya) had been evacuated. The exchange of populations had been almost complete. The government was soon in trouble with its racialist supporters who had been kept in order by the army, and could do little to soothe them except issue exaggerated reports of its firmness in dealing with the Tamils in Jaffna.

No commission investigated the disorders, no attempt was made to compensate the victims. The emergency lasted till 13th March 1959. The constitutional head of the state could take upon himself functions that lay outside his rightful sphere and administer the country, because he knew the people and could decide how he should act. Only the frequency with which Tamils in the west and the south found help and relief from Sinhalese and acquaintances who acted in full knowledge of the danger of reprisals helps to relieve the recollection of the shame of these three days.

In 1959 dissension between the two sectors of the Cabinet split it wide open, and Philip Gunawardena, the Minister responsible for the Paddy Lands Act (which had its teeth drawn) and the Rural Credit Bill left the Cabinet. A government familiar with crisis and near-disaster met with catastrophe on September 25th, when a *bhikkhu*, disappointed with his hopes of preferment in an *ayurvedic* college, emptied a revolver at point-blank range into the Prime Minister. Irresolution, infirmity of purpose, all the pitiful weakness of the last two years were redeemed by the courage and serenity with which he encountered death. The Governor General used his special powers to proclaim a state of emergency immediately. On the morning of September 26th S. W. R. D. Bandaranaike was dead.

EPILOGUE

Past, Present and Future

The body of the Prime Minister lay in state in Colombo and thousands from all over the provinces were drawn to participate in a catastrophe which had moved them profoundly. Nearly one-tenth of the population of the country is estimated to have gathered together at the funeral at Horagolla, the family seat twenty miles from Colombo on the road to Kandy. The grave in which the dead Prime Minister was laid has become a place of pilgrimage for the curious and for those learned in the lore of the country who see in his career and the violence of his death his connection with past heroes.

The Acting Leader of the House, W. Dahanayake, was called upon to lead the government. It would have been immaterial who took over, for the party to which S. W. R. D. Bandaranaike gave life could scarcely have survived his death without violent convulsions. In the last six months of his life it had had its seizures, and the coalition to which it belonged was over in May 1959 when Philip Gunawardena and his group left the government on the issue of the Co-operative Development Bill, which the right wing in the Cabinet resisted as fiercely as they had the earlier Paddy Lands Bill attempting to revise land tenures and give the agriculturist a new deal. The Prime Minister had to re-form his Cabinet and an all SLFP government was presented to the country in June. The Public Security (Amendment) Bill, discussed in the House in his lifetime, showed how disturbed the mood of the country was. It gave immense powers to the Governor General and the Prime Minister to deal with any situation they judged dangerous to internal security. It enabled the former to declare a state of emergency in any part of the country; the curfew could be imposed by the Prime Minister; armed forces could be called in if the Police failed to

298

maintain order; and strikes were to be forbidden if essential services were threatened. Though the Prime Minister was required to report to the House within ten days any action taken under the provisions of the Bill, there was sustained opposition to it, and it just got through the Senate by one vote. A one-day strike was called in protest against it by the Ceylon Federation of Labour.

When W. Dahanayake took over, the shock of the Prime Minister's assassination could keep the leaderless group together for a few months yet. What might have happened in a confused situation was prevented by the persistent barrage kept up by the Opposition, ably led by N. M. Perera, against the reticence of the government to expose the conspiracy responsible for the assassination, and its desperate expedients to keep itself going—the new Ministry of Internal Security and the censorship. This concentrated attack led eventually to the fall of the government and ensured that the House of Representatives which continued to meet during the emergency would have to be dissolved and new elections take place. It also forced action to be taken against seven accused, including two *bhikkhus*, who faced trial for conspiring to murder the late Prime Minister. That there had been a plot was clear, for too many in the pressure groups which felt that theirs was the credit for having put S. W. R. D. Bandaranaike in power had expressed themselves intemperately about his failure to satisfy them. It was in this atmosphere in the four months between the assassination and the dissolution of the House that talks of *coups* were freely bandied about.

The army and police forces in Ceylon are small and, on the whole, outside the political arena. The island is in the fortunate position of spending much less on its army than any other country in Asia. Army officers trained in England as a corps represent the tradition of the English educated. During the emergency in 1958 the army restored order and dealt joyously with mobs counting on the support of some member of the House to render them immune from harm. Through the smallness of its numbers and its parade-ground experience it has not won its spurs in any action which could give it a consciousness of itself as a distinct unit of importance in the country. That any political *coup* could be carried out by it seems unlikely. But a *coup* is not to be ruled out, for an army continually resorted to by the politician unable to govern the country on account of his political incapacity, can be carried away by its contempt for politicians into developing a sense of mission and using the powers delegated to it for political action on its own. In such an event its leadership is more likely to come from some 'hero' appealing straight to the ordinary ranker and not to the officer corps.

By December 1959 it was clear that the government was foundering. In the Cabinet the Prime Minister was expelling and dismissing his colleagues; there were frequent votes of censure in the House which the government barely survived and at last the Prime Minister advised the Governor General to dissolve Parliament. The General Election was fixed for March 1960. The Prime Minister left the SLFP which retaliated promptly by expelling him. It was in this atmosphere that he organized his own new party.

Dudley Senanayake, now President of the UNP, went into the campaign with a great deal of support for himself personally from the old oligarchy. The party could muster its forces through its influence with the urban man of property who distrusted the 'socialist' leanings of the SLFP, through numerous constituencies on the western coast and in the city of Colombo where Roman Catholic voters could swing the result of an election, and through dissatisfied elements everywhere. It could count on some support from the Sinhalese-educated rural voter disappointed during the last three years and confused about the situation in the country since September 1959. The success of the UNP in the elections to the Colombo Municipal Council in December 1959 pointed to its triumph in March 1960.

Its programme differed hardly at all from that of the SLFP. It would make Ceylon a republic, keep foreign policy neutral and replace English by Sinhalese. Like the SLFP it was against the nationalization of tea and rubber plantations, but it was careful to state that it would accept the nationalization programmes already carried out by the MEP government. The only difference between the two programmes was the UNP's readiness to continue State aid to denominational schools, without which item it would have lost its Roman Catholic support.

Past, Present and Future

The SLFP faced the elections without either its leader in 1956 or the group of young *bhikkhus* who had campaigned so manfully for it then. Since the assassination the *bhikkhus* were circumspect and had kept out of any activity even on the fringe of politics. Between 1956 and 1959 S. W. R. D. Bandaranaike had so dominated the party he led, sometimes going so far as to accept personal responsibility for the working out of the policy of an unpopular member of his Cabinet, that he was the SLFP. Without him or without some medium through whom he could be summoned his party could not exist. Mrs. Bandaranaike had refused to accept the Presidentship of the party, but when called upon in February to help in the election campaign, she certainly made the SLFP materialize.

The LSSP fought an election in 1960 which was the second instalment of 1956, with two parties as before claiming to lead the rural voter into the lost paradise. In 1956 the SLFP had been made to work by the transmission belts of *bhikkhu*, Sinhalese school teacher and *ayurvedic* physician which set the rural masses in motion on the power generated by S. W. R. D. Bandaranaike's call for the rehabilitation of Sinhalese—the language, the culture and the nation. In 1960 the UNP were beating the war drums of the threat to the nation since the Bandaranaike–Chelvanayakam pact. In this situation the success of the LSSP as an opposition group in Parliament, which lay in its support by the urban worker, could not get across to the voter in the countryside. As it campaigned for both Sinhalese and Tamil as official languages, it carried too heavy an impost to finish strongly.

The election was fought out by the UNP and the SLFP. Philip Gunawardena with his MEP stood outside both groups. A number of parties, some hastily put together and enlisting no more support than that of their founders, confused the issue further, with the result that there was only one straight fight between the UNP and the SLFP. The Ceylon Constitution (Amendment) Act had extended the franchise to those over the age of 18, but the new registers were not ready and they could not vote. The elections took place all on one day, and 75 per cent of the electorate voted in an atmosphere of calm. The UNP won 50 seats, the SLFP 46. The FP. were next with 15 seats, the LSSP and the MEP getting 10 each. The Prime Minister,

W. Dahanayake, was defeated and his new party routed. His four supporters in Parliament were asked to support Dudley Senanayake who was just able to form a government.

Once in power Dudley Senanayake lost no time in trying to steal the thunder of his opponents. He had ridiculed the LSSP for promising to reduce the price of rice in their election manifesto. No sooner was he in office than he reduced the price of rice himself, but without any of the accompanying fiscal and development measures which made it meaningful in his opponents' programme. On the question of Sinhalese he was inclined to be stiffer than the SLFP. So with the Left solidly against him, and nothing to be expected from the FP, his government could not last. It was defeated in April, Parliament was dissolved and the General Election fixed for July 20th.

The UNP campaigned for the July election as it had never done before, for to form a government it had to have an absolute majority over practically all other parties in the House. Every weapon in the armoury from gingals to Sten guns was thrown into the fight by supporters who did not care how the campaign was conducted provided the election was won. With its band of election agents and veterans in full blast, and one section of the press not above adding vulgar noises not officially set down in the score, the UNP drowned the wind with the noise of its electioneering. Such a campaign had to have results. It did. The UNP polled more votes than any other party. It increased its support in the election, in which again 75 per cent of the electorate went to the polls, from 829,636 in March to 1,143,290 in July. But it lost the election. It began it with 50 seats to 46 of the SLFP; it ended up with 30 seats to 75 of the SLFP.

Two factors decided this result. Mrs. Bandaranaike had accepted leadership of her husband's party and, though she did not contest a seat in the election, she announced that she would be ready to form a government if the SLFP was returned. She was not ready, as she said, to contest a seat only to be leader of the Opposition. It was a straight appeal to the voter to put the SLFP into power.

Further, an electoral agreement between the SLFP, the LSSP and the CP forced the voter into a straight decision between SLFP and anti-SLFP. Again there was little substantial difference between the programmes of the SLFP and the UNP, the latter was again determined to wear the whole armour of defence against the Tamil and the Indian 'menace'. On the side of the SLFP was the magic both of the name of S. W. R. D. Bandaranaike and the formula of carrying out his programme. With no such missile on its side and in straight fights with the opposition to it, the UNP lost seat after seat, though it polled more votes in the election. The SLFP with 75 seats and some others gathered from Independents could form a government on its own. The difference between the coalition S. W. R. D. Bandaranaike led in 1956 and his party after the July election in 1960 was that it could now form a government without any agreement or compromise with any party or any pressure group. The electoral agreement and Mrs. Bandaranaike had helped to put the government in power.

Mrs. Bandaranaike was asked by the Governor General to form a government, and became the first woman to be the Prime Minister of a country. She was nominated to a seat in the Senate and took the portfolio of Defence and External Affairs. The new Prime Minister is in her middle forties, a member of the Kandyan *élite*, her family belonging to the upper stratum of 'somebodies' in British times. She makes up with female single-mindedness and firmness of will for political inexperience. Her greatest asset seems to be the confidence she has inspired in the rural people whom she understands. Her government, with its large majority and assured of Left support for a progressive policy, is in a position which any parliamentary group must envy. It can implement almost any programme it chooses to adopt. It could certainly initiate discussions with the Tamils and arrive at a reasonable settlement of outstanding differences between the two groups. This so far it has not done.

The crudity of the election campaign fought by her opponents, some of it directed personally against herself by one section of the press, must be held responsible for one of the earliest statements on policy made by the new government—the take-over of the press from its private owners, not by the state but by corporations in which monopoly control will be impossible. The Bill has not as yet come before Parliament. It will certainly go through when it does, and in the country generally there will be no great opposition to it. The other legislation of the SLFP has taken up the serious and difficult problems of the country's financial situation. The schools take-over and the Language of the Courts Act of 1961 have both led to trouble in the country. Roman Catholic opposition to the schools take-over was called off, according to a statment in London by the Deputy Speaker of the House of Representatives, through the personal intervention of Cardinal Gracias who visited Ceylon at Nehru's request.

The Language of the Courts Act with its refusal to allow courts' records to be kept in Tamil in Tamil-speaking areas was deliberately vexatious. It brought the FP out on a *satyagraha* campaign. This was inexplicably allowed to gather momentum before once again a state of emergency and a curfew were imposed on two provinces and press censorship over the whole island. Once again the army came in to maintain order and carried out its duties with unnecessary vigour in the north. Although communal violence on the scale of 1958 was feared, it did not break out. The plantation workers who threatened to come out on strike in sympathy with the *satyagraha* in the end did no more than stage a one-day strike.

The status of the plantation worker—despite the attempts of every single Prime Minister in Ceylon since D. S. Senanayake to have this population group accepted as Indians by the Indian government—has not altered since the Indian and Pakistani (Citizenship) Act of 1949. Some few may succeed through the tardy processes of administration in registering themselves as citizens of Ceylon. But it has never been established how many of them are third-generation settlers in the island. The Jackson Report in 1938 offered no help at all. It stated it as a 'fact recognized by all that some proportion of the Indian population, originally immigrants, have severed their connection with India and have become permanently settled in Ceylon'. All the figures it dealt in was the statement that 'if an estimate of 60 per cent is taken for purposes of illustration, it will be seen that at the end of 1936 there were in the island approximately 400,000 Indian estate workers who had become part of the permanent population of the island'.

The majority of plantation workers will have to continue as they are at present—stateless. Their legal position exposes the hollowness of the proposals put forward to solve their 'problem' by political leaders. To offer them 'inducements' to leave

Ceylon is an evasion of the reality in a world of visas, travel permits and passports. Where should they go, even if an 'inducement' (which must cost the Ceylon government several million rupees since there are over 800,000 of them) were accepted by them? Their numbers will increase with the natural rate of growth, and those who can secure citizenship of domicile will slowly trickle into the electoral register in the future.

It is the electoral register, the vote, which will in the foreseeable future decide the shape of things for everybody in Ceylon, not only the plantation worker. In this sense a democratic procedure will arbitrate, in spite of the absence in Ceylon of the specifications of the English model: a streamlined party system which smooths away the sharp edges of difference between parties, so that one becomes indistinguishable from the other; Cabinet and Parliamentary conventions which allow a party group secure in the House to disregard the mandate of those who put it there; and the near-impossibility of anyone's standing for election unless adopted by a party machine. It is a wilful exaggeration to claim that the people of Ceylon are devoted to democracy, or that in 1947 they achieved Independence democratically. Such portentous capital letter words, hateful at most times, are the stock in trade of official spokesmen. It would be juster perhaps to say that in 1956 the voter showed his independence. If the capital letter word ought to be used only when the mass of people decide for themselves, as a result of their own experience, how they wish to govern themselves, then perhaps Independence has still to be won in Ceylon.

The frequent states of emergency, the rigour of press censorship, the powers assumed by the head of the state and the Prime Minister, have convinced foreign observers that democracy in Ceylon, as elsewhere in Asia, has failed to work. It might be asked whether the democracy of which these critics are so proud has been working during the last twenty years in just those countries in Europe where its values are presumably enshrined. Democracy—the big capital letter word—is encountering heavy weather in most countries in Europe at the present time too. As for the other big words like Freedom, in whose name countries East and West have been, and are, ready to commit crimes daily out of their rage to save the world, it is profitless to speak. Much more mundane tasks than saving the world face the people of Ceylon.

The vote which the Donoughmore Constitution gave the adult in Ceylon has become in the course of thirty years the most important possession of everybody anxious for the future. In 1956 villagers, working on colonization schemes far from their original homes where they had been registered, travelled nearly a hundred miles at their own expense in order to influence the future course of affairs. There is no apathy about elections in Ceylon. The average voter is much more political-minded than the voter in the West. He is interested in argument, he is a devotee of meetings, but those which draw the largest crowds provide no index of the sympathies of their audiences. Flags in the colours of the rival parties flutter from house- and tree-top. But again it would be rash to base any prediction of the result on the number of flags to be counted by the roadside. Processions conducting candidates with drums and music from one point in the village to the other, garlands compelling them to wear their chins bravely in the air, are unreliable guides to the way in which the vote is going to be cast.

The greatest guarantee of real democracy in Ceylon seems to lie in the absence of two features of the political scene in the 'West': commercialized mass-media and the tired conventionalities of official party organization. Of course newspaper proprietors know all the tricks of the trade, but so far all their subterfuges have been countered by rank and file workers who are in better touch with the voter than a newspaper in Ceylon can be with its readers. The very uncertainty of the result of elections may be the best hope of democracy, since the resolution of the ordinary voter to keep his own counsel and express his opinion without aid from newspaper and party machine is essentially democratic.

During the tenure of office of the MEP government (1956–9) the Prime Minister took up the subject of the appropriateness of the present constitution to the country's development and its needs. Constitutions, however carefully composed, can be altered at will. They have, besides, belonged to the recent past, and may on that account weigh no more in the present and the future than the division of a hair. More important than forms of government are the human beings to be governed. The

306

greatest difficulty besetting Ceylon at the present time is the fundamental need of discovering who are the people of the country waiting to be governed. Is there a nation, and who compose it? To restrict the words 'nation' and 'national' to significances given them in the last few hundred years in Europe is to be a trifle pedantic. Various peoples have lived in Ceylon in the course of its long story. They have contrived to co-exist as people generally do co-exist, in a state of mutual irritation with each other which sometimes erupts into war. Whatever these people are called—tribes, races, communities—the two major ones among them have both had a consciousness of an identity, of a distinctiveness, of a culture, of beliefs and institutions which do give those who hold them the character of a nation. In this sense there have been two major nations in Ceylon—the Sinhalese and the Tamils. They have, wherever exactly from the sub-continent of India they may have come and whenever exactly in the past they arrived in the island, lived together in it, maintaining themselves as identities apart from India however close the link with it has been.

Whatever the history of the distant past has been, for the last century and more Ceylon has been one. Its political shape—a colony ruled over by the British—has been less important than its human character. As a result of British rule the human beings living in Ceylon developed a mobility which they did not possess before. Forest, mountain and river no more restricted their movement. Roads, railways and the bus have put an end to the segregation of people. They have migrated from the south to the central hills, from north to south, to the east from the west, and everywhere from village to provincial centres which have grown into towns. This mobility has been a gain, for it has enabled the people inhabiting the island to draw naturally closer to unity.

The changed human pattern of life in the island was one result of the economic system for which the British were responsible. The name given to it is immaterial; it was the product of self-interest and commercial enlightenment. S. M. Hardy has drawn attention recently to the *Letters on Colonial Policy* written by Philalethes (Sir Robert Wilmot-Horton) in the *Colombo Journal* during his governorship of Ceylon in the 1830s. There is nothing in the outlines of the economic structure designed since his time which his five *Letters* do not anticipate.

His description of what Ceylon could be is roughly what Ceylon economically is at the present time: 'a valuable portion of insular territory under the tropics, where certain products *having an exchangeable value* are to be found in great abundance, but where the natives must form the great bulk of the population with all their indigenous feelings and prejudices. . . . Tanks, water-courses and roads are the sort of "*Capital*" which is *in the first instance* most required; these can only be created under the direction of the Government; these improvements being made, the opportunity of employing private capital commences. . . . Increasing population is the most desirable object in a country, where the application of capital *furnishing ample return* of profit, is alone required to make the land produce twice as much as it now does of human food.'

Both the mobility of people in Ceylon and the economic structure belong to what is given. They cannot be neglected in any calculations about the past, the present and the future. All the schemes for fashioning a new world, or of abjuring the present for the greater glory of the past, or maintaining the gains of the present in the interests of a class, bear the distinctive pressure of the social and economic situation of contemporary Ceylon. These might be set out as follows: an increasing population of close upon 10 million, the majority of whom, nearly 70 per cent, live in rural areas and are dependent on the land; a third of its rural population landless, without even the exiguous plots of the rest; its commercial crops of tea, rubber and coconuts its major resources; more than 65 per cent of its food imported; its lack of raw materials; its lack of industrial development; its *per capita* income £40, nearly a tenth of that of the United Kingdom.

What is given, as string of facts or table of statistics, is a statement of what has been accumulated in the past and is not available in the present. It could, of course, be radically altered in the future. What is most important in what is given is not its character of a fixed asset lodged in Ceylon, immutable and eternal whatever happens in the world. What is given exists as part of the world to which the island belongs and to which it is committed. Nothing in it, not even the small plot the peasant-owner in the Dry Zone tills for his own use, is being worked, or can be worked, by a man and his family insulated from the changing world around them. They may continue to use the techniques and the tools of their ancestors, but the seeds they plant, the water irrigating their fields, the grain they sell, and the price paid for it, depend on government spending, and that depends on Ceylon in the world economy, and not only on a particular small unit in a particular part of the Dry Zone.

It may be that, in a world in which great powers push themselves and others remorselessly towards war, all futures are irrelevant. If this is so nothing that the people of Ceylon can do has power to be anything but a puny gesture. The world would then be explicable only by the clearness of perception of the chief of the Latookas, Commori, who discussed the immortality of the soul with Samuel Baker, one of the pioneers of European colonization in Ceylon. It was the opinion of this 'naked savage' in Africa a hundred years ago that 'most people are bad; if they are strong they take from the weak. The good people are all weak; they are good because they are not strong enough to be bad'.

For all his cynicism Commori himself planned for the future for he certainly thought of himself as strong. In spite of the threat of war most human beings plan for the future too. The minimal demand we make of it is economic security and emotional satisfaction.

The latter, sometimes, is easy enough to come by. In Ceylon the positive achievement of the MEP government was the euphoria it developed in the rural voter. It gave him the feeling that he counted too, that his status had improved. This did provide immeasurable spiritual sustenance. Desperately low living standards borne for decades and regarded as irremediable can be mitigated by the dram of increased self-esteem. Once this is given other needs arise, and out of this comes the hope that having tasted his draught of 'status' the rural voter will thirst for water of a clearer spring.

Emotional satisfaction has been derived from a belief in a myth about the ancient past far different from the reality of the present. Present conditions can still nourish it because attention can be diverted, wilfully or unconsciously, from reality, or, as it seems more likely, one single feature of its pattern can be so magnified in a familiar way that the background of the ancient myth is recalled. The strength of the feeling aroused against the

309

Tamils, for instance, owes more to the conviction that some intangible hostile force is responsible for genuinely felt economic distress, than to communal feeling as such. It is part of a general exasperation and resentment, the anger of the under-privileged against the oligarchy (the 'nobodies'), and among the 'they' to be detested and feared are Sinhalese, Catholics, and the 'gentlemen' in trousers as well as the Tamils. Grievances against a group have taken both communal and class shapes. The former have been much more readily available receptacles of feeling than the latter. For a time there were more English-educated Tamils in the lower grades of the bureaucracy than would have been proportionate to their numbers, and there always was the feeling that a caste or a community is over-solicitous of its kinsmen. The Tamils have therefore been an easier target than others, also vulnerable. In the course of time the English educated will disappear as a group, but the balance of forces will not be altered if they or those who replace them keep their privileges, even though they may not speak English.

A more recent myth was the statement that the school-child of the previous generation knew his classmates by name, whereas now he knows only that X is a Tamil, Y a Sinhalese, and Z a Burgher or a Moor. One can be sure that the speaker is a 'nobody' reminiscing about his secondary school education. The truth most probably is that, in the economic group of the English educated a generation ago, the community to which one's fellows belonged was immaterial in the classroom. Outside it sooner or later there would be social conventions against which one would bark one's shins. These depended on the inescapable fact that X was a Tamil, Y a Sinhalese and Z a Burgher or a Moor. The clearness of differentiation between these communities was blurred in the small group of the privileged. If common privileges bestowed by the administrative and political unity of the country could have done this, the future could, if the people of Ceylon so desire, produce a similar effect with no restriction of its benefits to a class.

The story of the last thirty years in Ceylon has demonstrated the modifiability of what has been given. Whatever the shape of the future, it will hardly be a superstructure on the base of an unaltered and unalterable present. Discussion has raged incessantly on the extent of change, possible and permissible, on the pattern of what is given. There have been as many plans as there have been governments in the last fifteen years. There have been those who have planned for chaos, believing firmly that after the deluge comes their turn. Planning is in fashion and the very magic of the word 'plan' sets fervid imaginations to work. It also promotes the sober industry of the purveyors of doctoral theses and research papers. But 'planning' generally inhibits the thinking of both, for in one it projects notions of infantile grandeur, and in the other an induration of the pia mater. Both reactions to 'planning' in Ceylon are plentifully in evidence. The schemes of Heads of Departments and Ministers would provide some examples of the first; of the other there are the labours of scholars who issue questionnaires, count heads and prepackage the 'cultural reactions' of the inhabitants of Ceylon for the supermarket of research. The Planning Secretariat in Colombo, set up in accordance with the recommendations of the International Bank for Reconstruction and Development, has very different schemes from either of these types for the future of the island.

There can be no effective planning, however, unless it is based on a political assessment of the kind of society towards which the people of the country wish to move. Whatever that future may be, only the dull-witted can believe that it will be provided for out of the generosity of contemporary programmes of aid to under-developed countries. The various plans which advertise the good intentions of the 'West' or the 'East' cannot be depended upon to install the millennium of either dispensation. The intentions of these planners are clear and logical, the political character of their generosity is manifest. Such aid should always be accepted in the spirit in which it is offered—that of sober political calculation. All it can help to achieve is little, but even that temporarily may help. The soundest comment on such schemes as technical assistance to under-developed countries was made by an American professor in 1952 in Chicago, when he remarked that 'it may be doubted that the rules laid down by the present-day technical assistance missions would have permitted, for example, the rapid development of a country like Japan, whose status in the last century and the early years of this century closely resembled many of the under-developed countries today'.

More is required than such programmes can devise. To expose a country's planning to the changeable weather of the cold war is to risk frostbite. Within limits foreign aid has enabled a few things to be done. The Colombo Plan, for example, has been responsible for all sorts of oddments in the way of free services. 'Oddments'—because requests for aid have come from government departments, or a government, working haphazardly and without any co-ordinated schemes to which foreign aid could in the long term be linked. In the single field of peasant colonization programmes in which the government of the UNP under D. S. Senanayake was most interested, B. H. Farmer lists the following: 'Experts had been provided . . . Australia had sent tractors, lorries and agricultural equipment which were used in colonies and other places; and New Zealand had provided funds to develop a dry-farming station.' He goes on to say that the colonies discussed in his book were 'almost entirely financed from internal resources, no mean feat for a country of the size and character of Ceylon and a point to be borne in mind by those who imagine that help for Asia arose because Asia would not help herself'.

But the point is: what does Asia want to help herself towards? To patch up a broken-down economy? The feat of the Agricultural Department in Ceylon, placed in the setting of what needs to be done on the land, resembles the strategy of today's high command fighting the battles of the war before the last. Planning for the future, not in agriculture alone, but for the whole of Ceylon's economy, needs vastly different equipment and changed strategy. The Report of the International Bank for Reconstruction and Development could scarcely be accused of being rash in its conclusions. It expressed 'grave doubts whether increasing production in the old patterns can any longer keep up with a greatly accelerated population growth'. 'Accelerated population growth' has never been a spectre haunting the producers of food. Only those to whom 'the old patterns' are the laws of nature are unwilling to grant that even the latter have to be reformulated. The significant words in the sentence above are 'the old patterns'. On the basis of the old little can be achieved. Only drastic land reform can effectively increase the productivity of Ceylon's rice-fields. Without it neither extensive colonization schemes nor improved techniques of cultivation can be more than palliatives for a deep-seated disease. Agrarian reform could make possible other changes in the existing pattern of production which would increase the national product *per capita*. Together with it programmes of industrialization could work successfully. Without either, Ceylon must continue among the under-developed and hungry areas of the world. Josue de Castro, once the head of the FAO, had a forthright answer to the correspondent of *L'Express* who inquired how he proposed to solve the world's problem of hunger: 'There is no specific remedy against hunger and famine. The struggle against hunger is the struggle against under-development. It can only be resolved by the elimination of colonial economic structures, by agrarian reform and industrial development. But the two sectors —agriculture and industry—must be handled as parallel.'

The financial crises of today, the fall in Ceylon's external reserves, present-day inflation, all of them transform the 'grave doubts' of the Report of ten years ago into the conviction that new patterns must be traced. Even those who could be content if the future were no more than the quasi-feudal order of the ancient past towards which the militant Buddhism of the present beckons, must themselves figure out new patterns too, or lose themselves in the mazes of their thinking.

The future towards which Ceylon wishes to move must decide its planning. The modes employed will depend entirely on this. So far not one of the plans of governments has considered what kind of economy or society it was planning for. And not Ceylon in isolation in the Indian Ocean has to be considered. As the trend in the world is towards larger units, and the need to survive forces both states and commercial undertakings into newer and larger groupings, it is difficult to see how Ceylon can hold itself outside the regional confederations of the future. A few miles to the north lies the sub-continent of India (now India and Pakistan). As countries with a common background of culture and economic structures which are a survival of similar evolution move towards co-operation and confederation, it is possible that Ceylon too will be drawn in the same direction. If this should be so, it will repeat the story of the past with a difference.

What is given, where all ladders start, is the comparative poverty of Ceylon. Though its *per capita* income is higher than that of other countries in Asia except Japan, Malaya and the Philippines, by any reasonable test it is a poor country. Only 35,000 of nearly 10,000,000 people in Ceylon pay income tax, the lowest taxable income being about £360 per annum. With no likelihood of foreign aid or private capital on the scale needed, no satisfactory planning is possible without the deployment of the powers and resources of the state. Only the state can finance the investment necessary to increase productivity and so provide a better life for its growing population. The state can be moved to use its powers only by a population aware of what is given and how it can best be changed to meet economic needs and to provide emotional satisfaction. People will grow tired of imagining that they have been eating cake. They will ask for bread, and be no longer satisfied with stones.

Bibliography

This select bibliography has been compiled for the benefit of the reader wishing to know more about the story of Ceylon. As most work on the subject has been published either in Ceylon or in India, it is unfortunately not always easily available elsewhere.

Most histories of Ceylon have been written specifically for use in secondary schools in Ceylon and are therefore unknown outside the island. H. W. Codrington's *A Short History of Ceylon* (Macmillan, revised edition, 1947), not intended as a school text, is a simple unravelling of the main threads of the story up to 1833. There is hardly anything available in the intermediate category between school text and learned treaties except for Sydney D. Bailey's lively sketch, *Ceylon*, written for Hutchinson's University Library (1952). Résumés of the story of the island, as a background to books of travel, reminiscences or general information, do not really provide the interested reader with what he is looking for.

Of source-books on the early history of Ceylon the most eminent are the Pali Text Society's three volumes of Geiger's edition of the *Mahavamsa* (1912) and the *Culavamsa* (1929–30) in an English translation. Would that they were newly rendered in a form expressive of their literary value!

The pioneer work in examining the ancient records from a scientific and critical point of view was G. C. Mendis's *The Early History of Ceylon* (Y.M.C.A. Publishing House, Calcutta, 1932). Bhikkhu Rahula's *History of Buddhism in Ceylon: The Anuradhapura Period* (Gunasena, Colombo, 1956) is a useful treatment of early literary records. The learned and authoritative *History of Ceylon*, Volume 1, Parts 1 and 2 (University of Ceylon Press Board, 1959 and 1960), covers the ground ex-

315

haustively from the earliest times to the end of the fifteenth century, but is likely to be too weighty for the general reader. *A Concise History of Ceylon*, its one-volume abridgement by C. W. Nicholas and S. Paranavitane (University of Ceylon Press Board, 1961), is much more practical and useful.

Numerous scholars—notably P. E. Pieris and Father S. G. Perera—have worked on the history of Ceylon in Portuguese and Dutch times. The forthcoming Volume 2 of the *History of Ceylon* (University of Ceylon Press Board) should, as it embodies more recent research, place the subject in better perspective. Two recent studies of the early Dutch period: K. W. Goone-wardena's *The Foundation of Dutch Power in Ceylon* (1638–58) and S. Arasaratnam's *Dutch Power in Ceylon* (1658–87), both published under the auspices of the Netherlands Institute for International Cultural Relations (Amsterdam, 1958), provide an interesting pointer to the results of investigation of Dutch sources.

The British period was first systematically investigated by L. J. B. Turner in his *Collected Papers on the History of the Maritime Provinces of Ceylon 1795–1803* (Colombo, 1923). Colvin R. de Silva's *Ceylon Under the British Occupation 1795–1832* (Colombo Apothecaries, 1942) did for the early British period what G. C. Mendis's book already referred to had done for the ancient period. The latter's *Ceylon Under the British* (Colombo Apothecaries, 3rd edition, 1952) is still the best concise account of the British period available. Leonard Mills's *Ceylon Under British Rule 1795–1832* (Oxford University Press, 1933) is a study of the administration during the period.

Since the appearance of the books in the preceding paragraph a number of young researchers have published work on the British period in learned journals in Ceylon. An interesting assemblage of lore and tradition about Kandyan Ceylon in the second decade of the nineteenth century will be found in P. E. Pieris's *Sinhale and the Patriots* (Colombo Apothecaries, 1950).

Among studies of contemporary Ceylon, apart from magazine articles, should be mentioned the 3rd edition of Sir Ivor Jennings's *The Constitution of Ceylon* (Oxford University Press, 1953) with its account of how the present constitution came into being, and W. Howard Wriggins's *Ceylon: Dilemmas of a New Nation* (Princeton University Press, 1960), an American researcher's detailed assessment of events in Ceylon since 1947 and their bearing on the future. T. Vittachi's *Emergency 1958* (André Deutsch, 1958) has some interesting material on the communal disturbances in Ceylon in that year.

Index

Index

Kirigalpotta, 20
Kirti Sri (King of Kandy), 130
Kirtisrimeghavanna, 73
Knox, Robert, 21, 150, 170–85 (*passim*)
Kohomba Kankariya, 90
Kotelawala, Sir John, 268, 287, 289–90
Kotte, 72, 73, 74, 85, 99, 102,103,104, 106, 107, 108, 153
Kottiyar, Bay of, 130, 131, 171
Kshatriya, 51
Kurunegala, 72, 162
Kuveni, 37, 38, 39
Kuvera, 93

Labour Party (of Ceylon), 245,246, 247, 275, 280; (of Great Britain), 267, 271
Lake House (newspapers), 269, 281
Landraad, 128
Language of the Courts Act (1961), 304
Lanka (Sri Lanka), 32, 34, 36, 37, 38, 39, 40, 41, 47, 55, 62, 63, 68, 153
Lanka Sama Samaja Party (LSSP), 251, 252, 253, 255, 256, 275, 277, 280, 281, 282, 288, 289, 292, 293, 295, 296, 301, 302
Lawrence, D. H., 24
Layton, Sir Geoffrey, 261–2
Leach, E. R., 170, 208
Legislative Council, 168, 199, 213, 215, 226, 228, 239, 240, 241, 242, 245, 246, 249
Lenin, V. I., 251
Lima, Don Francisco de, 118
Linschoten, J. H. van, 117, 118, 120
Lisbon, 117, 118
London, 137, 193, 250, 256, 284
London County Council, 248
London University, 217, 243
Lopez de Souza, Pedro, 107–8
Low Country Products Association, 237

Maatsuyker, Joan, 146
Macao, 100
Macdonald, Major, 158
MacDowall, General Hay, 143, 144
Madagascar, 130
Madras, 130, 131, 132, 133, 137, 139, 140, 141, 142, 231
Madugalle, 159
Madura, 130, 168, 264
Mahadeva, Sir Arunachalam, 268
Mahajana Eksath Peramuna (MEP), 292, 293, 294, 300, 306, 309

Mahanama, 34, 41
Mahasena, 67, 68, 70
Mahathupa (Ruvanvelisaya), 64, 83
Mahavamsa, 32, 34, 40, 43, 44, 47, 48, 49, 52, 53, 55, 57, 58, 60, 62, 63, 64, 65, 67, 68, 70, 83, 85, 93, 315
Mahaveliganga, 16, 62, 70, 144, 163
Mahavihara, 41, 45, 64, 67
Mahayana, 68
Mahinda, 41,43,45,46,47, 48, 49, 52,53
Mahinda, IV, 68
Mahinda V, 70
Maitland, Sir Thomas, 148–9
Malabar Coast, 104
Malabars, 102, 126, 130, 153
Malacca, 100, 105, 110, 120
Malaria, 164, 249, 250, 276
Malaya, 23, 24, 69, 104, 205, 244, 260, 261, 262
Malays, 143, 144, 224
Maldive Islands, 103, 264
Malvana Convention, 108–9
Manaar, 39, 113, 126, 132
Manavanamma, 70
Manning, Sir William, 241
Manoel Dom, King of Portugal, 104
Marco Polo, 111
Maritime Provinces, 127, 137, 138, 139, 140, 141, 157, 164, 181, 190, 202
Markham, Sir Clements, 203
Marshall, Henry, 156, 158
Marx, Karl, 53, 251
Marxism, 250; (Marxist Left), 282, 292
Matale, 162, 194, 203
Matara, 113, 137
Mauritius, 130, 158, 165
Mayadunne, 107
McCallum, Sir Henry, 243–5, 238–9
Mediterranean, 76, 82, 112, 261
Melo Coutinho, Diogo de, 107
Melo de Castro, Diogo, 110
Mendis, Dr. G. C., 13, 14, 165, 168, 315, 316
Meuron, Charles de, 132
Meuron, Brigadier-General Pierre de, 139, 141
Mills, Leonard, 316
Milton, John, 5
Ministers (House of Representatives), 284
Ministers (State Council), 245, 248, 249, 252, 254, 256, 258, 259, 267, 271, 272, 280, 283

324

Index

Index

Index

DATE DUE

MR 10 '64	JY 2 '70		
JY 7 '64	JY 6 '70		
JY 21 '64	SE 30 '70		
OC 19 '64			
OC 29 '64			
MY 12 '65			
NO 2 '65			
AP 12 '66			
AP 19 '66			
MY 2 '66			
JY 9 '67			
JY 10 '67			
RESERVE			
OC 10 '67			
MY 15 '68			
OC 12 '69			
JE 27 '70			
GAYLORD			PRINTED IN U.S.A.

CPSIA information can be obtained
at www.ICGtesting.com
Printed in the USA
BVHW050005090223
658191BV00002B/79

9 781014 195616